CHAGRIN FALLS

Gary L. Palmer

PublishAmerica
Baltimore

First printing

ISBN: 1-59286-337-X
PUBLISHED BY PUBLISHAMERICA BOOK PUBLISHERS
www.publishamerica.com
Baltimore

Printed in the United States of America

DEDICATION

Many people have influenced my life in a positive way but eight of them have been very special. I would like to dedicate my book to those eight people.

In my childhood and adolescent years: Grandmother Mamie Kelley, Coach Ralph Quesinberry, and my two foster mothers, Vivian (Bee) Crawford and Florence (Non) Davis.

In my adulthood: My father-in-law Anthony Foderaro, my two sons, John and Jeff and my loving wife, Barbara.

This picture was taken in Chagrin Falls around the time that I was born (1940). Front, left to right: My brothers, George (age 9) and Kenny (10). Back row, left to right: My mother, Kathryn (28), Grandfather Fred Jones, and Aunt LaGoldendrina, "Goldie" (25).

Chapter I
The Early Years

My parents met as many lovers do, on a silky spring day when the perfumed air and warmth of the newly-returned April sun bring all of the senses to life. A great deal would come out of their union, little of it good, but they didn't know that then. They were young that bright afternoon in 1929 and under the spell of the weather. It gives me some comfort to know that at least on the first day, the day their paths crossed, no shadow of pain darkens the memory. Instead, it's all light and heat. For Kenneth Palmer and Kathryn Jones, the beginning flashed fire like the head of my father's match as he struck it against the sole of his riding boot. Neither one of them saw the invisible fuse attached, the inevitable, eventual explosion. They saw only each other.

There he leaned back touching against the plate glass of Wolf's Harness Shop, one foot propped on the window's lower edge just behind him. He looked like a dandy on this day as he stood in front of a store devoted to horsemen, his trade. The stock market hadn't yet crashed, but when it did he had a job at the stables that he would keep through the Depression. Kenneth Palmer felt he had the world bridled, the future yet to run. This fellow casually smoking his Lucky Strike in front of the horse shop on South Main Street caught Kathryn Jones' eye. She was 17, naïve and easily flattered, but knew that men who frequented the Harness Shop usually represented the macho breed. This fellow curved against the wall as sleek and cunning as a cat. He wasn't tall, but his slim build and spit-polished riding boots, sparkling in the bright sunshine, gave him an air of height, power and maturity. His pants were freshly pressed, his light blue shirt clean and tailored to accentuate his wiry form. As she strolled closer, she noticed the steel blue of his eyes, his brown curly hair dressed in aromatic oil. He didn't take his gaze off her for a second and she felt unable to look away from those eyes, the orange bloom of the cigarette hanging lazily from his lower lip.

For Kenneth's part, Kathryn Jones was the best thing this newcomer had yet seen in Chagrin Falls, Ohio. He was a horseman from the East, New Jersey, who'd come from Virginia to work on an estate in Gates Mills, a few miles outside of Chagrin Falls. He loved the horses, he had his life ahead of him, and he thought he held his independence in his hands with the same sure grip he reined in the young mares. Perhaps my father thought he could subdue my mother as he did those young female horses; perhaps he thought she'd so love the touch of his hand that he could guide her down any course. Likely, however, he thought nothing but that this girl was the loveliest young woman he had ever seen. She swept up the street with the scent of apple blossoms, her hair blacker than a raven's wing in the sun. She was a few inches shorter than his 5'8" frame, but deliciously proportioned; her icy blue eyes sparkled like the water sailing over the nearby falls. He could hear that water now, on the breeze; she grew closer and the scent of flowers nearly unmanned him.

Kenneth Palmer was 25 and no fool, but he was love-starved and lonely. Gin mills and cigarettes had provided the extent of his social life in Ohio and when Kathryn Jones strolled close to him, he felt his testosterone rise like a stallion in the mating pen. He politely but deliberately stepped into her path. "Hello," was all he said, but she felt the man's desire swirling beneath the surface, like ice floats under the Chagrin River in the spring torrents. She smiled and returned the greeting. He interpreted her response as an invitation. That's when it all began; the spark, the flame, the long, slow burning fuse that eventually detonated and blew the Palmers apart, throwing me clear of Kenneth and Kathryn, clear of their first two sons Kenny and George, clear of anything you might call a normal family.

This is my story, but it's also the story of America in the 1940s and '50s, and of one small town in particular: Chagrin Falls, Ohio. It took me half a century to realize how aptly named my home town was or, rather, my "no home" town. Norman Rockwell could have painted scenes from our little 2.7 square mile village, too, but they would never have included people like me, or like my parents. We were the ones who couldn't make it to the middle class let alone the typical upper middle class that inhabited the village. We were the ones who fell down before the Great Depression and succumbed to the bottle. Our lives were filled with chagrin, also rage, grief, and despair. The Palmers lived in Chagrin Falls without ever really being a part of it, just as I grew up in one household after another, but never really felt a part of any of them.

But I'm jumping ahead of this tale, which begins with these two blue-eyed young people on a bright spring day. Did I say that they're going to marry each other? They did, less than a year later. The soft-spoken horseman and the beautiful teenage brunette pledged to the local justice of the peace to spend their lives together, for better or for worse. In America during the Depression, the future for them looked likely to get worse: neither had completed high school and the bottom had dropped out of the economy.

My parents' marriage was a spontaneous reaction, not a planned event. The Depression and their drinking habits caused their pockets to be continually empty in a town where most people were well off.

Chagrin Falls, a logging town at the time of its origin, flourished primarily as a bedroom community for professional people that worked in Cleveland, a short drive away. The small town divided by the rushing waters of the Chagrin River, characterized by successful, happy, educated, community oriented Republican and Protestant citizens, did not even have a Catholic Church until the 1950s. But the churches in this small town didn't matter; to the best of my knowledge, my parents didn't have a religion.

In 1929, fewer than 3,000 people resided in the village of Chagrin Falls. Cleveland, however, located 18 miles to the northwest, with its steel mills and automobile factories, by the time the Depression began had built itself into an industrial giant. With a population of 900,000, it ranked as our nation's fifth largest city, tripling the population of the rest of Cuyahoga County.

For people who fit the white upper middle class stereotype, Chagrin Falls flourished as a nice place to grow up. Unfortunately, acceptance did not come easily for people who fell outside the stereotype, and my parents sat on the bottom rung of the socio-economic ladder in the charming river village of Chagrin Falls.

Even today, from the merchant shops and bandstand in Triangle Park to the older well-kept Victorian-style homes, Chagrin Falls appears like a transplanted New England village. The quaint and cared-for houses, each one unique, nestle among rows and clusters of old maple and oak trees that overshadow quiet, friendly streets.

In the 1930s, too, most of the friendly people in Chagrin Falls emitted an air of community pride, sometimes bordering on provincial arrogance; a feeling that if you weren't from this town you didn't quite measure up. Unfortunately, a small minority of people living in town fell short of Chagrin Falls' standards; Kenneth and Kathryn Palmer fell into this category.

In 1930, the same year Congress passed the minimum wage law at 25 cents an hour, my mother gave birth to my brother, Kenny, and then George arrived a year later. In June of 1940, nine years after George's birth, my mother brought me into the world. Franklin Delano Roosevelt won his third term in office in 1940, the minimum wage rose to 43 cents an hour and the

United States teetered on the brink of war.

By 1940, the marriage that had been sparked by the loveliness of a young girl in the springtime and fanned by infatuation had burned out. My earliest vivid memories did not depict family picnics, Christmas trees and puppies, but scenes far less pleasant.

"You goddamned son-of-a-bitchin' whore! I'll kill you!" yelled my father amid the sounds of lamps breaking, pots and pans crashing, and anything my mother could get her hands on to deflect the flying fists of my father. The drunken brawl raged in the upstairs living room of our rental house in Chagrin Falls.

I will never forget that muggy summer evening in 1945, shortly after my fifth birthday and a few weeks before the end of World War II. Loud, chilling screams from my mother after my father beat her in a drunken rage obliterated the sounds of chirping crickets and croaking bullfrogs from a nearby pond.

My 15 and 14 year-old brothers and I squeezed together like sardines on the creaky old bed that we shared. Frightened by the sounds of violence, I sat up and cried out for my maternal grandmother, who lived less than a mile away.

"Lay down and be quiet," said my oldest brother Kenny in a soft but authoritative voice.

With my head buried under a pillow, the sheets absorbed my tears. I pushed the pillow tightly against my ears to muffle the mangled cries: It sounded as though my mother might be killed on this dreadful evening. The nightmarish ordeal finally ended when the police showed up at our doorstep; a neighbor had called them.

Even though the violence only lasted a few minutes, it seemed like it would never end. In reality, for me, the sick feelings of abuse never did end. The next day brought more sadness when I looked at my mother and saw the black and blue bruises covering her face. Her battered face made me want to throw up, and even then I knew that I would never beat up a woman or anyone that I loved. At five years old, I learned what it meant to be helpless: I could not stop my father or save my mother from the terrible pain that she suffered.

During these times of turmoil, we lived in a two-story rented house. The outside of our home resembled an old barn that had been remodeled into an artist or writer's studio. Downstairs consisted of a kitchen, bathroom and utility room. The upstairs portion contained a living room and two bedrooms.

Except for the normal messiness of a boy's room, the bedroom that my brothers and I shared gave no clues that it provided the living space for three boys. It had an old mahogany chest of drawers that stored our limited supply of clothes and a wood floor that creaked with each step, sounding more like the haymow of a barn than a bedroom. No nightstands or lamps graced our bedroom. Moreover, one of the two bulbs from an overhead light seemed to always be burned out, casting a dim glow over the room. No pictures relieved the drab walls, though white see-through curtains muted the screened window. The reeking smell of cigarette smoke from my chain-smoking father clung like leeches to everything in the room.

Before moving to our home on High Street in 1944, we had lived in several locations around town. Either because my parents fell behind on rent payments or the landlords and neighbors could not tolerate their violent behavior and lifestyle, my family skipped from shabby house to shabby house. The homes we lived in would not be considered shabby in most communities, but by Chagrin Falls' standards, they appeared that way.

The verbal abuse in our household happened daily, but the physical abuse usually occurred on Friday or Saturday nights. Luckily, I missed much of the violence because I spent many weekends with my grandmother.

The bar scene served as the catalyst for the violence, according to relatives and people that knew my mother and father. When I grew older, they told me a few stories. In their scenario, my mother flirted, danced and sometimes left bars with other men.

"She flirted with other men because she loved the attention they gave her, she also liked that it made Dad jealous," said my brother George.

The fights and beatings took place during the wee-hours of the morning, after the bars closed. I often wondered why my brothers didn't try to stop my father's violent behavior. They probably got used to the routine abuse, and feared retaliation if they intervened. They may have thought that my father would throw them out of the house, or possibly they just didn't have the fortitude or confidence to stand up to him. Maybe they looked at themselves as being too young, but as I look at this some 57 years later, they appeared old enough at 15 and 14 to stop their father. Perhaps the real obstacle was their mixed allegiances. I didn't know at the time, but later discovered that Kenny had been close to Mom, and George especially close to Dad. I was close to my grandmother and after the comparatively stable time that I spent with her, I did not have warm feelings for either of my parents, but I did feel closer to my mother than my father. I felt sorry for her because of the way she had been treated by my father.

I didn't look up to the skinny, alcoholic runt that I called "father," and the only time I respected him happened when he threatened to apply his belt to my tender little ass. He always seemed to be angry, drunk and abusive, especially to my mother. We didn't do anything together as a family, and because of his alcoholism, there never seemed to be enough money for anything.

In the 1930s my father worked at nearby stables, grooming horses and cleaning out their stalls. In the 1940s he worked on the assembly line at the Chevrolet plant in Cleveland. I remember him carrying a black metal lunch pail, and riding off to work with someone who picked him up. I don't remember him driving, but he might have had a car sometime during the early 1940s. Most people that lived in the village of Chagrin Falls during this period didn't need a car. The merchant shops in town were clustered together and in less than ten minutes a person could walk from our High Street home to the far end of the small business area in town.

I have visions of my mother dusting the furniture and lampshades and sweeping the floors. I don't remember her doing much cooking, but I'm sure she must have. I do remember one Sunday dinner in 1944 or 1945. On the table sat mashed potatoes covered by streams of melted margarine and accompanied by a bowl of rich, dark, gravy; a dish of steaming peas and carrots; and a large platter of sliced roast beef with a pleasant aroma that had been drifting through our house for several hours. My brothers and I drank tall glasses of cold, creamy homogenized milk delivered every other day from Dean's Dairy. We spread thick slabs of margarine over white Wonder bread and folded it into sandwiches. We even had blackberry pie for dessert. It was so delicious; I didn't even mind the seeds that stayed crunched between my teeth, what seemed like forever. It was the only pie that I remember having the first six years of my life. That pie made a lasting impression on me; to this day it ranks as my favorite pie. I've had visions of that meal my entire life, but it wasn't just the good tasting food that made such a lasting impression. No one argued or fought, something very unusual around our house and that made the food taste so much better. I especially liked the mashed potatoes, milk and the blackberry pie, but most importantly the peaceful togetherness made the occasion special and unforgettable.

I kept glancing at my mother and father, wondering if they would have meals like this more often. That Sunday dinner remains the most pleasant family experience from those bygone war years that I can remember.

Something else stands out about that dinner. We had a houseguest, a friend of George's; I remember him sitting at the table between George and Kenny. I don't remember his name, but I recall feeling good about someone coming to our house for dinner. Except for the police and the landlord, I can't recall seeing anybody else in our house, not even my grandmother.

The bill collectors wanted to come in to collect the money that never seemed to get paid. They would knock at the door several times, look around for signs of life, get discouraged and leave. Our jet-black curly haired cocker spaniel Asta's sharp, loud barks sometimes caused the bill collectors to stay longer hoping that someone might be home. They would wander around outside, looking for signs of life, and it seemed like forever before they would leave. My mother always took me into a room away from the windows and told me to be quiet. I would watch the bill collectors pull away by sneaking a peek out of the window. I thought it was a neat game, hiding, and my mother not having to pay those rich men that came dressed in suits and wearing hats.

Despite the fugitive memories of a pleasant Sunday dinner and hiding from the bill collectors, violence dominates my early childhood memories. It lingered in the air like barroom smoke. My mother always flirted with danger, especially after visiting the bars, but none of us were ever out of the woods. When my father pulled off his belt, it signaled that someone would be whipped or intimidated. The big brown Western belt with a shiny silver buckle would fly off with one pull of my father's thin right arm, and hang from his side like a whip ready to be cracked. The belt whippings occurred as a result of something my brothers did or didn't do, or something they said that disagreed with my father. He would fly off the handle at the drop of a hat, especially when he had been drinking.

"You bucktoothed bastard," my father, Kenneth Palmer, would sometimes say to Kenny, his namesake, just before he began belt whipping his oldest son.

"I remember welts and blisters forming after some of the beatings. I got whipped more than George and you hardly got whipped at all; you were too little," recollected Kenny.

I probably did escape the beatings because of my age, but I do remember getting hit with the belt. I don't remember experiencing much pain, and I never got beaten with the belt the way Kenny did; mostly I recall the threats.

Despite the vivid, unpleasant early childhood memories from 1944 to 1946, I also remember some happier times: Climbing trees, fishing, hiking in the woods, staying at my grandmother's house, playing football with my brothers, and frolicking with them and Asta in the raked-up piles of autumn leaves.

One time my brothers and I built an airplane by putting cardboard wings on an orange crate. Because the plane would have a better chance of flying with a lighter pilot, they told me to be the pilot. Fortunately, the homemade airplane got hung up on tree branches and never found the ground. A couple of small branches pierced through my body, one in the knee and the other the scrotum, but the latter had no effect on my manhood. If it hurt I don't remember the pain; I think I learned to numb out physical pain.

A story that George tells involves another crash landing; it's a story that my brother has told over and over: "I was pushing you along the sidewalk on High Street in a baby buggy. My first girlfriend was with me and I was tryin' to impress her; I wanted her to think I was responsible enough to take care of my baby brother. I hit a crack in the sidewalk and the buggy went flying out of my hands and was heading down the side of a hill toward the paper mill and the river. I went chasin' after you and the buggy crashed into a tree. It's damn lucky the tree stopped you cause you were headin' right for the river." George hesitated, laughed and continued, "Or maybe you would of got lucky and crashed into the paper mill."

Other memories of those bygone years have stayed with me a lifetime. I vividly remember, through the open bedroom window, the soothing and peaceful sounds of rain falling on the leaves of the large maple tree outside my bedroom window and softly tapping on the roof, a refreshing change from the sounds of yelling, swearing and fighting.

I felt secure listening to the rain, but my hopes and dreams centered on two things: I wanted the next day to be nice so I could play outdoors; and most of all, I didn't want my mother to get beaten up.

In retrospect, my brothers must have felt the same way. Even though they didn't stand up to their father, I felt safe around them. I looked up to Kenny and George as pillars of strength that I could count on.

George played basketball and ran track before dropping out of school in the ninth grade. I always wanted to see him play, but nobody would take me to his games or track meets. He also trapped muskrats at the swamps near the millpond, a short distance away, and sold the hides to haberdashers for a dollar a piece. The thick, light brown muskrat fur was used to make women's coats.

Kenny also dropped out of school in the ninth grade, but he didn't play organized sports. Shooting his .22 rifle surfaced as my oldest brother's favorite pastime. One day he got me laughing when he told George and me that he could "shoot a squirrel off the wing of an airplane." I had toy guns, but I always wanted to shoot a real gun. I remember Kenny's response when I tried to convince him to let me shoot his rifle.

"I'll teach ya' how to shoot when you get a little older, you little squirt."

Some of my most prominent early childhood memories involved Kenny. Once he buried some money under a tree in our front yard. He told me he had hidden the money so we could spend it at a nearby store. We would buy potato chips and pop to keep from going hungry when our parents didn't leave us any supper, which happened quite often.

Kenny, unlike George, always talked about the war, especially the war in the Pacific. He talked about the Silver Star cousin Stanley won on Iwo Jima, and how we were going to "whip the Japs' ass," just like we did the Germans. At age five I didn't understand much about the war, but Kenny at age 15 liked to regale me with stories about the great military victories in the Pacific and in Europe.

I will never forget the victory sirens signaling the end of World War II, and the events that followed. I was playing outside when the news came that we had won the war. Shortly after the sirens began whistling Kenny slammed open the screen door, ran outside with his arms extended skyward and yelled, "The Japs surrendered! The war's over, we won!"

The sirens, compliments of the Chagrin Falls Volunteer Fire Department, blared for several minutes. Sporadically in the distance through the clusters of oak and maple trees, I heard faint sounds of people shouting with happiness. I remember wondering if people felt happy everywhere or just in Chagrin Falls.

The happiness of many northern Ohioans continued in 1945 when the Cleveland Rams won the NFL Championship, and Hall of Fame pitcher, Bob Feller, returned from his Navy war years to once again pitch for the Cleveland Indians.

The war years and post war era stand as nostalgic times in the history of our country. Families gathered around the radio to listen to half-hour mysteries, sitcoms as they are presently called, or other types of shows that entertained them. The most popular mystery shows of the 1940s kept Americans glued to their radios: *The Shadow, The Adventures of Ellery Queen, Gangbusters, Sherlock Holmes, Boston Blackie, Mr. and Mrs. North, Mr. District Attorney,* and *Richard Diamond, Private Detective. The Shadow* and *Gangbusters* became my favorite shows. A scary, vivid image of a man's shadow sent chills up and down my spine. I liked *Gangbusters* because of the name and the screeching sounds of tires when police cars were chasing crooks.

Equal in popularity were the sitcoms: *Edgar Bergen and Charlie McCarthy, Fibber McGee and Molly, The Life of Riley, George Burns and Gracie Allen, The Great Gildersleeve, Jack Benny, Our Miss Brooks, Abbott and Costello, Red Skelton, and The Adventures of Ozzie and Harriet.* I especially liked *Edgar Bergen and Charlie McCarthy* and the western radio shows, *The Lone Ranger* and *Roy Rogers.* Also popular; the great entertainers and variety shows: Kate Smith, Arthur Godfrey, Bob Hope, Bing Crosby, Perry Como and Frank Sinatra were household names across the land. Kate Smith singing her famous rendition of God Bless America made Americans burst with pride. And everybody loved America's most popular quiz show, *Truth or Consequences.*

I remember some favorite songs that I listened to on the radio in the middle 1940s, and I still remember most of the words: *When The Red Red Robin Comes Bob Bob Bobbing Along, Don't Sit Under The Apple tree, You Are My Sunshine, Home On The Range, I Wonder Who's Kissing Her Now,* and *White Christmas.*

I also remember doctors making house calls carrying their black, textured leather medical bags; Dean's and O'Brock's delivering milk and collecting the money from the glass returnable bottles that were left near the front door.

Most families in the 1940s had only one car or no cars at all. During the war years gasoline and many food products, most notably butter and sugar, had been rationed. Since steel and gasoline were so critical to the war effort, automobile production came to a near standstill. To conserve fuel, 35 mph became the speed limit on highways, none of which were interstates or divided highways at that time. The big band sounds of Glen Miller, Tommy Dorsey, Benny Goodman and Duke Ellington became the rage; movies, like *Gone With the Wind* and *Casablanca,* were heart-felt, emotional, entertaining experiences, not episodes of sex and violence; our men and women in uniform returning home from the war looked forward to peaceful, happy and prosperous futures; and finally, family values and people that worked hard to achieve success were revered, and patriotism pervaded all.

My parents did not factor into the family values and achievement mainstream like most people in Chagrin Falls. As if to prove how out of touch with those values they were, in the spring of 1946, several months after the war in the Pacific ended, my mother and father separated and abandoned my brothers and me. People in our family never referred to my mother and father's irresponsible deed as abandonment, but what else can you call it when your parents split and leave their children behind?

I remember my mother hurrying to leave our High Street home. The sun shone mightily as we rushed outside, my arms hugging a large brown grocery bag stuffed with my belongings as I ran to the waiting arms of Grandma.

"You're going to be living at our house now. Come on Gary let's go," she insisted.

With her arm draped over my shoulder, Grandma and I walked away. I don't remember saying goodbye to my mother, but I do remember being happy that I was going home with my grandmother.

There was a sense of urgency in my mother's departure; a need to vanish before my father returned from work. She told me in my adult years that my dad threatened to kill her if she left him. This may have been true because my mother changed her name and lived in secrecy in Cleveland to make sure my dad and the authorities could not find her. She wanted independence without going through a divorce.

I would miss the relationship with my brothers, especially our trips through the woods to a mysterious swimming pool nestled in a field not far from our house. The concrete pool, void of water had a diving board and cracks that ran along the sides and at the bottom. Weeds seeped through the cracks like they had been planted there. The walls, bleached white by the hot summer sun, buckled from the cracks. A pond sat next to the pool where we used to catch blue gills and my brothers fired Kenny's rifle at targets in the field.

My brothers and I spent much of our time back by the pool and pond, but the abandonment changed our way of life. I wished my brothers could have lived at Grandma's too. But my grandmother and her second husband, Bill Kelley, didn't have the means or the room for three boys. Being the youngest by nine years, I got most of the attention.

My brothers had a rough go of it after the abandonment. At 16 and 15 years old they were left to fend for themselves. Temporarily, until they found a permanent home, they stayed at a horse estate where my aunt and uncle lived and worked.

"When we first lived at the stables George and I slept together in a small bed and then we took turns sleeping in the tack room on a cot," said Kenny.

George, after a brief stay at the stables did something more adventurous.

"I hitch-hiked to Maryland with three-dollars in my pocket. I went there because I heard I could get a job working with horses. I was fifteen when I went to Maryland," said George.

My dad referred George to the horse estate where George worked for his room and board and a small salary. Then George moved to Westbury, New York, a Long Island suburb of New York City where Dad had lived since the separation.

My father and George worked on the Clark Estate in Westbury until around 1960, at which time George, his wife Marge, son Gregory and my father, moved with the Clarks to Aiken, South Carolina. My brother purchased a small, brick, three bedroom, one-story house in Aiken. My father lived there with George and his family.

Kenny worked and lived on a horse estate in Hunting Valley, near Chagrin Falls, with Aunt Goldie and Uncle Harold. After paying room and board to my aunt and uncle, in Kenny's words, "There wasn't much left."

I considered myself lucky to be living with my grandmother, but I regretted that my brothers could not live with us.

I already had fond memories of the weekend stays at my grandmother's house on West Orange Street. I can remember as far back as 1944 and especially 1945; the year the Cleveland Rams won the NFL Championship and the first year the Chagrin Falls Tigers played their home football games under the lights. I can still feel the goose bumps from the music of the Tiger Marching Band when they paraded from the nearby high school to the stadium. The sounds of the band at the stadium, less than a mile away, could be faintly heard from my grandma's house. That distant music made me fantasize about someday going to the games, and growing up so that I could be a football player.

I cherish other nostalgic reminders of days gone by at Grandma's house: Her warm touch, the nighttime sounds of whistling freight trains passing through town, and the peacefulness that I felt when the curtains from my screened bedroom window drifted back and forth in a soft summer breeze.

Plagued by health problems and financial hardships, my grandmother extended herself in a time of need. She and her husband Bill were on the verge of a total collapse when I arrived on the scene in 1946. They had to leave their home on West Orange Street and move into a three-room apartment above the Kroger Grocery Store. Later, in the depths of despair, they moved into a substandard one-room shack.

My maternal grandmother, a tall, thin, native Texan of German and Irish descent had mostly gray, straight hair with streaks of black, a long narrow face and sky blue eyes. She became a mother at age 17 and a grandmother at

35. Grandma, in her early fifties in 1946 and battered by poor health, saved me from being an orphan.

"Your grandmother was nicknamed 'Slats' and smoked a corn cob pipe," said Stanley Davis, who had the task of being my foster father from 1950 to 1958.

"Slats" didn't surprise me because of Grandma's tall slender build, but I never saw her smoke a pipe. But my grandmother did not pretend to be a typical lady of the 1940s, and may have been a chip off the old block.

Her father, Eugene Erastus Allshouse, born in 1855, served as an Indian fighter with the U.S. Army's 18th Infantry Division in the Montana Territory during the 1880s. His Montana tour of duty occurred a few years after Custer's Last Stand at Little Big Horn, in 1876. My great grandfather's exploits against the Blackfoot and Sioux helped pave the way for western settlers.

The Allshouses' American military roots go back to the American Revolution. My grandmother's great-great-great grandfather fought as a patriot during the Revolutionary War.

"Grandma was six feet tall," George told me, which may have been somewhat of an exaggeration, and then he added, "You got your size from somewhere."

I may have inherited some of Grandma's characteristics, but at this stage of my life I was a skinny little boy. I had dark curly hair and blue eyes.

My looks differed noticeably from my brother's. Besides having darker hair and darker features, in due time I became much bigger in stature. Our light colored eyes seemed to be the only trait that we shared.

Brimm's Beer Garden on Main Street, just north of the river, became Grandma's favorite hang out. Rough talking, beer drinking, blue collar-workers from the paper mill were Brimm's best customers, but that didn't stop Grandma. She often went there alone to drink beer or to insist that her alcoholic husband, Bill Kelley, come home and stop drinking up his meager paycheck. My grandmother's bar appearances always turned some heads. In the 1940s, attending gin mills unescorted was not a socially acceptable practice for women.

"Grandma went to the bars because she liked drinking beer. Other women went there for other reasons, but not her," said George.

Sometimes my grandmother would take me to Brimm's. The dark atmosphere of the small town bar exuded the familiar smell of cigarette smoke that lingered in the air like an early morning fog. I hated cigarette smoke so much that a brief whiff of smoke from a cigar or pipe seemed pleasant and refreshing.

When my grandmother and I walked into Brimm's and word got around that a lady was present, the profanity seemed to diminish. The beer drinkers, cigarette smokers and tobacco chewers always sat on the old-fashioned, round, backless bar stools anchored to the floor of the saloon. The bartender posted spittoons at each end and in the middle. The spittoon arrangement made it convenient for the chewers to spit out their juice. There were no tables in Brimm's, but instead four or five booths pressed against the wall opposite the bar.

The taste of cold Coca-Cola from a bottle, and crunchy potato chips that I smothered with salt from the same shaker that my grandmother used for her beer helped make the smells of the barroom more bearable.

The sizzling sound and tempting smell of hamburgers frying on the kitchen grill adjacent to the bar always made me hungry. But we never had enough money for hamburgers; they were an inflated 15 cents in 1947.

One summer day at Brimm's, Grandma seized an opportunity that enabled us to buy a couple of those delicious hamburgers that I dreamed about. It happened while we were sitting in a booth, sipping our Coke and beer. Grandma noticed that a man at the bar had carelessly pulled money out of his front pocket, and unknowingly dropped a bill into the spittoon. Her eyes zeroed in on the bill as if she had just opened her favorite Christmas present. She told me to hurry and get the money. When I retrieved the dollar bill, Grandma wiped it clean with a paper napkin and told me I could have another Coke, a bag of potato chips and a hamburger. I covered the burger with raw onions and mustard. It remains one of the most heavenly treats that I can remember. I wanted to be rich some day so that I could buy hamburgers at Brimm's.

The lessons learned from taking the dollar and other similar experiences made me realize that stealing was an acceptable practice and sometimes necessary for survival. Through much of my life, stealing and dishonesty surfaced as a bad habit and was not easy to shake.

Despite the unpleasant experiences of my early years, I benefited from growing up in a closely-knit, small town like Chagrin Falls. People didn't get upset when kids walked through their yards and many people didn't lock their doors at night. Good Samaritan deeds were performed almost daily and the church bells chimed on Sunday morning. Good old down-home activities like strawberry festivals; the fourth of July parades, the band concerts in the center of town at Triangle Park and Memorial Day parades were a tradition.

Almost the entire student body rallied around their school colors, and community pride had found its way to the majority of people in Chagrin Falls.

Chagrin Falls had many charms, but acceptance did not come easy for people who did not fit the white, upper middle class stereotype. As a shy, withdrawn six-year old, lacking in self-esteem, I didn't fit the mold in Chagrin Falls. Nevertheless, my grandmother tried very hard to get my life turned around.

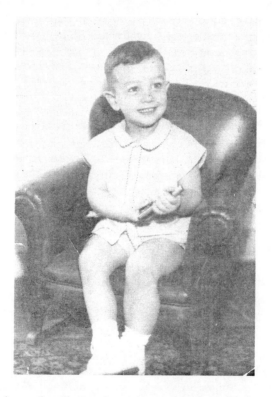

This is the only picture that I have of myself as a little boy. I look to be about 3 or 4 years old so it was taken in 1943 or 1944.

Chapter II
My Grandmother

During the post war, 1946-47 school year, I lived in a three-room apartment above Kroger's grocery store with my grandmother and her second husband, Bill Kelley. My first grade teacher, Miss Fletcher, was young, enthusiastic and serious about her mission to educate children. I remember her soft-colored summery dresses, reddish brown hair, freckles, pleasant smile and devotion to such things as the Red Cross, the March of Dimes, and collecting tax stamps.

"Children don't forget, tomorrow is the last day for bringing in tax stamps! Also children, remember...there's a special prize for the student who brings in the most tax stamps and the class that brings in the most," Miss Fletcher proudly announced.

During the 1940s, people received stamps equivalent to the amount of tax paid on purchases. Large numbers of stamps could be redeemed for merchandise. The tax stamps collected by our school would be used for educational materials. Grandma had saved hundreds of stamps for the final collection day. The sun shone warmly that spring morning when she gave me a large shopping bag full of tax stamps; they were almost too bulky for my six-year-old body to carry.

"Don't lose this bag! Take it right to Miss Fletcher, and Gary try to remember to bring back the shopping bag," Grandma said, and then reached down with her long thin arms and gave me a hug.

Nothing short of getting mugged could have caused me to lose the large bag. When I got to the school playground, I noticed that no one else had many stamps. My large shopping bag of tax stamps became another reminder that I differed from the other kids. When the bell rang I withdrew from the anxiety-filled task of giving Miss Fletcher the stamps. When no one seemed to be looking, I hid the tax stamps behind a tree. A few minutes later a safety patrolman came into our class, held up my bag of stamps and asked, "Did anyone lose this bag of tax stamps?" I did not claim the lost stamps nor did I tell Grandma the true story. It would have gotten her Irish up because she could have redeemed the stamps.

Grandma had been divorced from my grandfather, Fred Jones, for several years. I only saw Grandpa Jones a couple of times, but he didn't speak to me on either occasion. I wondered why he wasn't nice like Grandma. Everything about my grandfather seemed strange, especially his cold personality and the fact that he stood at least four inches shorter than Grandma. Remarkably, my father, Ken Palmer, looked more like Grandpa Jones than my mother did. My grandfather and father's similarities could be found in their height, complexion, the color of their eyes and hair, and the shape of their faces. I didn't notice these similarities as a youngster, but I did when I grew older, especially after looking at old photos. Maybe my mother felt attracted to my father because he resembled her own father.

My grandmother's second husband had the misfortune of being handicapped by alcoholism. His whole existence consisted of frequenting the taverns and working the late shift at the paper mill. Bill and Grandma walked everywhere; they didn't own a car, nor did they need one. They didn't have a driver's license between them. Occasionally, Bill took me on walks in the woods and along country roads. Sometimes we picked mushrooms and brought them home for Grandma to cook.

Things took a turn for the worse in 1947: Bill developed hip and back problems and started using a cane; and my grandmother was diagnosed with cervical cancer.

Our financial problems steadily worsened as Bill Kelley continued to spend his money on the drinking problem of which he could not rid himself. His alcoholic habits left little and occasionally no money for food.

With crumbling health, no place to live, no money and the responsibility of a six-year-old grandson, life suddenly became unfair to my grandmother, her husband and me. We were forced out of our apartment in town, and unless someone quickly came to our aid, we would be homeless.

Florence Savage, Bill Kelley's sister, offered help. She gave us a one-room house, literally a shack, located next to her small, three-room home on North Main Street. We were only supposed to live there for a short time, until Bill found us a home, but it didn't work out that way. Bill's alcoholism and Grandma's cancer resulted in serious problems.

To make a bad situation worse, Florence Savage suffered from paranoia. Suspicious of everyone, she slept with a loaded pistol under the pillow and kept her doors locked day and night.

Florence's son Clifford lived with her, but died in his twenties of a rare disease shortly after we moved in. Years later I learned that Clifford had a little daughter that mysteriously disappeared. I don't know if she disappeared because someone took her and raised her or for some other reason. I'm also not sure if a connection existed between Clifford's daughter's disappearance and Florence's paranoia.

Despite Florence Savage's problems, her house had electricity, one more convenience than we had. I remember my grandmother's comment when we moved into our substandard home, "At least it's a roof over our heads."

A kerosene lamp burned day and night giving our dark and dingy windowless home its only source of light. We used candles when we ran out of fuel. The lack of sanitary facilities became much worse than not having electricity. Bottles and buckets replaced a toilet at night and on blustery winter days. Grandma used a bedpan and counted on me to help whenever Bill wasn't around. I would push my grandmother's thin, fragile body up on one side and slide the bedpan under her. When she finished using the bedpan, I removed it and dumped it outside. Since Bill wasn't always around due to the night shift job at the paper mill and his drinking habits, it became my duty to help Grandma with anything that she needed. During the day when I went to school, Bill took care of Grandma. I don't remember hearing about Bill's sister, Florence Savage, helping Grandma when Bill and I weren't around, but maybe she did. Bill and Florence seemed far removed from each other; I don't even remember them talking, and I only recall being in Florence's house once or twice. None of us ever went to Florence's to go to the bathroom, so I'm not sure that she had sanitary facilities either.

As Grandma's condition worsened, she passed the time by lying flat on her back, staring at the dark, sometimes leaky ceiling. She could move her arms and head without assistance. That enabled her to lock and unlock the door by extending a crutch to the L-shaped hook. But as the cancer progressed, she became incapable of locking the door. When we left Grandma alone, Bill or I leaned a tree branch against the door to keep it from blowing open.

Our single room home measured roughly 24 feet by 12 feet. It had a small kitchen table with two chairs; an icebox that seldom had ice or food in it, and a single and double bed that were within two or three feet of each other. Of course we had no telephone, and it was too dark to have read a newspaper.

In retrospect, the thing that amazes me most is that I don't remember the shack having a source of heat. We didn't have a wood-burning stove, and I don't remember having a space heater, but we must have had some source of heat because we didn't freeze to death. On cold winter nights, I wore my clothes to bed. I wrapped myself in a blanket and hugged my pillow for warmth and comfort. I remember the bitter cold and I often wonder how we were able to stay warm enough to survive.

To add to our problems, we never had enough water. From spring to fall, I caught raindrops in a large, round, aluminum tub. With a scrub board and a bar of soap, I used the captured rainwater for washing clothes and to wash my hands and face. For drinking water, I filled up bottles mostly from the neighbor's garden hoses. In the winter, I brought water home from Grandma's brother, Uncle Frank and Aunt Jo Allshouse, who lived about a half mile away. One day I remember being so thirsty I drank a bottle of vinegar. I'll never forget Grandma's words when she found out.

"Don't drink vinegar, it'll thin your blood."

Then she told me to get help from our next-door neighbors, "Go ask Crawfords if they'll give us some water."

Every Saturday I took a bath at Uncle Frank and Aunt Jo's. They lived in town, but they never came to visit. I think they were embarrassed by our living conditions and just wanted to stay away. Except for Florence Savage, Uncle Frank and Aunt Jo were my grandmother's only relatives living in Chagrin Falls. But her youngest daughter, Lagoldendrina (Goldie) Bywaters, lived nearby in Mayfield Heights.

Grandma suffered through the hardships without complaining or blaming anyone. Her inability to care for me hurt my grandmother more than anything. I could see it in her eyes when she talked. Grandma's words, barely heard through her crackling voice, comforted me.

"Everything will be all right, Gary."

Actually, I survived my misfortunes well; I stole candy bars, packaged food that would fit into my pockets, fruit from trees and bushes, garden vegetables and money. Sometimes Grandma encouraged it, other times I just knew I had to do it.

One day when our food supply ran low, my grandmother asked, "Is Crawford's car in the driveway?"

Since our home had no windows, I became Grandma's eyes and ears. We lived back by the woods, right next to Crawford's large vegetable garden.

"Yeah, Grandma," I responded.

"Wait till their car is gone and then go to the garden and fill up that grocery bag," said Grandma.

I watched Crawford's driveway and looked for their car. When they left I made my raid. Even though we didn't have a stove to cook on, we had fresh and free vegetables. We ate the tomatoes like apples. At the age of seven I became a master of survival.

"Gary, when you were here the other day, did you see a five dollar bill anywhere? It was on that table over there," said Bee Crawford, my friend Lee's mother, as she pointed to an end table next to the couch.

"No," I responded.

"Are you sure you didn't see the money?" Then Bee hesitated, looked at me and said, "Did you take the money?"

"I didn't take it," I said.

Even though Bee knew the truth, I wouldn't admit guilt. It would be embarrassing and I would have to give the money back. I had already given the five-dollar bill to Grandma and told her I found it. Actually, I did find five dollars once, but I kept the money on that occasion.

The food shortage kept getting worse, and to my knowledge Grandma received no medical treatment from doctors or any health officials. But because of her toughness and her conditioning to hard times, she never gave up fighting the cancer.

For most of our meals, we ate bologna or peanut butter sandwiches, and sometimes just plain bread. Despite my meager existence I never felt deprived. When I got hungry everything tasted delicious, especially milk, which we didn't have very often. Besides being expensive, it didn't keep in Grandma's sometimes ice-less icebox.

Before my grandmother became bedridden we would occasionally be invited to Aunt Goldie's for Sunday dinner. My mother's sister probably made the dinner arrangements with Grandma through the mail. I don't remember Goldie or my mother ever coming to visit Grandma, only my brother, Kenny.

Aunt Goldie and Uncle Harold would drive to the top of the hill a couple hundred feet from our home and beep for Grandma to come to the car so they could take us to their house for dinner. They waited in the car, and sometimes Grandma struggled to get there. With my right arm reaching up for Grandma's waistline and her left arm draped around my shoulders, I remember slowly walking to the car. When her condition worsened, we walked slower and slower.

Bill Kelley never got invited to Goldie's for dinner with Grandma and me. Aunt Goldie blamed Bill for Grandma's poverty-stricken environment and therefore she cruelly excluded him from the privilege of a hot meal.

Grandma and I always looked forward to the occasional Sunday afternoon hot meal at Aunt Goldie's. My mouth watered just thinking about the delicious food. It almost rivaled the memorable meal with blackberry pie that I had enjoyed on High Street. The anticipation of a delicious meal heightened when Grandma and I walked through the back door of my aunt and uncle's one-story, framed home on Lander Road. The heavenly experience of smelling and seeing hot mashed potatoes, meat and vegetables, bread and butter, milk, and green olives is impossible to describe.

Outside of the few hot meals at Aunt Goldie's, the adults in our family turned their backs on Grandma. I have always felt that if my grandmother had money, people in my family would have been falling all over her. But because of her destitution she would never be able to help them financially, so they were content to see her suffer.

The spirit of Christianity did not find its way to my family. Most of my family, including myself at this stage of my life, never saw the inside of a church and thus never knew about the teachings of Jesus. I never saw Grandma attend church, but family members told me that she had once been a devout Catholic, having gotten her religion from her mother, Kathleen O'Brien, an Irish immigrant.

I never went to church with Grandma or anybody else, and I don't remember her going to church. But Chagrin Falls didn't have a Catholic Church during the 1940s anyway. The nearest Catholic Church, St. Rita's in Solon, was about five miles away. I don't remember, but she may have ridden to Solon with her sister-in-law, Aunt Jo, to attend mass.

It probably explains why no pastors came to our house to visit, to pray for my grandmother or to bring food, a Christian thing to do when somebody is going through such horrendous suffering. Had they known about Grandma's suffering, they probably would have helped.

My Aunt Goldie, who scorns Catholicism, later in life claimed that Grandma converted to an Episcopalian, which I find hard to believe. St. Martin's Episcopal Church along with St. Joan of Arc Catholic Church established their parishes in Chagrin Falls in the 1950s, well after my grandma's death in 1948. If she became Episcopalian, I'd like to know with whom she went to church, when and where. I think my aunt made this up because of her anti-Catholic sentiments. Her hate for the Catholic Church was never more offensive to me than in later life when she said, "Your grandmother left the Catholic Church and became Episcopalian because the priests and nuns were having sex."

In school, the ways that I differed from the other kids became increasingly more obvious. My second grade classmates were clean, cheerful and wore different clothes each day. Most of the other children lived in nice houses and had moms and dads. They were brighter, more attentive and seemed to like school. Much of my time in school I daydreamed about food, what I would do after school, and the tribulations faced by my grandmother. I also daydreamed about the great outdoors, animals and sports.

My second grade teacher, Mrs. Maiden, was older, taller and stricter than my first grade teacher. She was very businesslike and intolerant of children that were not achievers, and she did not like my continual habit of daydreaming. One day Mrs. Maiden angrily took me out in the hallway away from the other kids. I didn't know what I had done wrong until she started lashing out at me.

"Why don't you take a bath and put on clean clothes? You wear the same dirty clothes every day and you smell awful! You are a disgrace to the other children! You never have your lessons done! You don't pay attention. What am I going to do with you?" vocalized Mrs. Maiden, while pointing her finger at me in an intimidating manner.

Several fifth graders passing by glanced over and then turned away, pretending not to be interested in the tirades of Mrs. Maiden.

I had never seen Mrs. Maiden so upset. Speechless and terrified, I hung my head in shame. For the first time, I had been singled out as unacceptable. I didn't tell Grandma about the incident; she could do nothing to change my environment and lack of motivation in school. Besides, I rationalized, Mrs. Maiden will get angry with me again, because there will be other times when I won't have enough water to wash the dirt off of my hands and face.

Despite the unpleasantness of my school experiences and living conditions, I found a way to cope with my adversity.

When I wasn't taking care of my grandmother, I retreated to the outdoors. I would sometimes play with my next-door neighbor and only friend, Lee Crawford, but usually I played by myself. I took hikes in the woods and did normal boyish things. Climbing trees, throwing stones, and following the creek to the river became my favorite pastimes. I drank water from the "crick," tried to catch butterflies, and pretended to be an explorer lost in a sacred wooded wonderland that only I had ever seen.

The trips in the woods and the games that I played alone during my growing up years kept my spirits alive. I created the games and made up the rules. A common thread ran through all the games that I played; there had to be a winner and a loser. My competitive instincts helped form my character and became the stepping-stones of my hopes and dreams. The only thing I thought about or cared about was winning. It didn't matter what I was doing, picking cherries, killing mosquitoes or throwing snowballs at trees; in the games that I played, both real and imaginary, I created a competitive atmosphere that emphasized winning.

One of my games involved throwing stones and rocks at designated targets. Sticks floating down the river became enemy ships. I had to get a direct hit in order to sink the ship and win the battle. If the enemy got down the river unscathed, they won the battle and there would be an ensuing battle. Whoever won the most battles won the war. Meanwhile, so that I could play by myself and not get bored, I played modified versions of football and baseball, my two favorite sports during this time period.

When I came inside from playing my imaginary games, Grandma would ask, "What were you doing outside, Gary?"

"Just playing," seemed to be my usual response, and then I would ask, "Do you need help with anything, Grandma, or can I go back outside and play?"

"Go outside and play and have fun, Grandma will be fine. You go ahead and play," Grandma would say.

I knew she was trying to be nice and I also knew that she just didn't seem right. I worried about Grandma, but I didn't want her to know that I worried about her. I went out to play and tried to erase her sickness from my mind. When I left Grandma alone I wanted her to be all right, but nothing could have been further from the truth. To my knowledge, not only did she not receive medical attention, I don't remember ever giving her pills of any kind. But maybe Bill had given her pain pills, or other medication that I didn't know about.

Outside of our home, I played my imaginary baseball and football games in a sloping field that served as our front yard. I used sticks and stones for bats and balls and a tied up rag or an imaginary ball, for a football. I played the games with enthusiasm and imagination, imitating both teams and adding excitement by announcing the game. When playing football, the ground became my companion at the end of each play. I mimicked the ball carrier, quarterback, receiver, and tackler. When the snows came I threw snowballs at trees. A direct hit on a tree represented a completed pass. I pretended to be involved in the most important football game ever played. Football, especially in the snow, had an exciting and magical effect on me.

I'm not sure if I played these games as an escape from the harsh reality of my environment or just because I loved them. My deepest feelings are that I would have played them even if my environment had been different; most boys like competition, athleticism and achievement. I would have used real footballs, baseballs, bats and BB guns, and I may have had more friends to play with, but the instincts for playing undoubtedly would have been the same. Of course, necessity being the mother of invention, I might not have been as creative if things had been normal.

I had only been to a few movies, but the newsreels of football games were worth the price of admission. I didn't know that players wore shoulder pads. I thought they hunched their shoulders to look big and tough. My favorite teams always won the imaginary games; Ohio State crushed Michigan, and Notre Dame rolled over every opponent. Next to Ohio State, Army and Navy, I liked The Irish of Notre Dame because they always had such powerful teams. Those were the teams along with Michigan that I heard about most often, and sometimes saw in the newsreels. As I grew older, Georgia Tech and Maine got added to my list of favorite teams because I liked their fight songs and Oregon State because I liked the sound of their name. Also Oregon State's colors, orange and black were the same as the Chagrin Falls Tigers.

I liked the Buckeyes the best, but the brigades of midshipmen and cadets marching and rallying themselves for battle on the gridiron sent goose bumps up and down my spine.

Many times in my imaginary games the two service academies squared off against each other and usually fought to a tie. From 1947 through the next seven years of my life I played and announced imaginary games, especially football. I tried to model myself after the athletes and sports announcers. The following is a reconstructed rendition of the last minute of college football's greatest and most traditional rivalry, the Army-Navy game.

"Army has the ball on Navy's one yard line. The score is tied, 27-27. Both teams are undefeated. There's less than a minute left. The Cadets led by Blanchard and Davis, have taken the ball all the way down the field. It's fourth down. Army's great team comes up to the line. Navy's pride and courage will try to stop the Army team. A Navy player yells out, 'If we're strong and brave, we'll stop them, just like we stopped the Japanese.' Doc Blanchard plows into the line. Billy O'Brien, a Navy player from Chagrin Falls, Ohio, flies like superman over the Army line throwing Blanchard for a loss. But wait, there's time for one Navy play. The Navy quarterback goes back to pass. It's the Statue of Liberty play. Bulldog Benson breaks into the open field. Joe Perini, a brave Army player, comes out of nowhere to make the tackle. The game is over! Folks, this game will go down in history as one of the greatest football games of all time! It's Army 27, Navy 27!"

"On brave old Army team, on through the fray, fight on to victory, for that's the fearless Army way.

"Anchors away my boy, anchors away, cheer Navy down the field and sink the Army sink the Army gray!"

I also imitated the Chagrin Falls Tigers; in my imagination, the Tigers always steam-rolled their opponents, Solon, Orange and Mayfield, the teams I heard adults talking about. In post-war Chagrin Falls, like other small towns across the country, football represented the main cultural event. Tiger football games brought the community together and established a common bond of spirit and pride.

In 1947, the Tigers were unbeaten. I felt proud of their greatness, even though I never saw them play. They were legendary in the village of Chagrin Falls. Some day, I wanted to be part of a great team like the 1947 Chagrin Falls Tigers. The names of some players from that team are still special to me . . . Danciu, Skeel, Miraglia, Green, Smith, and the Plazak brothers, one of which died fighting for his country on the battlefields of Korea.

Paul Brown and the Cleveland Browns did not become favorites of mine until the 1948 season. I couldn't listen to games at home because we didn't have a battery radio. Occasionally I would hear portions of a football or baseball game at Aunt Jo's or at a neighbor's house.

Harry S. Truman, our President in 1948, became our Commander-in-Chief in 1945, near the end of World War II, when Franklin Delano Roosevelt died. President Truman, short in stature, wore a gray ten-gallon hat and glasses, hailed from Missouri, and gave the orders to drop the atomic bombs on the Japanese.

The saddest day of the first eight years of my life occurred in the spring of 1948 when my dear grandmother died. The details of that day have been blocked out of my mind, but I do remember some of my thoughts. Being close to my grandma, I didn't understand why she had gone away forever. I struggled trying to imagine life without her, and I wondered if I would still live with Bill or go somewhere else. What will I do without a mother, a father, a grandmother or a grandfather? Why does everybody else have a family except me?

I remember Grandma praying and talking about God, who seemed to live in the sky. I didn't know what he did up there or how he got there or even if he existed. If God really existed, why would he want to make Grandma sick and take her away from me? Why wouldn't he see to it that I got a real baseball, a bat and maybe even a glove, a real football and some toys like other kids? Why did he make Grandma so poor that we couldn't get enough food to eat? And why did he want me to have parents that drank and fought and hated us kids? And why did he give me a teacher that hated me? And a family that never took me to football games? This attitude, plus the fact that I had never been to church, made me a non-believer, and I would soon be eight years old.

Losing the only person that I loved at this point in my life came as quite a shock, but disappointments and tough times had always shadowed my existence.

At Reed's Funeral Home, I put some second-grade artwork in Grandma's casket, so she would have something to remember me by. Fifty-four years after her death I wrote this poem:

> *I don't know where my Grandma's gone,*
> *a soft wind took her away.*
> *She slid from my grasp like a floating butterfly,*
> *a doe gliding gracefully through the woods,*
> *a rabbit's scurry to the briar patch.*
> *Gone from my sight like the leaves and the snow,*
> *the sunset, and the soft summer rain.*
> *Like the birds and the clouds,*
> *she's now just a memory in my mind.*
> *Wasn't it just yesterday that she was smiling,*
> *and laughing and dreaming and loving.*
> *She's gone like the sand, the dust, and the tide,*
> *to be replaced by the fresh and the new.*
> *I don't know where my grandma's gone.*

Chapter III
A Boy on the Move

My less than two year impoverished existence came to an end with Grandma's death.

"You're going to be staying with the Davises across the road. I can't take care of you here," Bill Kelley told me.

In retrospect, my assumption is that Florence Davis stepped in and offered to take care of me when Grandma died.

I didn't know the Davises very well, but Florence Davis had always been nice to me, and I dreamed of playing with their English springer spaniel, Tippy. I didn't know Florence's husband Stanley or Grandma Davis (Agnes), Stanley's mother, the live-in owner of their old farmhouse. I had never spoken to Stanley and Grandma Davis and had only seen them a few times.

Living with the Davises transformed me. I had plenty of food to eat, wore clean clothes to school, took baths at home, and became a lot warmer on winter nights. Davises' turn-of-the-century farmhouse had a coal-burning furnace, a cellar, electricity, a bathroom and a radio.

Having a radio fascinated me the most. I listened to football and baseball games and some of the programs that were popular when I lived with my parents. Three songs I especially remember hearing and liking when I lived with the Davises in 1948: *Buttons and Bows, Dear Hearts and Gentle People,* and *Doin' What Comes Natur'ally.*

The Davises were not the typical Chagrin Falls family. Stanley Davis drove a truck, a big tractor-trailer rig for General Electric, and by Chagrin Falls' standards they lived in a somewhat shabby house. But to me, after living in a one-room shack, their house seemed like a mansion.

The Davises' seven room, two-story house had a screened-in porch overlooking the back yard. Directly behind the house, about a hundred feet away stood a barn that had been converted into a garage, and beyond that, a chicken coop. To the north a few hundred yards away sat the hilly woods. A rushing creek separated a nearby sloping field from the woods on Davises' 18 acres.

My new home seemed exciting and wonderful, but I needed to make certain adjustments for my survival. Florence Davis was a warm and caring person and treated me like a son, and Tippy and I became instant buddies. But even though the chemistry flowed between Florence and me, it never did with Stanley or Grandma Davis.

"Get away from those pies; they're too hot to cut, let alone eat!" snarled Grandma Davis.

"I'll call you, Gary, when they cool off and are ready to eat," said Florence.

"I wish he'd get out of here and go outside or somewhere. There's lots of work to be done around here. He shouldn't be eatin' any pie anyway, whyyy that'll ruin his supper!" cackled Grandma Davis to Florence, loudly and clearly so that I could hear.

"Not with Gary's appetite; he's hungry all the time," interjected Florence, with a glance and a smile.

Always wanting to get in the last word, Grandma Davis spoke, "He'd eat a whole pie if you'd let him!"

"Goddamn knucklehead would eat every one of those pies if you'd let'im," chipped in Stanley as he entered the room. Then he blurted out his patented half sarcastic laugh, "Ha! Ha!" and directed a question to me, "Why the hell don't you do some work around here?"

The pleasant smells of Davises' kitchen overrode any harassment that could be thrown at me. The appetizing smells surpassed the food at Aunt Goldie's, or even the famous High Street meal that I fondly remember. The real difference at the Davises' centered on Florence and Grandma Davis always cooking good food. The drifting sensual smells of homemade bread, fresh fried eggs from the henhouse, dumplings, pot roasts, and fruit pies cooling on top of the stove, made inhaling a heavenly experience.

Florence and Grandma Davis never baked one or two pies at a time. When the rhubarb, raspberries, blackberries, strawberries, cherries and peaches were harvested in the summer, and apples in the fall, Florence and Agnes baked three to five pies at a time. They usually gave one or two pies to their relatives and froze one or two.

Whatever fruits didn't go into pies, including gooseberries and currants, were canned for the winter, and stored in the cellar, a dark area off of the basement that had a firmly packed dirt floor. The Davises used glass mason jars covered with wax for the preserves, jams and jellies and larger glass jars for the garden vegetables. They used larger glass jars to can the vegetables from their half-acre garden.

There were several things that the Davises, victims of the Great Depression, didn't have to buy. Besides growing fruit and garden vegetables, and raising chickens, they made bread and sauerkraut. During hunting season when Stanley bagged ducks and pheasants, less money needed to be spent on meat products.

My room sat right next to Stanley's gunroom, convenient if my masculine eight-year-old body ever had to shoot an intruder. The painted walls of my bedroom had little or no insulation. When the temperatures dipped into the 20s, ice formed on the inside of the windows. The creaky, dark brown wooden floor reminded me of the bedroom on High Street where my brothers and I slept. Having a double bed to myself, covered with a thick quilt stuffed with feathers that Florence made, seemed like pure luxury. The bedroom overlooked the field, the woods, and the creek. It faced the northern sky where Lake Erie lay, 20 miles away.

In June of 1948, after a few weeks living at the Davises', the school year ended, and I got my second grade report card. Mrs. Maiden passed me to the third grade probably because she wanted to get rid of me or maybe deep down she felt sorry for me because of my bout with poverty, and the death of my grandmother.

The highlight of the summer of 1948 happened one July evening, the same year the Cleveland Indians defeated the Boston Braves in the World Series. I saw my first major league baseball game, a night game at Municipal Stadium. Florence, Bee, Lee and I watched Gene Bearden pitch a 2-0 shutout against the Chicago White Sox. The excitement of being at a major league game, especially a Cleveland Indians' game is indescribable. In awe of my experience, not wanting to leave the stadium when the game ended, for several minutes I stood and gazed at the field.

Besides the Indians winning the World Series in 1948, the Browns won the American Football Conference title and the Cleveland Barons, a professional hockey franchise, joined the parade of championship Cleveland teams. With all three professional teams winning titles in 1948, around the sports world Cleveland had a new title: The City of Champions.

When the school year began in 1948 I soon proved worthy of being in the third grade. The quality of my school experience turned completely around. I even got A's in two subjects, writing and spelling. My third grade teacher, Miss Lemmer, deserves the credit for my academic turn-around. She had a pleasant demeanor, a positive attitude, and her learn-by-doing approach made school fun and meaningful.

"Everyone will help build a Pueblo Indian village. We will learn how these southwest Indian people lived," said Miss Lemmer.

Despite having an ancestor (my great-grandfather) that fought in the Indian Wars, Miss Lemmer instilled in me a respect for Native Americans that I have maintained my entire life. Their history and culture is interesting and meaningful. Currently on trips out West, I visit historical Native American landmarks, reservations and trading posts.

My father paid an unexpected visit during my short stay with the Davises in 1948. He called and asked if I could meet him privately out by the mailbox, a ploy that allowed him not to have to come face to face with the Davises.

When I saw my father he looked the same as he had two years earlier when we lived together. He continued his habits of wearing neatly pressed clothes, keeping his face clean-shaven, and not being able to force a smile. With no pats on the back, handshakes or hugs, he began speaking when he was several feet away, "There's something I want to tell you."

I had mixed emotions about seeing my father; I didn't miss him or my mother. Still, I remember his words as if he had spoken them yesterday. When I grew older, I realized that his words didn't sound like something a father would say to an eight-year-old son.

"I came to say goodbye. I'll probably never see you again. You be a good boy," he said.

When my father slowly walked away, tears began trickling down my cheeks. I stood and watched him because I had difficulty swallowing his words. The thoughts raced through my mind that I would never see him again.

After taking several steps, he turned to see if I still remained and repeated the words, "You be a good boy."

My father may have been gone forever, but I became accustomed to disappointments. And since eight-year-olds have short attention spans, his departure and words of farewell only bothered me the rest of the day. I had other things in my life to worry about, such things as playing with Tippy, wondering what time we would eat supper, and strategizing my next hike in the woods with Tip. Most importantly, I worried about getting along with Stanley and Grandma Davis so that I could continue having a roof over my head.

At the time, I didn't realize the physical differences between my father and me, as I did when I grew older: I became a much bigger person than he; his brown hair and fair skin was distinctly different from my dark hair, and my skin turned mahogany in the sunshine. My father's features were much like Kenny and George's and very different from mine. Amazingly, my mother's father looked like he had come from the same genetic pool as my father, Kenny and George. All of them were small in stature and had similar features.

A few months after my father's farewell, my life would change again. In January of 1949, halfway through the third grade my brief stay with the Davises came to an end.

"Gary, your Aunt Goldie wants you to come and live with her. She will take good care of you," Florence said.

"I can't stay here anymore? Will I ever see you and Tippy again?" I asked.

"Oh yes," Florence said as she hugged me, attempting to contain her emotions.

I only lived with the Davises for a few months, but I had grown to really like Florence and Tippy. But, I figured living with my aunt and uncle might even be better. I knew for sure that they liked dogs and horses, and my cousin Susan was only a few months younger than me.

My aunt and uncle's small, one-story framed house had a living room, kitchen, three small bedrooms, a basement and an unattached one-car garage; it was the same home on Lander Road in Mayfield Heights where Grandma and I had occasionally gone to for Sunday dinner.

When I went to live with Goldie and Harold I thought that they were just being nice and wanted to take care of me. I found out quickly that my aunt had a different objective; she planned to move me along as quickly as possible. I had no idea where my next home would be, and my aunt didn't give any clues.

The warning signal went up when Aunt Goldie wouldn't allow me to go to school. Every morning from the front window I watched Susan, a second grader, cross the road and walk to school.

"Aunt Goldie, will I ever be able to go to school like Susan?" I asked.

"You're not going to be here that long. I have to get some things worked out and then you'll be leaving. It's really your mother's responsibility to take care of you," said Aunt Goldie.

"Why couldn't I stay at Florence's?" I asked.

"Ohhh I don't know, but Florence isn't your mother either," countered Goldie.

"But I don't want to live with my mother," I said.

"Oh, you won't be living with your mother. Nobody knows where she is. She doesn't want to take care of you or your brothers," said Aunt Goldie.

35

"I can't take care of you here, either," continued Aunt Goldie. "We have such a small place here and Harold has an awful drinking problem. We can't afford much of anything because of him."

I wondered why she took me from the Davises' in the first place. I also wondered where my next home would be. My aunt made it clear that I would be leaving, but didn't give me any clues where I would be going or when.

Being an eight-year-old, I could not read the minds of adults, but as I grew older Aunt Goldie's motives were easy to figure out. It's conjecture, but I believe she brought charges against my parents for child neglect thinking she could get welfare money for taking care of me or possibly she tried to use me to get money a different way, maybe from a source that I did not know about. My guess is, when Goldie discovered her scheme wasn't working, she decided to give me up. Maybe she convinced Florence that she had my best interests in mind. Of course, the other possibility is that Stanley and his mother may have lobbied for my departure.

Nevertheless, I learned very quickly not to like or trust Aunt Goldie as much as my grandmother and Florence, but I did like her better than my mother and father. One thing I didn't like was Aunt Goldie's relentless attacks on Uncle Harold over his drinking problems, and the way she always made fun of him. He always seemed like such a nice man. I don't recall ever seeing him drink and I certainly never saw him drunk. But if Aunt Goldie said these things, there must be something to it. A laid-back southern gentleman, my uncle's personality allowed him to cope with my aunt's verbal abuse. My well-liked native Virginian uncle happened to be married to a very strange woman.

Aunt Goldie passed her time by telling ghost stories.

"When Harold and I lived in Cleveland, we used to hear chains rattling in the basement. Harold didn't want to go down and see what was down there, but one night he did. He came back and said he didn't see or hear anything," Aunt Goldie said.

Aunt Goldie was smiling and laughing as she rambled on, "Of course he didn't see anything. Ghosts are invisible! They can see you but you can't see them unless it's the dead coming back. My mother came back to see me you know. She stood at the foot of my bed and kept repeating my name softly, 'Goldie, Goldie, Goldie!'"

If Aunt Goldie wanted to scare me, she accomplished her objective. Sometimes I would lie awake at night scared shitless, wondering if ghosts would come in my room and spook me. I remember hiding under the sheets hoping the ghosts would not come, or would go to Susan's room instead.

When Aunt Goldie would talk about the supernatural, Uncle Harold's body language told it all; he just shook his head from side to side.

"Just because you haven't seen ghosts and talked with the dead doesn't mean anything," Aunt Goldie said to Uncle Harold.

When Aunt Goldie got on the ghost story bandwagon it made me think back to something very bizarre that happened in Virginia. It gave Aunt Goldie's belief in the supernatural some credibility. This event occurred on a horse estate near Danville, Virginia, when I was four or five years old. The Palmers and Bywaters went to Virginia because of my father and Uncle Harold's job–working with thoroughbred horses. Uncle Harold was back at home in the beautiful, mountainous countryside of southwest Virginia.

One afternoon the Palmers and Bywaters, and the people who owned the estate gathered in the living quarters. The room, larger than any I had ever seen, had a large fireplace made out of stone.

My brother George ran over to the fireplace looked up the long chimney and then scurried away. He acted startled by what he had seen.

"The devil's at the top of that chimney! Gary, look up that chimney and you'll see the devil," George said after he got as far away from the chimney as he could.

Several people in the room began laughing and encouraging me to look up at the devil. Afraid at first, my curiosity and the constant encouragement, especially from George, got the best of me. I crept over to the fireplace and poked my head inside the chimney and looked straight up, directly into the eyes of Satan. The devil's face, one of the most recognizable in the world, appeared at the top of that chimney looking straight down at me. George, Kenny and some of the adults in the room had me convinced that I saw Satan. My imagination played tricks on me, or did it? In retrospect, someone may have placed a painting of the devil's face in the chimney.

"He's there! He's there! I saw the devil! I saw the devil! The devil's there! I saw him!" I said in a frenzied and frightened way, scared out of my wits.

"We told you he was there," George said as the room broke into laughter.

To several people scaring a little boy was funny and cute. By age 13, I could have whipped anybody in that room, including Satan.

On that Virginia trip, tragedy struck the horse estate where we stayed. The stables burned to the ground. Men battled the blazes with hoses and buckets of water in a desperate attempt to save the horses. From a window of the house, I watched the roaring fire. Some of the horses died a terrible death in the inferno. I knew many of the horses by name, and had been hoisted into the saddle of one of the mares that perished in the fire.

After the stable fire I'll never forget what Aunt Goldie said to me, "Maybe you did see the devil."

Quite possibly the stable fire may be responsible for a lifelong obsession that I have with matches and certain other things. I can't stand to touch or be around matches; if they are near food I completely withdraw from eating. I have the same obsession with pencils and certain types of pens that other people have touched. If I touch these items for any reason, I have a compulsion to immediately wash my hands.

In the 1950s in Chagrin Falls people burned their trash. Burning the trash became my least favorite chore. I always ran in the house and thoroughly washed my hands after burning the trash in the old rusted round barrel out by the orchard. It's only speculation, but the Virginia stable fire in 1944 or 1945 may have been the catalyst for my obsession with matches and things that were burning.

As for the pens and pencils, in the ninth grade, someone accidentally stabbed me with a pencil in shop class. It left a small black mark on the palm of my left hand, but I'm not convinced the stabbing accident had anything to do with my pens and pencils obsession. During my school years I had a sickening feeling whenever I saw pen or pencil marks on people's skin. Occasionally, it accidentally happened to me and I would rush to the boys' room and scrub it off. I don't recall it happening, but possibly someone wrote on me as a child, or maybe on my mother.

I remember the fire vividly, but I do not remember two other Virginia stories that my aunt told me.

"We realized that you were gone and everyone went looking for you. We came across a well somewhere in the woods and we thought you fell in the well because you didn't answer our calls. We couldn't find you anywhere. We finally found you but you scared a lot of people," said Goldie, then she paused and continued.

"On that same Virginia trip, I saved your life. You ran in front of a car. I ran out and knocked you down, away from the car. Both of us nearly got killed!"

Nobody else has ever confirmed that these two claims by Aunt Goldie actually happened. She may have made them up to make herself a heroine, especially the one about saving my life.

On January 10, 1949, Aunt Goldie filed charges against my mother and father for child neglect, a polite term for abandonment. Being a resident of Cuyahoga County, my aunt turned me over to the social welfare services in Cleveland. The police issued a warrant for my mother and father's arrest.

Initially, the authorities failed to locate my mother; she lived in Cleveland under the alias of Catherine Rink.

On January 28, 1949, in Juvenile Court, my father pleaded guilty to child neglect charges. The courts ordered him to pay twenty dollars twice a month toward my support.

On February 25, the courts caught up with my mother. She pleaded guilty to child neglect charges and received a sentence of 60 days in the county jail. She got a suspended sentence when she chose the option of paying five dollars a week in child support.

I don't remember most things said in Juvenile Court, but I do remember my father saying, "My mother in New Jersey will take care of Gary and raise him."

Kenneth Palmer saying that his mother in New Jersey would take care of me sounded like something that a father would say. Those words echoed in my ears much of my life. More than anything else, it made me realize that Kenneth Palmer, despite our obvious differences, could be my father after all. Why would Kenneth Palmer want his mother to raise me if I were not his son?

I remember the judge's response to Kenneth Palmer's request, "Gary is a ward of the state of Ohio. Under law he cannot leave Ohio."

I found out later in life that Florence Davis had been in juvenile court through all of the proceedings. The obvious question remains, why didn't she try to get me back? I strongly feel that she wanted to, but the resistance from Stanley and Grandma Davis overrode her. I remember later in life Stanley eluding to the fact that he hesitated taking me in because, "I didn't know if I could handle you." Understandably, Stan had reason for concern; the mold had been set.

Since no one could or would take care of me, the Juvenile Court judge assigned me to the welfare home in Cleveland. My new place of residence had two departments separated by a hallway: one department for neglected, homeless, or abandoned boys, and other for delinquent boys. When I arrived, the homeless section that some people called the orphanage had no vacant bunks.

"You'll be staying on the other side (Detention Home) until we have room for you over here," said one of the officials.

The person who came for me said, "There's no beds anywhere right now."

"What are we going to do with this boy?" someone else said.

"He's going to have to stay in that solitary that's open until a bunk opens up," an official commented.

I spent a couple of days and nights in the solitary cell, but after that my luck ran out again. The orphanage section of the children's home had no room for me. I got assigned to the Detention Home section of the welfare facility commonly referred to as the "other side."

The U-shaped two-story brick building had a fenced in playground located between the orphanage section and the Detention Home. Black vertical iron bars kept us from the outside world. We lived in a large barracks-type room with bunk beds and a footlocker. A large shower area, several sinks, a urinal, and a few private stall toilets sat next to our living quarters. We ate cafeteria style and most of the time the food tasted good.

I learned very quickly about living in a communal setting with juvenile delinquent kids and even colored boys, who were definitely in the minority at the Detention Home. The first person that I met in the DH, an overweight ten-year-old colored boy named Bailey, hit me like a ton of bricks because I didn't know anything about colored boys.

"How old are you and why you in here, boy?" said Bailey.

"I'm eight and my mother and father can't take care of me. Why are you in here, boy?" I asked, letting Bailey know that I caught on quickly to saying boy.

"I ran away from home and my parents don't want me back. Y'all must have done somethin' bad to get in here with us," said Bailey.

"They didn't have room for me on the other side," I responded.

"But wait a minute boy, you had to be bad to be put in here with us. We all bad boys!" said Bailey, before continuing.

"Besides, eight year olds aren't supposed to be in here. We all nine and ten."

"I stole things when I lived with my grandmother. Maybe that's why they put me in here," I responded.

"Why you lookin' at me like dat? Ain't you ever saw a Negro?" asked Bailey.

"I saw em' before, one or two times, but I never talked to any and I never heard em' called Negroes," I said.

"Yeah I know what you heard us called, we called everything–niggers, colored boys, burrheads, coons, jungle bunnies, everything. I know white folks think our color will rub off on y'all!" said Bailey, with a slight smile.

"I don't think it'll rub off! You're jist tryin' to be funny," I said.

Bailey touched his arm to mine and tried very hard to avoid laughing.

"Look, you gonna be a nigger!" said Bailey, pointing at my arm.

I looked at my arm to make sure it had not turned black. Bailey laughed like I had never seen anybody laugh before. First he bent over and almost fell down, then he raised his arms up in the air as if he wanted the whole world to know what had just happened. He got the attention of almost the entire Detention Home.

I noticed some differences between the white and the colored kids. Most of the Negroes were louder and they smelled different than the white kids, especially when they worked up a sweat. I never liked to get too close to them when they were sweating. I didn't realize it back then, but we white boys must have smelled awful to them too.

I noticed on the playground how fast some of the colored kids could run, but Bailey, one of the few colored boys that I could beat in a race, couldn't run a lick. And man, did some of those colored boys have hard heads. I knocked heads with one kid on the playground and saw stars; the colored boy acted like it didn't even faze him. But it didn't matter how somebody smelled, the color of their skin, how fast they could run, or the hardness of their heads; I could relate to the colored kids because of their poor backgrounds. I also understood them when I heard them talk about parents that didn't want to take care of them.

Most of the colored kids seemed friendly and fun to be around. They laughed at almost anything and they didn't seem to mind being black or being in the Detention Home. They just rolled with the punches and made the best of it, just like I did.

I asked some of the colored kids why they were there. I remember two responses.

"I stabbed my mother with a butcher knife, but I didn't do it on purpose," one kid said.

"I stole my uncle's car. I was gonna bring it back but I knew if I did, dat man (uncle) would kill me," said another.

When it came to talking, laughing and having fun, Bailey wore the crown as the prince of the Detention Home. I could never understand why his parents wouldn't take him back after he ran away. He seemed like such a nice kid—conniving, mischievous, always up to something, but nice.

Although most of the kids were friendly, some were antagonistic. Being

41

new and younger, I had to do something to prove myself in order to gain respect. A small growth of skin about the size of a piece of macaroni that I had since birth contributed to my susceptibility. It hung in front of my left ear and flopped every time my head moved. By the time I entered the Detention Home the piece of skin had grown to about three quarters of an inch long and continued to grow in proportion to my body. In the summer of 1949 at the same time that I had tonsillectomy surgery the growth was surgically removed.

The nurses that tended to me at Lakeside Hospital could not have been nicer. In retrospect, I think they felt sorry for me because I came from the welfare home and did not have any visitors during my stay in the hospital. I didn't have a guardian, but somebody in my family had to give their approval to the surgery, probably Aunt Goldie. I didn't expect any visitors when I was in the hospital, and the way the nurses treated me, I didn't need any. They won my heart over when they brought me ice cream after the surgery, and then granted me a wish.

"If you had one wish, what would it be?" asked one of the nurses.

It was a question that would only be asked to a younger boy and I responded like a younger boy, "Could I listen to the Cleveland Indians' game on the radio?" I asked.

Almost immediately, a nurse brought me something I had never seen before, a very small radio with headphones. But I felt happy that I had a chance to listen to Jack Graney and Jimmy Dudley broadcast the defending World Champion Cleveland Indians' baseball game. I also remember switching stations between innings during the Erin Brew commercials, and hearing one of my favorite songs, *Buttons and Bows*.

Getting that piece of skin removed improved my self-esteem. Sometimes I got into several fights over my "earring," as some kids called it.

The first fight in my new environment resulted after a brief argument; it occurred before the surgery. My front tooth got chipped and my mouth was bloodied when I got slammed against a bunk bed in the large barracks-type room. I'm not sure who won the fight, but not backing down against one of the white boy bullies caused me to have more friends when it ended.

In June of 1949, I turned nine, and only in retrospect do I recall that no one visited, called, sent a card, or made a cake for me. Being nine and equal in age to some of the other boys made my birthday a happy one.

Mandatory church attendance at my new place of residence did not stand in good favor with me, but many kids wanted me to attend chapel with them.

"Are you Protestant or Catholic?" asked one of the officials.

"I don't know," I said.

"You have to be one or the other," said the official.

I never heard the words Catholic or Protestant before. I did not have the slightest idea what they meant, and except for my grandmother, I had never lived with anyone long enough to get established in a church. Besides, I had such a non-believer attitude that I thought if God favors one of these religions, then maybe I should join the other.

My Protestant friends said, "Be Protestant," so I could attend chapel with them.

My Catholic friends said, "Be Catholic," for the same reason.

The authorities contacted Aunt Goldie and asked her about my religion. My family had both Catholic and Protestant roots, but mostly they subscribed to no religion. Aunt Goldie didn't have a religion, even though she considered herself a Protestant, which seemed to be a common practice for people not affiliated with a religion. Aunt Goldie told the Detention Home authorities that I should be considered a Protestant. They informed me of my new religion.

Going to chapel became a unique experience for me because I had never been to church and I didn't believe in God. But I did believe in two people that came to see me, Florence Davis and Bee Crawford. They didn't come during visiting hours. The two ladies from Chagrin Falls just popped in whenever they could. It seemed obvious they felt sorry about my plight. In fact, they may have been more upset about my fate than I was. My life had always been a struggle; I rolled with the punches, figuratively and literally, and carried on. Besides, the Detention Home didn't seem that awful; three squares a day and a warm bed, and I got used to having juvenile delinquents and colored boys as friends.

One day I noticed Bee and Florence standing behind the locked gate at the end of the playground, waving and smiling. I went over to the gate and said, "Hi." Due to shyness and nervousness, that's all I said. They just smiled and asked how I had been doing, and then someone came and got me. Bee and Florence stood by the gate outside the black vertical iron bars that surrounded the playground, and watched me play. I kept glancing over and wondering why they came to see me. When recess ended, Florence and Bee slowly walked away.

On another occasion I looked through the windows of the two-story building where I lived. I saw Florence and Bee standing and looking up, outside of the high-wired fence that surrounded the Detention Home as if they knew my exact location. When they spotted me, they began waving and smiling. I waived back and watched them for several minutes. I can clearly see the images of Bee and Florence standing outside the security fences of the Detention Home in the summer of 1949; it's an image that I have carried with me an entire lifetime.

I wanted to go talk with them, but I couldn't. We could only talk with outsiders during visiting hours. But Florence and Bee's presence brought hope and joy to my life. I could not put into words the feeling that I experienced when they came to see me. They turned out to be the only people that came to visit during my eight-month stay at the Detention Home. Florence and Bee caught me by surprise because I didn't expect any visitors.

When I went to chapel the following Sunday and the minister began talking about Jesus, it got me thinking. All these great things that they claim that this man Jesus Christ did, I wonder if he had anything to do with Florence and Bee coming to see me. Probably not, how would he know about some cruddy third grader like me? Besides he went to places like Jerusalem, Galilee, and Bethlehem. I thought to myself, "How in the hell would he ever be able to find Chagrin Falls or the Detention Home?"

Maybe Jesus couldn't find Chagrin Falls, but he may have found Cleveland. One day during the late summer of 1949, after what seemed like an eternity being locked up, my social worker came to talk with me.

"How would you like to go back and live in Chagrin Falls?" she asked.

I didn't expect to be getting out of the Detention Home, but suddenly I had this wonderful feeling about living with Florence, Stanley and Tippy again. Then my social worker informed me that it wouldn't be the Davises that I would be living with.

"The Crawfords would like you to live with them. They would be your foster parents. What do you think of that?" asked my social worker.

Happy and puzzled, I don't know what I said to my social worker, but I remember my thoughts. Why would the Crawfords who lived next to our shack; the people that I stole money from, want me to live with them? Why didn't Florence want me to live with her again?

It may be conjecture on my part, but I think Florence did want me to live with her, but faced stiff opposition from Stanley and his mother. Florence and Bee both wanted me out of the Detention Home, and since Florence couldn't take me in, Bee stepped forward.

Even though I never stayed anywhere for very long, I remember thinking that maybe this would be different. Disappointed that my friends at the DH had to stay, I said goodbye and told them that I hoped they would get put into foster homes too.

Through the adversity of the children's home came lessons that served me well. I learned that colored kids acted and smelled different than white kids, but are just as human as us, despite what some people thought. I also learned to relate to the colored kids because I had the same concerns and circumstances as they did, mainly poverty and parents not wanting them. I learned to dry between my toes after taking showers and not walk around bare footed after taking showers. Lastly, I learned that because of the adversity that I had already experienced in my life, I could cope with just about anything that people threw at me. I've been on the other side of so many bad fences, nothing will ever seem bad again, at least that's what I thought.

I looked forward to going back to my hometown; playing baseball and football, hiking in the woods, going down to the river, and living in a real house with a family and a dog named Skippy. I felt lucky to have such an opportunity. "The Crawfords are nice people, and Florence and Tippy live right across the road." I felt like the luckiest boy in the world and I didn't want to do anything to screw it up.

Chapter IV
The Crawfords

Coming from the fenced in playground, brick buildings and polluted industrial smells of the city, Chagrin Falls could not have looked more beautiful than it did on that summer day in 1949. Shortly after arriving at Crawfords', I ran down town to see the river and the falls.

The steady waters of the Chagrin River flowed gracefully under Main Street directly through the heart of my hometown to the falls, a beautiful and historical landmark. The river, especially powerful after melting snows and spring rains, empties into a rocky bed below the falls and turns white rippling over rocks as it winds its way past the west edge of town. It felt great to be back home; I remember feeling that I never wanted to leave Chagrin Falls again.

I brought some drawings from the welfare home to show the Crawfords. They were sketches of the buildings and things around the welfare home that someone gave me when I left. I remember my foster brother Lee's fascination over the artwork. He thought it was "neat"–our term for cool back then.

Albert Lee "Butch" Crawford got his nickname from his father because of his haircut. Lee always seemed to have a Butch haircut, short, flat on top and combed up on the sides. Unlike me, Lee looked good with a Butch because he had a round-shaped head.

My new roommate/foster brother and I had many differences: Lee was left handed, a year behind me in school and 15 months younger. He was considerably shorter, and compared to my skinny body, he appeared a little on the chunky side. "Butch" was a better student, but not as good in sports.

Despite our differences the Crawfords warmly welcomed me into their home, and soon Lee and I became much like brothers. We played football, basketball and baseball, rode the fire trucks in parades, and went swimming and hiking together. Lee and I picked blackberries and strawberries and sold them at a stand we set up by the road.

On summer nights when the Cleveland Indians were playing, we went to a neighbor's house to listen to the radio broadcasts of the games. We sat on the porch with Mr. and Mrs. Briggs and listened to the dynamic and legendary

Indians' broadcasters, Jack Graney and Jimmy Dudley. At the end of every broadcast, native Virginian Jimmy Dudley always said the same thing, "So long and lots of good luck, ya' heah!"

Mr. Briggs scored every game in his green Erin Brew scorebook; Erin Brew was one of Cleveland's largest breweries. I still have a scorebook that he gave me from the 1948 season when the Indians won the World Series. Annually, the Briggses went to Tucson to watch the Indians spring training practices and games. Mr. and Mrs. Briggs did not have children of their own, but during my growing up years, they were two of the nicest people that I knew.

Lee and I shared a bedroom adjacent to the living room and right next to John and Bee's bedroom. Because of the smallness of Lee's bedroom, before I moved in, my social worker insisted that bunk beds be installed, an exciting idea to Lee and me. We didn't care about the extra room it gave us, but sleeping in bunk beds added thrills, adventure and excitement to our lives. I'll never forget that first night at the Crawfords'. Bee told us to get our pajamas on so she could tuck us in and we could say our prayers. Nighttime prayers were not an option at the Crawfords', but instead a ritual. Before we said our prayers, we had to get snuggly in bed. The real question of the night and for future nights became an emotional issue, one I will never forget. Who will be the lucky one and get to sleep on top? Being a guest at the Crawfords' and feeling very lucky to be there, I did not want to be choosy about which bed I slept in or about anything else. Whichever bunk Lee decided on, I would gladly slide under the covers of the other bunk.

After Lee and I put our pajamas on and brushed our teeth, I waited for my foster brother to choose which bunk he preferred, and he did so with gusto.

Lee yelled out his preference, "I got the top bunk!"

Then he zoomed up the ladder as if a rat trying to pinch-bite his heels had chased him. When he got to the top he flopped down, acting exhausted from a hard day on the farm. I noticed the mattress sunk down making me think that I would wait each night until Lee landed in his bunk, before I climbed into mine. I didn't want my skinny nine-year-old body to get crunched by a flopping, flying eight-year-old. I especially worried what would happen if Lee came down full-force and landed on my dick and balls; that would really hurt, and then maybe I wouldn't even be able to go to the bathroom.

After I slid into my bottom bunk, I kept looking up, wondering if Lee would start doing bed-bouncing acrobats like my friends at the Detention Home. He seemed unrealistically quiet; I soon found out why when I heard

Bee's soft voice as she entered the room.

"Are you boys ready for your prayers?" she asked.

Oh no, another thing that I wasn't required to do at the DH; say my evening prayers.

Bee, a warm and loving foster mother, taught me *The Lord's Prayer, The 23rd Psalm*, and many other things, some, including the prayers, I never forgot.

"Gary, it's hate not haint. It's spelled H-A-T-E."

"People are healthy. The food that we eat is healthful."

"It's who *art* in heaven, not who *aren't* in heaven. God is really up there."

"I before E, except after C. There are some exceptions to this rule, but I won't confuse you with that right now."

Bee also taught me about hygiene. I remember my gums bleeding when I first lived at the Crawfords'; I wasn't used to brushing my teeth very often or very well. And when I took my first bath at Crawfords', Bee reminded me to wash my penis really well. I told her I never heard it called that before. Having spent eight months in a home for boys, every expletive imaginable had been used to describe the male organ, but "penis" didn't ring a bell.

I learned many things from Bee, but my foster father, John, represented the role model that I desperately needed; I really looked up to John.

John Crawford, a kind and easy-going man grew up in Jewett, a town much smaller than Chagrin Falls. Many of Jewett's residents worked in the steel mills of Steubenville, Ohio, a river town about 20 miles from Jewett. Steubenville and the West Virginia panhandle city of Weirton, another steel town are right across the Ohio River from each other, and are about halfway between Jewett and Pittsburgh.

John, a rather large man at 5'11" and well over 200 pounds worked at the paper mill, The Chase Bag Company, as a foreman. He showed his loyalty to the community through his work as a volunteer fireman and an Emergency Medical Technician. John loved fishing, hunting, bowling, playing cards, clambakes, football, baseball, and a beer with the boys at Racketans'; the same bar that my parents once frequented. John smoked cigars and chewed Mail Pouch tobacco religiously. He could hold a big wad of tobacco in his mouth and still carry on a conversation. I wanted to be a Mail Pouch tobacco chewer just like John when I grew up. I once mimicked him by cramming several pieces of bubble gum into my mouth to get my cheeks puffed out like his; my jaws got real sore.

John, a craftsman with tools and a handyman could build and repair just about anything. He converted the attic portion of the Crawfords' one-story cape-cod style home into a bedroom for boarding. Edna Morris, a boarder at the Crawford's during part of my stay, slept in the newly converted attic bedroom. Sandy, Edna's seven-year-old daughter, lived with her aunt at the time, but eventually moved in with her mother.

Religion surfaced as one of the disciplines I learned from Bee. I attended mandatory Protestant Chapel at the Detention Home, but because of what happened to my grandmother, I still had my doubts about God. However, Bee's strong belief in God had me thinking that our savior Jesus Christ might be for real.

Bee spoke often about predestination; she believed in the teachings of John Calvin and the Presbyterian philosophy that our fate had been laid out for us as part of God's plan. But, since Chagrin Falls had no Presbyterian Church, I became a bible-toting Methodist: "A Baptist that can read" like the Presbyterian minister said in the movie, *A River Runs Through It.*

For Lee and me and most kids in Chagrin Falls, Sunday school and church service were not optional. Dressing up and spending two hours worshiping God became a new experience, and I didn't like it. Everyone looked forward to the half hour break (10:30-11:00), between Sunday school and church service and gathered at the Standard Drugstore on the corner of West Washington and Franklin Street. I liked orange phosphates and fountain cokes, and the seldom-affordable delicious treats: Grilled hamburgers cooked right before your eyes, golden french-fries and extra thick milk shakes.

I remember trying to decide in Sunday school if Jesus could really perform miracles like the Bible taught us. One day in Sunday school I told our teacher, Mrs. Crittenden, "I can walk on water, too...when it's frozen."

Not having to fear low achievement or failure is what I liked most about Sunday school. On the other hand, regular school loomed as a difficult, frightening experience. In the Detention Home, the expectations for achievement had been low, but in Mrs. Ransford's fourth grade class at Chagrin Falls Elementary School, high expectations became the rule. My teacher's straight forward, no nonsense, "You will learn this" approach, woke me up. It made me aware that I had fallen behind when I left Chagrin Falls Schools, nine months earlier, and that I had a lot of catching up to do, especially in reading.

The holiday season, always a welcome relief from the rigors of school, became a special occasion in 1949, the happiest Christmas of the first nine years of my life. Lee and I opened all our presents and found out we had not gotten the present that both of us had dreamed about, a new bicycle. John asked us to pick up the wrappings and take them to the basement. When we got to the basement, two bikes with ribbons neatly tied around the handlebars sat beautifully on their kickstands. Lee got a green and white twenty-four inch Schwinn; the look on his face and the smile when he got that bike would have been a great picture for Boys' Life magazine. My shiny dark red twenty-six inch Western Flyer, purchased at the Western Auto store in town, immediately took the prize as being the nicest Christmas present I'd had since getting a tricycle of the same color in 1944.

Lee and I ran upstairs and gave John and Bee a big hug; then we hurried downstairs and rode our new bikes around the basement. Another indication of Bee's character surfaced: She and my brother both told me that Kenny purchased the bike, but years later I found out that my brother and the Crawfords shared the expense fifty-fifty.

During the Christmas season of 1949, my 19-year-old brother Kenny still paid room and board at a horse estate, either Zettlemeier's in Hunting Valley or Merry's in Gates Mills. Uncle Harold had worked and lived at both places, but in the late 1940s and early 1950s, my aunt and uncle lived in Mayfield Heights. As a stable hand Kenny did not make much money, but he still chipped in for my bicycle.

Easter Sunday of 1950 is another holiday that I remember at the Crawfords'. We drove 100 miles to Jewett to spend Easter with John's family. I got carsick from the drive and from eating too many jellybeans.

St. Patrick's Day of 1950 left a lifelong impression. I thought everybody wore green on St. Patrick's Day because I remember Grandma talking about how they should. I asked Bee if I could wear green to school on St. Patty's day and I'll never forget her response.

"You should be wearing orange not green. You're an Orangeman, a Protestant Irish," said Bee in reference to my religion.

I didn't understand all that Orangemen and Protestant stuff, and I didn't know why wearing green seemed so important to Grandma, and not important to Bee. I found out later in life why Grandma thought green was appropriate for St. Patrick's Day; my grandmother's mother, Kathleen O'Brien, was an Irish Catholic immigrant. I learned later in life that the Presbyterians and the Catholics, especially in Scotland, Ireland and England, weren't exactly kissing cousins.

The school year ended in June of 1950. Despite my troubles in school, Mrs. Ransford passed me to fifth grade. Failing had always been one of my greatest fears.

On June 25, 1950, the day after my tenth birthday, the North Korean Communists crossed the 38th Parallel and captured Seoul, the capital city of South Korea. President Truman sent U.S. forces to Korea, many of which were already stationed nearby in Japan and Okinawa. The objective of the United States military forces was to recapture Seoul and drive the communists back across the 38th parallel. In the months ahead, my brothers got drafted into the Army, and fought to preserve the freedom of the South Korean people.

George came to Ohio to bid farewell to family and friends when he got his orders to serve in Korea. I'll never forget what he told me when he came to say "goodby." His words reminded me of my father's words three years earlier, "I know I'm not coming back."

Kenny also came to say "goodbye" before his departure to Korea, but he showed more optimism about his chances of surviving.

"Those gooks aren't goin' get me, I'll be back," he said.

Kenny served as a combat engineer with the 5th Army, but George became the real grunt, an infantryman that carried a Browning automatic rifle, commonly called a BAR by GIs. George used to kid about being a BAR man; two things he said are unforgettable.

"Because I carried a BAR, the commies were hot after my ass," and "I was a BAR man, I never went past a bar without going in."

Toward the end of the summer I noticed Bee and Florence Davis spending more time together than usual. Bee seemed to be going across the road to Florence's quite a bit. In the past, Florence usually came to Bee's. I noticed the new trend, but I didn't think anything of it. One hot, August day in 1950, I found out they had planned something that would change my life again.

"Gary, what would you think about living with the Davises again? Florence would very much like you to live with her. We both love you but Florence can't have children of her own. It's really your choice but I know Florence really wants you to live with her," said Bee.

"I don't know what to do. What do you think I should do?" I said.

"It's really up to you, but I think it would be nice if you lived with Florence," said Bee reassuringly.

"Florence wants me to come back, but what about Stanley and Grandma Davis? I don't think they like me very much," I said.

"Well, they had to agree to you coming back or we wouldn't be having this conversation," said Bee.

There seemed to be a lot of resentment by Stanley and his mother toward me, but maybe that would change this time around. Stanley and Grandma

Davis may have had something to do with me leaving Davises' back in January of 1949 to live with Aunt Goldie before going to the welfare home. But judging from Florence's words and demeanor that cold, January day, I think my aunt initiated the scheme. Goldie probably thought that somehow she could get some money from somewhere or somebody for taking care of me.

Nevertheless, it sunk in that Bee wanted Florence to have me back. They were close friends and Bee wanted Florence to experience the joy of having a child Florence could call her own. Florence agonized her entire life about not being able to have children; Bee explained this to me years later.

Florence and Tippy gave me two pretty good reasons to move back with the Davises, and maybe Stanley and Grandma Davis would be nicer this time.

The few months that I had spent with Davises in 1948 enabled me to develop a favorable relationship with Florence, and I got very attached to Tippy. It didn't take long to inform Bee of my decision, a done deal from the beginning.

"If you think I should live with Florence, then it would be okay if I do," I said.

"We'll miss you, Gary, but we'll still get to see you all the time; Florence will be happy," said Bee.

After what the Crawfords had been through losing a child of their own, a foster child moving across the street would be a piece of cake.

At the age of two, JD died of polio in the early 1940s. His death devastated the Crawford family. The death of a child being the most crushing thing that could happen to a family, I have always respected and admired their determination to carry on.

Later in life Bee expressed her feelings about my decision to move back to the Davises'.

"I'll never forget that day. I watched you cross the street to go live with Florence. It was sad, but I was happy for Florence. Florence told me you were her last chance to have a child of her own," said Bee.

I kept wondering if I had made the right decision even though Bee assured me that I did. I spoke to Lee before leaving.

"I'll miss living with you, Lee, but whenever you want to play, I'll be right across the road. You and Skippy can go hiking with Tippy and me anytime you want," I said.

"You can come over and play anytime," said Lee.

Even though this became the first move that I decided on, it still wasn't my idea. I had guilt feelings about changing homes all the time; there had to be a reason why people didn't want to keep me very long. The move to Davises' became my seventh move in four years. Except for the Detention Home, every place I went I had high hopes that I would live there permanently, but things never worked out.

Every time I moved, the feeling surfaced again that I didn't fit in anywhere, and I would probably soon be moving. I remember thinking that anyone foolish enough to put a roof over my head might be fighting an uphill battle. No matter how hard anyone tried to make me feel part of their family, I never did. A voice from within kept telling me I didn't really belong.

Because I had been disappointed so many times, getting close to people became difficult. Suspicion and doubt always prevailed; I learned not to trust people. I always felt like an outsider, even around people as loving as Florence and Bee.

I only lived at the Crawfords' for one year, but I knew I would miss living with them. John and Bee may have been the best foster parents that anyone could possibly have. If it hadn't been for John and Bee, I may have been raised in the Detention Home and probably would have gone down the wrong path in adulthood.

I liked having Lee as a brother, riding on the fire trucks in the parades and going to the fire station and the paper mill with John, shooting baskets at the hoop attached to Crawford's garage, and playing knee-football, a game Lee and I took credit for inventing.

Realizing that we could still do these things together, I justified my loss by rationalizing that I would be just across the road. Lee felt the same way that I did, and expressed his feelings, years later.

"The day you left to live with Florence and Stan; I remember my mother sobbing after you left and me not understanding; after all, you had just gone across the street."

Chapter V
The Second Time Around

With the Korean War raging and the sun mightily shining, I moved across the road to the Davises' on that hot, muggy August day in 1950. But the war didn't enter my mind, I only thought about getting settled in my new home, and I wondered how accepted I would be by Stanley and his mother, the second time around.

When I walked across North Main Street carrying some of my belongings, the thoughts of a joyful reunion with Tippy floated through my mind. I remembered what Stanley used to say when I lived with the Davises before, "Tipper's the best damn birddog in these parts." When I burst through the Davises' kitchen door looking for Tip, he ran to greet me. His stubby tail wagged with joy and his tongue, dripping with perspiration, hung from of the side of his mouth. He appeared to be smiling, laughing and acting as though he knew that once again I'd be living with him.

There's something about relationships with dogs that's rightfully called unconditional love. I once heard a farmer talking about his sheep dogs. What he said left a lasting impression, "They're not pets, they're companions that are more loyal than people."

I felt the same way as the sheep farmer; I trusted dogs more than I trusted people.

Tippy's greeting contrasted sharply with Grandma Davis' response to my return. When I came in and began hugging and playing with Tippy, Agnes stood at the kitchen sink with her back to me, washing dishes.

"Hi, Grandma Davis," I said, continuing to hug Tippy while he tried to lick the sweat off of my face.

"You got all your stuff over here yet?" asked Grandma Davis.

"Not yet; can I play with Tippy for a while?" I asked.

"Never mind Tippy! They want you to get all your stuff over here!" said Grandma Davis in her predictable surly way.

"Are Florence and Stanley here?" I asked.

"They're around here somewhere," she responded.

"I'm going back to Crawfords' to get some more of my stuff," I said.

54

Judging from Grandma Davis' response to my return, I wondered if I had made the right decision. During our entire conversation, she never even looked around.

Florence greeted me in the front yard on my second trip back from getting my belongings.

"Gary, let me help you get your stuff," she said.

"I can get it, Florence; I have to get my bike and my football, and my mitt," I said.

"I'll see you over at Crawfords' when you get back", she said.

After Florence and I got the rest of my personal belongings across the street, I already felt a little homesick, and I continued to worry about how I'd be received by Stanley. Grandma Davis being the only clog wouldn't be so bad, but if Stanley also did not welcome my return there would be hell to pay.

After a hike in the woods with Tippy not long after I moved in, I got a dose of things to come.

"Where the hell you been, Herman?" Stanley asked.

"In the woods with Tip, sir," I responded.

I didn't like being called Herman, and I'm not sure why Stanley called me that, but I know how I perceived it. I felt it was Stanley's way of showing disrespect. He never called me Gary and when he was upset he called me Herman or Knucklehead, among other things.

"Jesus H. Christ, look at Knucklehead!" Stanley said with his patented partial smile, and then he continued.

"And Herman, don't call me sir! You're not in the Army or that goddamn welfare home anymore!"

Tippy and I stayed clean for only the initial few minutes of our hike. Once we got to the creek bed near the edge of Davises' property line, cleanliness and dryness became things of the past. When Tippy and I got home, it looked like we had rolled down every muddy embankment along the Chagrin River.

"You better get those dirty clothes off and get in the tub! You're not eatin' supper in this house lookin' like that! Look at him! He looks like he was rollin' in the mud!" groused Grandma Davis.

Taking a bath stood last on a list of things that my hungry, thirsty and tired body wanted to do. The soggy peanut butter and jelly sandwiches from my knapsack had been eaten several hours earlier. My canteen had been empty for more than an hour. I kept from getting dehydrated by drinking creek water on the way home. Numb and lifeless, my springer spaniel and I pushed on.

After arriving home and quenching my thirst at the kitchen sink, I just wanted to eat and lie down.

"You can take a bath later, before you go to bed. You must be hungry, just wash up for right now," Florence responded.

After washing up and returning to Florence's domain, the kitchen, Stanley started a conversation about one of his favorite subjects.

Stanley had an affectionate name for Florence—he called her "Non" and Florence's nieces and nephews called her "Aunt Non."

"So Herman wants some grub. If anybody in this house goes to bed hungry, it's their own goddamn fault! You're lucky, Herman; Non is the best cook in the world. Nobody makes sauerkraut and dumplings like Non," said Stanley.

"There's plenty of food left," said Florence.

"His eyes is always bigger than his stomach!" were familiar words from gruff mannered Grandma Davis. "Trouncin' in here this late, he's lucky there's any food left!"

Grandma Davis always directed her sarcasm towards me but spoke to Florence and Stanley. She always tried to get them to see it her way. Stanley rarely agreed with anybody; he had strong opinions of his own. I can't recall Florence ever acknowledging agreement with Grandma Davis. Except when she got mad, Florence either said something nice or remained silent, but Stanley and Grandma Davis always expressed their opinions.

"What the hell you talkin' about, Ma? His eyes bigger than this stomach," said Stanley. "Knucklehead's got a hollow leg. I've never seen anybody eat like Herman. I'd rather clothe him than feed him."

Stanley may have been right about my hollow leg. Among people that knew me, especially as a teenager, my reputation for eating had prominence. Once I ate 25 pancakes for lunch; on another occasion seven hamburgers for dinner, and at a General Electric Company picnic I scarfed down 17 hot dogs.

Despite my enormous appetite, I could not eat certain foods, and Davises' adherence to one of their codes does not bring back pleasant memories: "You're not excused from the table until you eat everything on your plate," rang in my ears. The Davises suffered through the Depression, and like most families that went through those years of deprivation they enforced the discipline of cleaning up your plate before leaving the table. The way that I cleaned my plate of food that I could not eat, especially beef tongue, would not win an award for originality, but it worked.

Tippy always hung out under the table and rested his head on my chair, or the top of my knee. I would bring the paper napkin up to my mouth and pretend to be using it properly. Then I spit the food into my napkin, slid it down to my four-legged pal and started talking so no one could hear my dog's eating sounds. The timing for the spitting had to be perfect. The only time I could transfer the food into my napkin occurred when no one was looking directly at me.

Once when Stanley and his mother made fun of how much I could eat, Florence entered the conversation, not realizing that she would open up a can of worms.

"Gary's a growing boy and he's very active," Florence countered.

"He should be more active doing chores around here, for one, that chicken house needs cleaning out," said Grandma Davis.

"Who, Herman clean out the chicken coop?" added Stanley. "Hells bells! Hell'll freeze over before that happens."

I always thought there should be a law against cleaning out hen houses without the use of a gas mask; chicken shit made me sick just thinking about it.

While I continued my thoughts about how much I dreaded cleaning out the chicken coop, Stanley and his mother continued their conversation.

"All he cares about is sports, food and that birddog of ours," continued Stanley.

"You forgot getting in trouble and always doing what he's not supposed to be doing," snarled Grandma Davis.

"Ha! Ha! Ha!" laughed Stanley before continuing. "Goddamn knucklehead!"

During the verbal assaults, Florence always came to my rescue.

"You have to admit he's all boy and 'Tip' has never been in better shape," added Florence.

Florence's tolerance of Stanley and Grandma Davis' attitude toward me must have been a trade off for them allowing me to live in my seventh home in four years (1946-50); the ninth if you count the three different locations with my grandma.

Despite Stanley and Grandma Davis' attempts at humiliation, I still considered living in the Davises' turn of the century farmhouse a good bargain. There were responsibilities, chores, and verbal abuse in my new home, but nothing rivaled living in the dark, dingy shack across the road with Grandma.

I had to make my bed, pick up after myself, burn the trash, cut the lawn, clean out the barn and the chicken coop, and sometimes collect the eggs. Three chores I hated the most, all for different reasons: Burning the trash, cleaning out the coop, and collecting the eggs. The latter, until I learned to treat it as a challenge and a game, scared the hell out of me.

"Gary, will you collect the eggs today?" asked Florence.

Because I tormented the rooster, collecting the eggs became a combative experience. My tormenting involved poking the rooster with sticks through the chicken wire fence, and throwing cherry pits at him from the tree overlooking the chicken-yard. I paid the price for my spiteful gestures.

On the way to the coop, I always stopped at the barn to arm myself with a garden rake for the impending fight. The rooster hated me so much he always initiated the attack as soon as I entered the hen house. With wings flapping and spurs flying, the courageous feathered warrior attempted to get even with me for my playful, but annoying assaults. When I knocked him down, he fought even harder; occasionally during the fray, I grabbed an egg and placed it in the basket. The rooster's relentless attacks continued until I left. I admired the courage and tenacity of that son-of-a-bitchin' redheaded cock. He taught me the real meaning of the words persistence and tenacity.

"You're the only person that I know that's gone to the chicken house for twenty minutes and comes back with five eggs. Last time it was three," said Grandma Davis scornfully.

"I don't know why he takes so long and what he does out there," muttered Grandma Davis to anyone who would listen. Only the rooster, hens, and myself knew the answers to Agnes' concerns.

My ineptness at collecting eggs did not concern Florence. She focused on helping me to develop a sense of values. It lingered as a big disappointment to Florence when I refused to attend her church.

"Gary, I'd like you to join the Federated Church," said Florence.

"Do I have to? I'd like to continue going to my church," I said.

"It's your decision, as long as you go to church, but I'd really like you to go to our church," said Florence. "You would really like Reverend Townsend, and a lot of your friends from school go to our church."

At this point in my life if someone had explained the philosophical differences between churches, I may not have chosen the Methodist religion. But children don't choose their religion, that's what parents are for. In my case, maybe I should have chosen my own religion; I had a prescription for how I would have done it. I would take a watch, a sheet of paper and a pencil, and each week attend a different Sunday school and church service in town. I would mark down the length of time I spent in Sunday school and church, and add those times together. My religion would be the one that had the least total minutes. I suspect that the Methodist or Federated Church would have had the highest total minutes since Chagrin Falls had no Baptist, Mormon or Catholic Church in town in 1950. There were two other churches in town, the Chagrin Valley Lutheran and The Christian Scientist Church. During the 1950s decade after St. Joan of Arc Catholic Church and St. Martin's Episcopal came to our little town of 4,000 residents, we now had six churches. That's an average of one church for every 666 residents. There wasn't six of anything else in town, not even close. Religion was a dominant force in Chagrin Falls and if you didn't partake you might get a frown, a stare, or not get spoken to when you strolled down the street.

Reverend Townsend's sermons drew people to the Federated Church, which is called the Church of Christ or Congregational Church in most communities. But Reverend Townsend knew I didn't go to church with Florence, and at the annual Strawberry Festival he made it a point to be nice to me. I thought he wanted the measly ten percent from my dollar a week allowance to go in the till at the Federated Church rather than the Methodist Church. He didn't know that sometimes I spent the entire dollar on baseball and football cards, Coke and potato chips. When I didn't have money for the offering plate at church, I would put my hand in the small basket with my fingers together, touch the bottom of the basket to make it sound like I dropped in money; then I would open my fingers and lift out my hand. Sometimes I took money from the offering basket, but I always prayed that night for forgiveness. I learned at the Methodist Church that Christians are blessed and that we are forgiven. Whenever I did something wrong, and that happened almost daily, I prayed for forgiveness.

Much to Florence's chagrin, based on the foundations established at the Methodist Church when I lived with the Crawfords, I continued going to Chagrin Falls' oldest church. With catechism and baptism on the horizon and being tired of constant changes in my life, I took the liberty to make my own choice. Florence didn't like my decision, however, she reluctantly accepted it. I do remember once acknowledging Florence's request to attend church with her–it was in the early 1950s.

"Gary, what would you think about attending Easter service with Stanley, Grandma Davis and me?" she asked.

With a smile on my face I responded, "In Stanley's words, 'not a snowball's chance in hell' of that happening."

To please Florence though, I did agree to attend Easter service with the Davises. It became one of the most embarrassing moments that I can ever remember. Stanley's loud, deep voice dominated the many hymns we sang that unforgettable Easter Sunday. Every time I looked in the church program and saw the next hymn, I got nervous, and when we began singing, I wanted to disappear. I happened to be sitting next to Stanley, on his right side, and I kept asking myself, "How did I get conned into this?" Two things I learned from the experience: Stanley had a deep voice, and I would never attend another church service with him. I couldn't wait to get back to the good old Methodist Church.

A few years later, during my high school years, Jack Richardson, one of my closest friends, and I made a guest appearance at the new Catholic Church in town, St. Joan of Arc. Mike Grubich, a friend from school, invited us. Mike didn't tell us the mass would be in Latin, a traditional practice of the Catholic faith during that time. I had never seen or used kneelers before and I never stood and sat so many times in one hour my entire life. Basically, Protestants, with the exception of Episcopalians and Lutherans, just stand for hymns. But I respected the Catholic faith a lot more after that service. It was more ceremonial and not laid-back like I was used to. It made me realize that the original Christians had to be Catholic. Sometimes I listened to the Catholic broadcast of the rosary on the radio and I even memorized "The Hail Mary."

Another thing I'll never forget about that mass at St. Joan of Arc: Felicia Miraglia, an attractive freshman girl that my friend Jack liked, and a few other Chagrin students looked at us in amazement. Felicia's comment to Jack and me became a classic memory, "What are you doing here?" she asked.

With catechism classes on Saturday and Sunday school and church on Sunday, I got more than my fill of religion. I started cutting church service quite often since my attendance could not easily be monitored. I would usually meet my friends at the Standard Drugstore, located at the corner of Franklin and West Washington Streets, next to the Methodist Church. I would get a church program from them, and a briefing on the sermon. One Sunday I forgot to get a program and talk to my friends about the sermon, and I nearly got hung out to dry.

"How did Sunday school and church go today?" asked Florence.

"Fine," I responded.

"What was Reverend Wyant's sermon about?" asked Florence.

I gave a pretty generic answer, "He talked about Jesus' attitude toward the poor; how much Jesus loved poor people and always helped them," I said.

"I'm glad you were paying attention and got something out of the service," said Florence.

Sometimes Florence would ask me to repeat scripture and I used to tell her I'm not too well "versed" in it. She always smiled when I said that. But I did memorize the Lord's Prayer, the 23rd Psalm, and two verses from the book of John: 3:16, *God so loved the world that he gave his only begotten son, and whosoever believeth in him shall not perish but have everlasting life;* and 14:6, *I am the way, the truth, and the life.* Even though I knew some scripture, I didn't read and study the Bible like I should have.

I also knew the Ten Commandments but I violated two of them without any guilt feelings whatsoever. Not only did I become a good liar, but I also continued my habit of stealing. The Standard Drugstore became the place where most of my thefts occurred.

From a counter at the front of the drugstore, customers received checks for food and drink purchases and paid the checks at a different location. The way they had it set up made dishonesty very easy; you could leave the counter with your check, browse a bit in the magazine area, and walk out without paying. The number of times I left the Standard Drugstore without paying surpassed anyone that I knew. Some people always paid; others only occasionally cheated the drugstore, but I became a perpetual cheater. One day, all the chances I took not paying my checks caught up with me.

"Gary, what are these unpaid checks from the Standard Drugstore doing in your pockets?" asked Florence.

I usually remembered to tear the checks into pieces and throw them away. Unfortunately, this time I forgot—when doing the laundry, Florence found the unpaid checks in my pockets.

When I told my foster mother my cock-and-bull story, "I forgot to pay," she responded angrily.

"You forgot five times?" Florence asked. "That's how many checks I found in your pockets. Five checks from three different days! I want you to immediately take these checks down to Mr. Stoa and pay them. If you don't have enough money, I will loan you the difference or you can work it off. Regardless, I want these paid immediately!"

I could tell by the tone of her voice, and by her expressions and body language, that she meant business.

"Yes Florence, I will pay. I have enough money," I said.

I really didn't have enough money, but I didn't want Florence to know.

"I don't want this to happen again," said Florence, looking directly into my eyes, and then she continued, "Gary, look at me! Do you understand?"

"Yes, Florence. I'm sorry for this embarrassment to you," I said.

"I'm not the one that's going to be embarrassed. You're the one that has to tell Mr. Stoa what you did," said Florence.

On the way to the Standard Drugstore, I tore up the three largest checks. I gambled that Florence wouldn't call Mr. Stoa to tell him about my five unpaid checks.

Nervous and embarrassed, I went to the pharmacy to speak with Mr. Stoa. I went to school with his daughter Karen, and I knew if he told Karen what I did everyone at school would know.

I prayed, "God in heaven, please help me get through this. I promise I'll be good from now on. Amen." This became my prayer whenever I got into serious trouble.

"Mr. Stoa, I found these unpaid checks in my pants at home; I forgot to pay them, here's the money, I'm very sorry," I said as I handed Mr. Stoa the checks and the money.

"Gary, I wish everyone was as honest as you," said Mr. Stoa. "This is quite a gesture on your part; I bet the Davises are real proud of you."

"Thank you, Mr. Stoa; I was in here so long the other day I just wasn't thinking about those checks; I'm sorry!" I said.

I only felt sorry about getting caught. The things I learned earlier in my life about survival never left my mind. I loved the risk and the adventure of stealing; the fact that I usually got away with it, and most importantly, I liked the idea of not having to pay. But I always wondered if Mr. Stoa knew from Florence about the checks that I didn't pay.

I knew that Florence would not tell Stanley about my check stealing episodes at the Standard Drugstore. She may have been irate over what I had done, but she wanted to see me in one piece and she didn't want me to get shipped back to the Detention Home. A laundry list of bad deeds might send me packing, despite Florence's objections. The lesser punishment might be something dreadful that I'd already experienced; a ban from listening to my favorite radio shows.

I never missed an Ohio State football game or the 1950 NFL Champion Cleveland Browns games on the radio, and rarely did I miss a Cleveland

Indians game. I had several favorite radio shows in 1950: *Sky King, Tom Mix, The Shadow, The Lone Ranger, Bobby Benson and the B-Bar-B Riders, the Edgar Bergen and Charlie McCarthy Show,* and popular music.

Stanley liked listening to the radio too, but by 9:00 in the evening with his head turned to the side, mouth wide open, he snored loudly from his favorite overstuffed chair, and everyone knew better than to wake him up. Personally, I wanted to stick a rag in his mouth so I could hear the radio shows more clearly.

Stanley stood the same height as John Crawford, 5'11", had a fairly big nose, and wore glasses. A true southpaw, Stanley did everything left-handed. When he rolled his big left hand into a fist it looked like a shot put, and when he got angry his piercing steel-blue eyes intimidated me. One time, shortly after I moved in, Stanley backhanded me across the face for not coming directly home after school, like he told me to do. I remembered being dazed from the smack, but I refrained from crying; I didn't want to give Stanley the satisfaction of knowing that it hurt. That same night, after thinking about the rage in my foster father's eyes when he hit me, I tucked my head under the pillow and let the tears flow.

Despite the missing rapport between Stanley and me, no one could deny his professional truck driving ability. He drove a 32-foot rig for General Electric for 25 consecutive years without having an accident.

One December day in 1950, Stanley asked me if I wanted to go with him to pick up something that would forever change our lives.

"Herman, Non says you want to go with me to get the television set," said Stanley.

"Can I go?" I asked.

"Yeah, come on you can tag along and give me a hand," said Stanley, almost as if he had given in by allowing me to go.

Excitement radiated in the air; we would soon be owners of one of the world's modern marvels. Stanley and I drove to a General Electric store in Euclid, Ohio, to purchase our new 13" black and white GE television set. The fantasizing that I had done about having a television set would soon become reality.

The thoughts of having a television set for Christmas made the season that much more exciting, but I felt uncomfortable with Stanley. During the one-hour round trip ride neither of us spoke a word.

Florence more than likely arranged the trip, thinking it would be nice if Stanley and I could do something together. But maybe Stanley wanted me to go because he needed my ten-year-old body to help with the television set.

I liked everything on our three-channel television set. With the exception of an occasional squabble with Grandma Davis, everybody liked to watch the same programs. There were only three channels, NBC (channel 3), CBS (channel 5) and ABC (channel 9). Everybody in the United States and Canada that had the good fortune of owning a TV set watched the same programs.

Amos N' Andy, Jackie Gleason, Groucho Marx, I Love Lucy, and *I Remember Mama* became family favorites. My favorite programs during those early years of television were *Howdy Doody, The Lone Ranger, Lassie,* and the only telecasted football bowl games in the 1950s, the Orange, Sugar, Cotton and Rose Bowls. I also liked *Victory At Sea*, a documentary about the famous battles fought in the Pacific theatre by the Navy and Marine Corps during World War II.

Stanley also liked watching *Victory At Sea*. Once while watching the show he explained to me why he didn't serve in the military. Born in 1904, the year after my father, both had been too young for World War I and too old for World War II.

Stanley had two favorite TV shows: *The Gillette Friday Night Fights* and *The Pabst Blue Ribbon Wednesday Night Fights.* A slugging left-handed amateur boxer in his younger days, he loved the fight game.

White people and colored people alike who watched boxing became partial to fighters of their own race, Stanley being no exception. Although Stanley's biggest partiality surfaced when white fighters fought colored fighters; his partiality extended to left-handed fighters, and white fighters when they fought Latinos.

Besides being an amateur boxer, my foster father also played football and basketball at Cleveland's now extinct Central High School. Occasionally, Stanley would sing a song that the students of Central High sang at football games during his high school playing days (1918-1921), just after World War I.

Our boys will shine tonight, our boys will shine.
Our boys will shine tonight, all down the line.
Our boys will shine tonight, our boys will shine.
When the sun goes down and moon comes up, our boys will shine.

Stanley talked often about boxing, football, basketball, hunting and fishing, and also about his father's ice business. He said the strength he developed delivering ice helped him perform better in sports, especially boxing and football.

"My father was in the ice business. I remember working day and night delivering ice. Refrigerators hadn't been invented yet so everybody had iceboxes. I used to pick up those blocks of ice with a clamp; you couldn't help but get strong carrying those goddamn things. My father bought a farm with the money he made from the ice business," said Stanley.

Stanley loved fishing and hunting, his favorite recreational sports. During the 1940s, he did a lot of fishing on Lake Erie, but thanks to a fellow General Electric employee, Frank Sculley, Stanley found a new fish camp for the 1950s. Brown's Cottages on Long Lake, in Alpena, Michigan became a summer tradition for the Crawfords and Davises during the early and mid-1950s. The Davises and the Crawfords, and occasionally another family from Chagrin Falls, the Hawersaats, went to Long Lake the last two weeks of July. Beautiful Long Lake extended north and south nine miles and ran two miles wide. It lay in a pine forest, a few miles west of Lake Huron. Brown's Cottages sat on a bay at the extreme southwestern end of the lake. The order of the day at the fish-infested lake in northeastern Michigan made the two week vacation an adventure: Fishing, swimming, boating, and just plain fun.

I didn't like leaving my summer league traveling baseball team, but the two weeks of vacation excitement more than made up for missing a couple of games; we only played one game a week in those days.

Stanley and John taught Lee and I the art of bass fishing and trolling. During evening trolling runs we caught walleye and northern pike, but I got "hooked" on bass fishing.

"Herman, give it a little more slack," said Stanley. "You got a strike! Don't set the hook until he stops running. Okay, Herman, set it! You got em'!"

"Wow! This is fun!" I rejoiced.

"He's putting up quite a fight. The small mouth bass are sporty fish. They'll fight you tooth and nail," said Stanley. "I got the net! That son-of-a-bitch'll start flopping when Herman gets him up by the boat."

"Gary, what a beautiful fish," complimented Florence. "That's the biggest one today so far. You're getting to be quite a fisherman."

"About fifteen inches," said Stanley. "That's about two pounds. We got small mouth, perch, and the walleye and pike that John and I latched on to last night. They'll be some good eatin' tonight. Damn, this is living! Hells bells Tipper'll be eatin' fish tonight!" laughed Stanley.

"Don't forget to count the Crawfords' catch," added Florence.

Lee, John and Bee spent the morning fishing somewhere else on the gorgeous water wonderland– Long Lake.

"John's way the hell out there today," said Stanley, pointing in a northeasterly direction toward Lake Huron.

We stayed in the same cottage with the Crawfords; when the Hawersaats came, they rented a separate cottage. Their son, Larry, was a year ahead of me in school and two years ahead of Lee.

Stanley and John fished in the morning, afternoon and evening. Bee and Florence would go fishing in the morning and sometimes they alternated going in the afternoons, so that at least one of them could be with us boys. Lee and I always went fishing in the morning, Lee with his family and I, of course, went with Florence and Stanley. Occasionally, Lee and I would go trolling in the evening with John and Stanley.

Swimming and frolicking in the lake with the girls who stayed at Brown's Cottages highlighted the sun-filled summer afternoons. A float sat invitingly in the water about 150 feet from the dock and served as a rallying point for good times.

Lee, Larry Hawersaat and I used air mattresses for racing, sunbathing and just plain having fun. Quite often some of us would end up in the lake whether we were wearing our bathing suits or not.

"Gary, did you push that girl from Dayton off the pier with her clothes on?" asked Florence.

The way Florence worded her question made my imagination run wild. I thought about how nice it would have been if I had pushed her off the pier with her clothes off.

"Yeah, but it's all right, Florence," I rationalized. "We kinda have a crush on each other."

"I bet she doesn't have a crush on you anymore," said a smiling Florence.

I didn't want to admit to adults my feeling about girls, but they lifted my spirits. Their luscious lips, long, soft shining hair, shapely and sun-tanned bodies activated my hormones. I tried to impress the girls so they would really like me. Sometimes I even acted like I didn't care about them so that they might think that they were more interested in me than I was in them, but nothing could have been further from the truth. I wanted to kiss some of the girls so badly I could hardly stand it. My adolescent fantasies ran wild in the presence of many of those young, beautiful girls.

Besides the gorgeous girls in their bathing suits at Long Lake lifting my spirits, so did my dog, Tippy. Our highly motivated water spaniel would retrieve anything. When I threw a rock or stone way out in the lake, Tipper satisfied his retrieving instinct by swimming out away from the shore, and bringing in a large rock to replace the one that I had thrown. He spent much of his vacation time pulling unusually large rocks out of the lake and piling them on the shoreline. People sat on their screened-in porches, or stood along the shoreline to see Tippy's determination and the strength of his teeth and jaws work their magic. His stockpile of rocks made him a favorite at our fish camp. At the end of our stay during those "dog" days of summer at our camp in Alpena, Stanley had me throw every rock back in the drink.

I still see images of Tippy's boat riding exploits in Stanley's 13-foot aluminum fishing boat; his paws resting on the forward part of the bow with ears flapping in the breeze and his tongue hanging from the side of his mouth dripping with perspiration from the hot summer sun. The air conditioning effect caused by the movement of the boat cutting through the water created just enough breeze to keep him from getting too hot.

One mess Tippy got into at Long Lake did not lift anybody's spirit, but rather left everybody holding his or her noses. A skunk underneath our cottage sprayed our beloved dog and it took many days of tomato juice treatments and shampooing to get rid of the awful smell, one that worsened when Tip got wet. Tippy's sulfur scented skunk smell made us all want to wear clothespins on our noses.

Something worse than the smell of skunk happened to me that summer in 1951. I found a wasp nest attached to a storage shed, and started peppering it with rocks. One of my throws hit the bull's-eye and the nest went flying to the ground. The wasps swarmed me when I tried to escape; I got stung on the back and neck several times. I yelled for help and got a lot of first aid attention from several kind adults. After the wasp-stinging episode, I couldn't lie on my back, take my shirt off in the sun or go swimming for several days. Fortunately, I had no allergies to wasp stings.

"Goddamnit Herman, maybe you learned a lesson, but knowing you, you'll do it again. Some people die from less stings than you got," commented Stanley.

One day while lazily rowing back in the lily pads, just across the bay from our cottage, Lee and I got scared out of our wits by something more threatening than wasp stings. About 200 feet directly in front of our boat, we spotted a black bear getting a drink along the shoreline. Too scared to row away because we did not want to get the bear's attention, we crouched down and kept a watchful eye on our furry friend. Suddenly, we felt the boat slowly drifting toward the shoreline. We did not drop anchor because it would cause a disturbance and would not be helpful to a fast getaway. But if we failed to stop our rowboat from drifting, in less than five minutes we would be shaking hands with a wild animal that could easily have us for lunch. Somebody must have been looking down at us; without even glancing in our direction, the burly black bear turned and calmly walked back into the woods. Lee and I looked at each other, gave the thumbs up, and then the adrenalin started flowing. Scared shitless, we sprung to our rowing positions and made a full speed getaway. I found out later in life that the probable reason why the bear didn't see us was because of poor peripheral vision. But one thing puzzled me; since the bear had been downwind from us, why he didn't smell us? In retrospect, he probably did and that's why he left. The feeling of fear is usually mutual, but it's never viewed that way in times of crises.

I had mixed emotions about coming home. The summer trips to northern Michigan were highlights of my growing up years; they created a lifetime of fond memories. I even got to occasionally see my classmate and friend, Bob Searcy; he spent much of his summer vacation at his aunt's trailer home, on the far side of Long Lake.

On two occasions, Florence, Bee, Lee and I left the confines of Long Lake and made a couple of side trips: Once we took a ferry to Mackinac Island; and another time we went to the famous Deer Country of northern Michigan, a drive-through wilderness trail where deer galore could be seen.

Despite the fun, adventures and the pretty girls at Long Lake, I looked forward to going home and playing baseball again, hiking in the woods with Tip, playing Army with Lee, and going swimming at the Chagrin Valley Recreation Center pool along side the gorgeous babes from Chagrin Falls. The "rec" center was the focal point of our existence during those memorable days of summer. Swimming and baseball were my favorite activities at the recreation center–back then none of us really knew how lucky we were.

When we got home from Alpena, only a month of summer fun remained before Lee entered the fifth grade and I became a sixth grader. Lee and I planned to make the most of the remaining four weeks of those memorable days of summer that seemed to pass so quickly.

Picture taken at Long Lake, Alpena, Michigan in 1950. Left to Right: My beloved English Springer Spaniel, Tippy; Lee "Butch" Crawford; Bee Crawford and me. Lee was going on 9, I was 10 and Bee 32. Because of poison ivy and a fear of snakebites, we always wore jeans in the summer.

Chapter VI
The Davises

Grandma Davis didn't go to Long Lake with us; she stayed home to tend to the house, the garden and the chickens. Along with the chores, she also could not separate herself from two radio programs: The Cleveland Indians baseball broadcasts, and a show that aired at 6:00 every Monday through Friday, called *Dinner Winner*.

Being an avid baseball fan, a taste she acquired in her later years, Grandma Davis rarely missed a Tribe game on the radio. She sat at the kitchen table with her ears attuned to a small, cream-colored, plastic General Electric radio with brown knobs. Everyone knew better than to talk to her during an Indians baseball game. When the Tribe lost, Grandma Davis had a classic expression of disgust.

"I don't know what's wrong with them! They make me mad! One game they play good and the next game they stink up the place!"

Her other favorite radio program, The *Dinner Winner* show, each day called several families in the Cleveland area. If you answered the phone by saying your favorite meal, you were a winner; that entitled you to receive a full course meal of your choice for four people, from your local grocery store. Grandma Davis never missed listening to *Dinner Winner*; it became a ritual. Since we never had steak because it cost 79 cents a pound in the early 1950s, Grandma Davis always said that if the phone rang during the *Dinner Winner* broadcast time, she would answer by saying, "STEAK!"

The chores around her 18 acres took precedence, and one July evening when we were in Michigan, the regrettable happened. Grandma Davis came inside to listen to *Dinner Winner*, and the phone rang as she walked through the door. She thought the program had not started yet, and she answered the phone by saying, "Hello."

"Oh! I'm sorry, this is *Dinner Winner*," the voice on the line said.

Heart-broken, I don't remember Grandma Davis ever listening to that program again, even after Stanley taunted her about her mistake.

"Well, Ma, goddamn it, since you listen to that program every night, why the hell weren't you listening?"

"Oh I don't know! I got in from the garden about a minute too late. But I know one thing, that was our last chance to have steak; Florence says it's seventy-nine cents a pound at the store!" replied Grandma Davis.

Stanley's disappointment surpassed Florence's concerning Grandma Davis not winning the steak dinner. He said he hadn't had steak in so long, he forgot what it tasted like, and then he continued, "Even the fat on a piece of steak tastes good."

Not only did Stanley have a passion for fishing at Long Lake and boxing, he also loved duck and pheasant hunting, and collecting guns. My foster father's gun collection may have been unsurpassed. He had a small arsenal of semi-automatic and single shot rifles, shotguns, automatic pistols and revolvers.

Stanley loved hunting, fishing, and his gun collection, but not near as much as he loved his hunting dog. He always talked to Tippy and then answered as if his springer spaniel could talk. He would look with glowing interest into Tippy's dark brown eyes, pretending to be figuring out his dog's thoughts before beginning his dialogue.

"Tipper's the best damn birddog around these parts, aren't ya boy? He says, 'Ya damn right I am.' Ha! Ha! Ha! He says, 'Boy could I use a rabbit to chomp on right now.' He says, 'No, I don't want a duck. I'm supposed to retrieve them not eat em.' Ha! Ha! Ha!"

Florence loved Tippy too, but she never allowed him to sleep on the beds or the furniture. Once, when Florence found Tippy's hairs and knew that he had slept on her bed, she sprung a surprise on him. Florence bought several aluminum mousetraps, and placed them on the bed when Tip was alone in the house. When she and Stanley returned home, their beloved dog rested in his box by the kitchen door with three or four mousetraps clinging to his long mostly white, and brown hair. Tippy never slept on their bed again.

Grandma Davis didn't show much affection for Tippy, but I know she cared about him. Her pride and joy centered on her three grandchildren (Stan's brother Earl's kids), the old farmhouse, her garden and the land that she owned.

Grandma Davis, short and stocky, and 69 years old in 1951, had snow-white hair, a rather big nose and hunched shoulders that were probably the result of bending over and working hard throughout her life.

Every year, Agnes planted, hoed and harvested a half-acre garden. The seeds for her strong work ethic were sown at an early age. Born in Nebraska in 1882, she grew up on a farm during the late nineteenth century horse-and-plow days, an era when every phase of farming had to be done by hand. Without the aid of tractors, balers, reapers, combines, and pickers, it took strength of character, body and mind to succeed as a farmer in those days.

Grandma Davis' isolated existence revolved around the farm and her 12 years of formal education in a one-room schoolhouse.

"There was just a handful of us kids in the schoolhouse, never more than ten or twelve; everybody came from farms, miles around. They came through snow blizzards and what have you. There was no such thing as not having school; whyyy these kids nowadays are spoiled; they don't know what hardships are. We had to get up at four o'clock in the morning, do our farm chores and then worry about the long wagon ride to school. Don't forget, everything was horse drawn back then," said Grandma Davis.

Obviously, Grandma Davis didn't think that my misfortunes in any way compared to hers; at least, on the surface she didn't seem to think so. Personally, I would have traded her existence for mine: Endless acres of land to call my own; fresh air and warm, friendly people; animals to care for; privacy, dignity, and the freedom of the great outdoors. I always fantasized about that kind of existence, even after hearing about Grandma Davis' tough times. She talked about the flatlands of Nebraska, survival, farm chores, poor harvests, cold winters, isolation, caring for animals, the one-room schoolhouse, Indians and Gypsies.

"Nebraska is flat and doesn't have trees like we have here. When those cold winter winds blew across the plains, it was cold," said Grandma Davis. "But, we had to keep the animals and ourselves alive."

"What about Indians?" I asked.

"The Indians that we knew was friendly, but there was trouble with em' in some parts. They were big on trading; they'd bring blankets, baskets, headdresses, and even those hatchet things, what do ya call em?" she asked, motioning up and down with her right arm.

"Tomahawks, goddamn it, Ma, you're losing your mind!" said Stanley.

"They wanted your animals and guns, they wouldn't try to steal from you. Now the Gypsies was the ones you had to watch. They'd steal anything, even your horses," said Grandma Davis.

"The Gypsies would come to the front door of our farmhouse and keep you busy begging for food and things while the others would be out back stealing our chickens. My father felt that a couple of chickens wasn't enough to shoot a man over," said Grandma Davis.

"I'd shoot any son-of-a-bitch that comes on my property and steals my chickens!" said Stanley.

Gypsies, like the ones Grandma Davis remembered, began migrating to the United States in significant numbers during the late nineteenth century. They came mainly from the Balkans and Russia, but the rugged mountain areas of India is their ancestral point of origin. The Gypsies traveled about in rural areas, setting up camps at strategic locations. They continued their rural vagabonding until the Great Depression of the 1930s. Their traveling and begging lifestyle did not lend itself to the hard times of the Depression. During the era of economic collapse in our country, most Gypsies settled in large cities on the East and West coast.

I enjoyed Grandma Davis' fascinating and interesting stories of gypsies in the late 1800s and her other memories of growing up on a farm in Nebraska.

I'll always remember her pronunciation of the state of Iowa–she said "Ioway." And when she wanted to make a point that someone was getting older, she would say, "He's no spring chicken." She always used the word *was* instead of *were*: "Now the gypsies *was* the ones you had to watch."

Stanley's mother put herself well above the norm when it came to good health and level of activity for the elderly in the mid-twentieth century. Besides working diligently in her garden, Agnes babysat for Mayor Gresham's son, played cards with friends, regularly attended the village Sixty Plus Club meetings, took care of the hens, and helped Florence with housekeeping and cooking.

Grandma Davis, Stanley, and Florence had their likes and dislikes, and their differences of opinion, but their nationality had always been a common bond. They were Bohemian-Czechoslovakians, Bohemians first, then Czechs. Bohemia is the region of Czechoslovakia that Grandma Davis and Florence's ancestors came from.

Stanley's father prided himself on being Welsh. Once Stanley explained to me about the origin of the name Davis.

"The name Davis is derived from the Welsh name Davies. A lot of Welshman changed their name from Davies to Davis, but there's a lot of Davises that are Jews," said Stanley, and then he continued.

"Speaking of Welsh; your grandfather was a Jones, and that's as Welsh as Patty's Pig is Irish!"

I became more interested in the Czechoslovakian thing because I heard on the radio about Slovak Village, the Czechoslovakian Slovak community in Cleveland that used to dance to Frankie Yankovich and his polka band.

"What's the difference between Bohemians and Slovaks?" I asked the

Davises. "Are they both Czechoslovakian?"

Florence, the Bainbridge High School Class of 1930 Valedictorian had an academic answer to my question.

"Bohemia is part of Czechoslovakia like Bavaria is part of Germany and the Ukraine is part of Russia, only on a smaller scale," said Florence. "Bohemia is a region in the western part of Czechoslovakia; Slovakia is in the east. Both peoples are Czechoslovakian, and at one time Bohemia was part of Austria, so some Bohemians speak Deutsch (German)," said Florence.

"Czechoslovakia became a Communist country after World War II. The Iron Curtain separated free people from the slavery of Communism. All mail behind the Iron Curtain, incoming and outgoing, was censored.

"It takes about three months for our relatives behind the Iron Curtain to get our mail, and another three months for us to get theirs," said Florence. "The communists read all the mail and will not allow any to go through that they think is detrimental to their cause. You really have to be careful what you say."

"Goddamn Communists!" muttered Stanley.

I related to Stanley's comments because my brothers fought in Korea against the spread of Communism.

When Kenny served in Korea, I remember sending him a picture of myself holding my baseball bat and glove. It was 1951, my first year of organized baseball; I played on the Chagrin Falls Little League traveling team. From an achievement standpoint, it turned out to be my worst year in sports. Besides being the youngest player on the Chagrin Falls community team of 11 and 12 year olds, I may have been the worst player in the starting lineup. My skinny, clumsy, not so agile or strong body wanted to do more than its capabilities allowed it to, and I missed several games because of poison ivy and our annual fishing trip. I loved the game of baseball, but winning is what I really enjoyed. I used sports as a vehicle to accomplish the ultimate objective–winning.

I remember the words of team captain John Thomas when I asked him why I always batted last. John, a natural leader, a model student-athlete, a future inductee into the Chagrin Falls High School Achievement Hall of Fame, and a psychologist at age 12, had all the qualities that I didn't have. John looked at me and said, "We need strength at the bottom of the lineup too, but you won't always be batting ninth."

John turned out to be right! After the 1951 season from Little League to Pony League and throughout my high school playing years, I never batted ninth again. Three of the four years from fifth grade through eighth, we won the five-team Chagrin Valley Little League and Pony League championship. The year that my team didn't win the title, we finished second behind the Bainbridge Bombers. Our rivals and neighbors to the south and the east were led by pitching ace, Don Bagley, a future pitcher for the Yale Bulldogs.

The leadership and role model skills of my two coaches, Coach Quesinberry and Mr. Kermeen, and teammate John Thomas made baseball a positive experience. I continued playing and coaching baseball for a good part of my life and became an avid student of the game. I even applied to several major league teams in the early 1980s. I wanted to land a position scouting or coaching in the minor leagues.

After Kenny received the picture with my bat and ball, he sent me his picture and a silky, colorful jacket with dragons on it that he purchased in Japan. I proudly wore the jacket during the sixth grade school year, 1951-52.

Having a jacket that was sent by my brother from far away was nice; I was the envy of my classmates, but not even that silky, shiny jacket could get me excited like sports did, not even close. My attachment to sports began when I was a little boy, and got stronger as I grew older.

Besides sports there was something else that I really enjoyed during my tenure in sixth grade. I looked forward to the Friday spelling bees in Mr. Grandstedt's class. Along with writing and geography, spelling surfaced as one of the academic subjects that I excelled in. Mathematics, the sciences, and subjects that required reading ability hindered my progress. It remains a mystery that I could spell so well and not be a good reader. I guess it was because I had a good memory; once I saw a word in print, I could usually spell it.

During the sixth grade school year Florence insisted that I play a musical instrument, so I took drum lessons. Florence thought that the discipline of playing an instrument would be good for me, but it became one of the horrors of my youth.

I practiced my rolls and flam-a-diddles on a piece of wood covered with hard rubber. The expense of snare drums made them prohibitive, and the noise from practicing at home would have probably forced me to find yet another foster home.

My instructor, the high school band director, did not major in psychology. On one occasion, he got so mad at me he broke a folding chair by slamming it several times over the top of his desk. Another time he broke his drumsticks by smashing them over a chair.

"Why can't you get this? This is so simple! You must not be practicing or maybe you're just stupid! You're going to keep doing this until you get it right!" yelled my instructor while breaking his drumsticks over a chair.

He scared the hell out of me, but the fear of his tyrant antics worked in my favor. I practiced harder and longer to become more proficient. I didn't want the instructor to break more chairs or drumsticks on my behalf.

My music instructor's anger tactics often worked against him. I always had to get even when somebody did me wrong. I got back at my drum teacher by letting the air out of his tires on a regular basis, causing him to bring an air pump to school.

Florence insisted that I play a musical instrument, but playing the drums became my choice. The next thing Florence had up her sleeve did not come with any choices.

"Gary, I would like you to take dance lessons," said Florence.

"I don't like to dance. It's a sissy thing to do," I said.

"How do you know? All you've ever done is square dance in gym class. The lessons are for ballroom dancing; you'll learn many dance steps. It'll be good for your social development; some day you'll appreciate it. The lessons are on Fridays from four to five o'clock at the Masonic Temple. A lot of your friends will be there with you. I've already signed you up; be a sport, curly top," said Florence, as she put her arm around my shoulders.

"The most embarrassing thing in my life would be to miss seeing the Tigers play because of dance lessons," I said.

"Gary, the football games don't start until 8:00," reasoned Florence.

"But Florence, will you please listen? I always go real early to see the Tigers warm up and to see the other team get off the bus; I can't miss that!" I insisted.

"There's plenty of time; I'll make you a deal. If you don't get to see Chagrin warm up and the other team get off the bus because of dance lessons you can eat lunch at Frizzell's on Monday. Gary, you won't be late; you told me you could walk to the stadium in ten minutes," said Florence.

Florence knew how much I liked hamburgers, French fries and Pepsi at Frizzell's. But she didn't know the main reason I went to the games early. The earlier my friend, Dick Gibson and I got to the games the more likely we would get in free. We dug a hole under the fence surrounding the stadium and neatly camouflaged it. The hole under the fence, located in a wooded area near the "rec" center swimming pool became the ticket to the most exciting experiences of my childhood—Chagrin Falls Tiger football. We avoided detection by going early when there were less people around. When Dick moved to California I lost a close friend. I went to his house the day that he left to bid him farewell.

"Dick, I'm going to miss you. Maybe we'll meet in the Rose Bowl," I commented, amid thoughts that I might not see him again.

"Maybe you can come to California and visit me sometime or maybe I can come back to Chagrin," responded Dick, behind his familiar wide smile.

I really did miss Dick. Going to the Tiger games and playing football with him ranked at the top of my list, drum lessons and dancing at the bottom.

Like most of the other eleven-year-old boys, dance lessons made me nervous. The three most popular girls in sixth grade were in our dance class, Joan Schuster, Judy Simons and Jean Kaserman.

Joan Schuster, a personable and attractive brunette, became a member of the homecoming court at Michigan State University, along with two other girls from my class, Holly Hurtt and Ellen McPeak.

Judy Simons, a blond beauty, eventually married Tom Matte, a football standout at East Cleveland Shaw High School, and a star quarterback at Ohio State University. Matte started at quarterback for the Baltimore Colts in the 1964 NFL title game against the Cleveland Browns. His best friend, Dave Banning, moved to Chagrin Falls from East Cleveland. Dave became an outstanding athlete and future teammate of mine.

Jean Kaserman, blond, beautiful, quiet and definitely not boy crazy, may have been the biggest challenge of the three girls. I wanted to ask Jean out, but my shyness and nervousness prevented it. I had never been on a date; I didn't know where to go, what to do, and how to act on a real date. These thoughts, the fear of rejection and something that I'll never forget raced through my mind. Why would Jean Kaserman, who lives in this real nice house want to go out with me, a foster child with a poor background who gets up every morning to a crowing rooster that he hates? And once Jean found out that I just wanted to neck, she probably wouldn't go out with me again anyway.

"I bet Jean would go out with you if you asked her," said Bill Blair who also liked Jean.

"I don't think she would go out with you," said Bill Stearns, who liked Joan Schuster.

"I'd be embarrassed to go up to her house for a date," I said.

"Ask her to meet you at the movies," said Bill Blair.

"Yeah ya chicken, ask her!" interjected Bill Stearns.

I hated to be called chicken. Somehow, I had to get a date with the girl of my dreams, Jean Kaserman. So I conjured up enough nerve to ask her. The worst that can happen is that she'll say no, but I'd really get teased about that.

"Jean, would you," I was so nervous my vocal chords stopped working. "Would you...well...would you like to go to the movies Saturday or some other time?" I asked.

Although she definitely did not do cartwheels over the prospect of going out with me, she didn't give me a flat out no answer either.

"Maybe Saturday, I'm not sure," responded Jean.

"I'll meet you there at quarter til two, okay?" I said.

"I'm not sure I can; I'll try, but I have to ask my parents," said Jean.

To me, "I'll try" meant that Jean would be there. Whenever Florence said, "We'll see," it meant yes. I couldn't wait to tell my friends about the date.

"I can't believe it! Jean Kaserman is going to meet me at the movies!" I said to Bill Blair and Bill Stearns.

The excitement that I experienced over having a date with Jean Kaserman is indescribable. I arrived at the Falls Theatre about 20 minutes early with 50 cents in my pocket. In 1951, no one needed more than 50 cents for a movie date–14 cents for admission and 5 cents for popcorn and soft drinks.

Bill Stearns and Bill Blair showed up at the Falls Theatre to see if I really had a date with Jean; unfortunately she did not show up. The embarrassment and fear of other rejections caused me to wait three years before my next date. Because I lacked confidence, dating became a nervous ordeal for me. I loved some of the girls, but I had a complex about not measuring up to many of them.

Anxiety also set in when I visited Stanley's relatives, another item on Florence's list of compulsories for me. Christmas Day became the only exception to Florence's rule. I always went to Aunt Goldie and Uncle Harold's for Christmas. My displeasure at attending family events did not make Florence happy.

"Gary, don't forget we are going to Earl and Elizabeth's for dinner on Sunday," said Florence.

"Do I have to go?" I said.

"You know you have to go," said Florence.

Stanley's brother Earl and his family lived in a small, one-story house in Eastlake, Ohio, a few blocks from Lake Erie. As much as Stanley's relatives tried to make me feel part of their family, I never did, especially around the older Davis boys, Bobby, Donny and Billy. The age difference accounted for a big part of the lack of rapport with the Davis boys. Adolescents don't have much use for "little kids," especially a poor, shy little foster boy that intruded on their grandmother and uncle.

Laid-back pipe smoking Earl, and Stanley always traded stories about their favorite pastimes, hunting and fishing.

"Tipper and I went pheasant hunting a few weeks ago. We got one bird and we should have bagged another. Goddamn it, if there's a ring-necked anywhere around Tipper'll flush it. He'll start pointin' and walkin' slow. Then he freezes," said Stanley, imitating Tippy to dramatize his point before continuing.

"When he knows you got a bearing on that goddamn bird, he'll flush it. His field instincts amaze the hell out of me. Non dressed that bird up, damn that was good eatin!" said Stanley.

The adults at Davises' always talked about how much I had grown and the size of my feet.

"What are you feeding this boy, Florence? He's growing like a weed; look at the size of his feet," said Earl's wife, Elizabeth.

"Those aren't feet, they're gunboats!" chuckled Stanley.

"If he keeps growing, you're going to have to cut a hole in the ceiling," laughed Earl.

Although Stanley's family tried to be nice to me, I always felt more comfortable around Florence's relatives: Her brothers, Frankie, George and Syl; her sisters-in-law, Mabel and Helen; Florence's nieces, Celia, Marre, Jane and Caroline; and her nephew, Joey.

"Gary, jak se mate (yok see mosh)," said Frankie

"Dough bray," I said.

"How are you" and "I am fine" (in Czechoslovakian) had always been a traditional greeting for many of Florence's relatives, especially Frankie.

I felt closer to Florence's family than to my own mother, who had plans of visiting me on my birthday, an experience that would add more anxiety to my life.

"Your mother's coming out to see you on your birthday," mentioned Florence.

"I don't want to see her! Why does she have to come out?" I asked.

"She wants to come out and see you. Be polite and nice when she comes."

The news that my mother had decided to visit me on my birthday upset me; I didn't want to see her. I had not seen her in five years; since the day she abandoned my brothers and me. She wasn't in Juvenile Court in January of 1949 because the authorities hadn't found her yet. She deserted her family and completely ignored my grandmother during Grandma's time of suffering and poverty. She went by an alias, and although I never thought anything of it at the time, she never came to see me in the welfare home. But now that I would be 12 years old and considered Florence my mother, why did she insist on seeing me? To add to this upcoming stressful ordeal, Florence agreed to my mother's right to see me. I wondered if my social worker had told Florence that my mother had the right to see me if she wished.

My mother came to Davises' dressed as if she were auditioning to be a call girl in a Hollywood movie. Her low-cut dress clung to her body as if she had been poured into it. Her long, dangling earrings sparkled like diamonds and her black high heels matched her jet-black hair. My mother wore expensive looking clothes and jewelry, and the strength of her perfume could be smelled in the next room. She applied her lipstick, makeup, and eye shadow so excessively it looked like she could peel it off. And to my amazement even then, her boy friend, Eddie, turned out to be younger than my brothers.

In contrast, Florence wore a housedress and slip-on, sneaker-type shoes. An apron that she always wore when cooking, canning and baking, covered the front of her dress. Florence removed her apron and stopped cooking when my mother arrived.

My foster mother had straight, well-groomed brown hair, very little makeup and no perfume. Florence could have been the cover girl for *Country Living* magazine. She was down-to-earth, moral, intelligent, creative and loyal. Her attitude toward education, work ethic, and devotion to family made her the perfect mother for me. I felt lucky having Florence as my mother, instead of the lady sitting across the room who had given birth to me.

My mother was a little shorter and heavier than Florence and slightly older. Florence came into the world on Flag Day, June 14, 1912, and my mother in September of 1911. Florence had been the valedictorian of her high school class, and during the Depression she earned a two-year degree from Dyke-Spencerian Business College in Cleveland. My mother dropped out of school, but despite their differences, Florence showed respect for my mother.

"Hi, please come in and sit down," said Florence.

"This is Eddie, my boyfriend, isn't he handsome? Okay, where's the birthday boy? I got something real nice for him. Oh, this must be the dog I heard about; don't get near my new stockings," said my mother to Tippy, followed by her loud cackling laugh.

She knew about Tippy because that's all I talked about when she called to confirm to me that she had decided to come out on my birthday.

"Tippy come here," said Florence. "Lie down."

Tippy responded obediently like he always did, and then my mother spoke, "Oh there's my son! Isn't he big and handsome, Eddie, and doesn't he look like his mother? Do you have a kiss for your mother?"

I really didn't want to kiss my mother and I didn't like that she referred to herself as my mother; I considered Florence my mother.

I didn't kiss my biological mother; instead I let her kiss me. I remembered that Florence said to be polite and nice to my mother, but I couldn't bring myself to kiss her.

The Davises sat and looked at my mother in total amazement. My mother rambled on about things that made no sense to anybody. She talked about herself as if the sun rose and set just for her. Her obsession with herself did not allow her to stop talking. She always wanted to be the center of attention, never caring about what others had to say.

My mother did not listen even when she asked a question. I found a way to deal with her questions, one-word answers.

"Have you been a good boy?" said my mother.

"No!" I said.

My mother responded again with her loud, cackling laughter.

"Yes, he has been good," said Florence.

Grandma Davis responded with her favorite contradiction, "Haa!"

"Do you miss your mother?" asked my mother.

How could I possibly miss my mother...I hardly knew her! And she seemed so flashy, un-motherly and disgusting compared to Florence. I kept thinking over and over and over again about all the things she had done to make me dislike her. This time even Florence did not refute my answer to my mother's question.

"No," I said.

Again my mother responded with her cackling laughter as if I didn't mean what I said.

"Do you like the present I got you? Isn't it nice?" asked my mother.

"Yes, thank you," I said.

"Look at the new clothes and jewelry that Eddie got me. Doesn't your mother look beautiful?" bragged my mother.

I knew, even at age 12, that someone who would ask that question has a problem, so I didn't answer.

Grandma Davis sat in her rocking chair and looked at my mother with contempt written all over her face, but did not say a word. Florence sat and looked at my mother expressionless and quiet. Stanley looked at her as if she had just landed from outer space.

The same question kept racing through my mind, why did my mother come out? It became clear as I got older that she wanted to show off and let the world know that she had a handsome boyfriend, 20 years younger than her, and he loved her so much that he spent all this money buying her expensive jewelry and new clothes.

Later that evening after my mother and her boyfriend left, I crept to the top of the stairs and overheard Stanley and Florence talking in the kitchen.

"Either the waitress business is thriving and her kid boyfriend has money or it's her money. You know what I think she is!" said Stanley.

"It would be absolutely devastating to Gary if she ever got him back," said Florence.

"After what she's done! She doesn't have a snowball's chance in hell of getting him back. Christ, Non, Herman would be a burden for her. She didn't come out here to get him back. She came out to show off," said Stanley.

Despite my good fortunes of having a foster mother like Florence, I fantasized quite often about running away. Maybe Florence loved me, but I wasn't her child. Besides, Stanley and Grandma Davis would not be disappointed if I left. Running away would also be exciting, adventuresome, and a real test to see if anyone really cared.

The first time I tried running away, Florence caught me packing my clothes. Without saying a word, she unpacked my clothes and put them back in the drawers, pretending not to know of my plan to leave.

This time when I decided to leave I had a better plan. It happened during the summer of 1952. I struggled with words and tears when I said "goodbye" to Tippy. I spoke to him as if he understood.

"You be a good boy. You're better off not going with me. Stanley and Florence will take good care of you. I'm going to miss you and Florence. Stanley will take you hunting and you'll still get to go to Alpena. I love you, Tip!" I tearfully said as I hugged and kissed my favorite companion.

This time I made sure not to get caught by Florence. I secretly packed my clothes and supplies, cramming my knapsack with canned beans, bread, peanut butter, snacks, a fish cleaning knife, and a small outdoor skillet. I put some clothes in my knapsack, and a rolled-up blanket in my duffle bag; packed my fishing rod, baseball glove, and 20 dollars that I had been saving for several months.

I sneaked out of the house early in the morning through the upstairs bathroom window so that Grandma Davis, from her downstairs bedroom, would not hear me or see me leave. With a knapsack, canteen, and a duffle bag hanging from the handlebars of my Western Flyer, I quickly rode away. I rode through the front yard so the Davises couldn't hear my tires crunching on the gravel driveway.

I planned to camp the first night on the banks of the Chagrin River in Gates Mills, about seven miles from home and only a couple miles from Aunt Goldie and Uncle Harold's. I would build a fire to keep warm, repel the mosquitoes, to warm the beans and cook the catfish that I planned on catching. The earthworms that I used for bait squirmed and dangled from the end of my fishing line, but did not attract any fish.

That evening with no fish or warm fire, I reluctantly contemplated my next move. My supper of beans and peanut butter sandwiches had been a far cry from Florence's home cooked meals. I thought about sleeping alone outdoors in a strange place every night and I realized that I should have snitched one of Stanley's loaded pistols for protection. I wondered how long my food and money would last. What would I do when cold weather came? How long could I last without seeing Florence and Tip? Besides, Florence would worry about me and probably call the police. Realizing that this didn't seem like a very good idea after all, I returned home that same evening about 14 hours after leaving. I rode home in the dark with no reflector or headlight on my bike. There weren't many cars on the secluded country roads, but whenever I saw one I got off my bike and went to the side of the road. Nervously, I walked into the house trying to act nonchalant and was greeted warmly by Tippy. I could tell immediately by the looks that I got from the entire Davis family that I was in deep shit.

"Where the hell you been, you goddamn knucklehead?! You had Non worried to death about you! You're nothing but a goddamn knucklehead!" yelled Stanley.

"We were very worried; I called all your friends. Chief Smith (Police Chief) has been searching everywhere for you," said Florence.

"Florence, can I talk to you alone?" I asked.

"Sure," said Florence, and we both got up and headed to my room.

"Don't let him talk his goddamn way out of this, Non!" warned Stanley, just before he got up to call Chief Smith.

Grandma Davis looked at me and just kept shaking her head. Everybody's body language indicated that my ass was grass, but I didn't care. Florence and I went to my room and closed the door.

"Gary, why did you run away?" asked Florence.

"Okay Florence, I'm going to tell you for the first time ever just how I feel!" I said.

Then the barrage began and I didn't care if I got kicked out of the Davises' house or not. I knew I could go back to the Detention Home–I knew the ropes better this time and I was bigger now. I spoke to Florence openly and honestly.

"I'm tired of being a problem for people! I'm tired of being forced to do things I don't want to! I hate going to Earl and Elizabeth's, taking drum and dance lessons, and wearing itchy wool pants to church! Did you know I wear pajamas under my wool pants and they still itch through; and about my mom coming out, you and her never asked me my feelings about her coming out. I'm never given a choice!" I paused before continuing as Florence gazed at me with the most troubled look that I had ever seen on her face, but she chose not to speak. She got caught off balance by my emotional outburst. I was on a roll; I had finally gotten someone's attention.

"I know Stanley and Grandma Davis don't want me here. No one really wants me because I'm not their kid. I don't know what I'd do if it weren't for you and Tippy. What did God put me on this earth for? You know something? Knowing what I know now, if I had a choice between being born and not being born, I would choose not being born!" I said, and then decided to listen to Florence's response.

Tears streamed down my cheeks. Florence struggled to hold back her tears, but they began trickling from the corners of her eyes. After I got everything off my chest, I looked into Florence's eyes. I never saw her cry before, nor had I ever seen her choked-up. When she finally started talking, I knew God would be brought into the conversation. Florence hugged me and then began speaking.

"I love you but not more than God does. You will know some day why he put you here. I think he put me here to take care of you," comforted Florence.

Florence continued, "There's a purpose for everything in this world. God has a plan for all of us. You came back because running away was not in God's plan for you. I know it's hard for you here, but I want you to stay. I consider you my son, Gary."

When Florence spoke about God's plan, it was like Bee speaking. They both believed in predestination and the sovereignty of God, almost as though they had gone to theology school and studied John Calvin. It made me realize that even though Christians have all these different churches, for the most part, they're united in their fundamental beliefs about God.

I didn't expect that Florence, Stanley and Agnes would change their ways because I ran away, and they didn't. To begin with, Stanley and Agnes didn't feel they had done anything wrong. In my twelve-year-old mind they hadn't done anything wrong–I was the one causing the problems. After all, the Davises had agreed to take me in on two occasions. Having discovered what a problem I became, I wondered if they would do the same thing over. I theorized that Florence would despite the uphill struggle that she had with me, but I knew Stanley and Agnes wouldn't.

Florence's conversation with me after I ran away had a real impact on my self-esteem. After that conversation in my room, I knew without a doubt that she really did love me like a son. I never ran away again–it was my way of proving to Florence that I also loved her. I was miserable at times and wanted to run away again but I never did. Hurting Florence like I had done when I ran away was the last thing in the world that I wanted to do–she was everything to me.

My foster father, Stanley Davis, and my dear foster mother, Florence Davis. Photo taken around 1950 at Brown's Cottages on Long Lake. Stanley at the time was around 46, Florence 38.

Chapter VII
Ole' Ben, Parks, and Sports

Now that I had gotten the bug to run away off my chest and had the assurance of Florence's love, I had a more positive feeling as I prepared to enter the seventh grade. Some new friends that emerged on the scene in the fall of 1952 helped bring out those feelings.

"How y'all doin' this mornin' young man?" asked the elderly colored man that I had seen on several occasions while walking through town.

He was a slight, gray-haired man, with long arms and skin as dark as strong coffee. I had spotted him before, washing windows at the hardware store and sweeping the sidewalks, but never had the occasion to speak to him directly.

I responded with my customary greeting, "Hi, how are you?"

The old gentleman flashed a partial smile, stopped pushing his broom and began leaning on it with both arms. His teeth shone so white against his shiny black face I was convinced that he brushed after every meal, just like I was supposed to do.

My new acquaintance threw a gaze at me with warm curious eyes the color of bittersweet chocolate, and then responded, "I's fine too."

"I'm Gary, named after Gary Cooper," I offered.

"I'm Benjamin, I don't know who I wuz named afta, maybe Benjamin Franklin. You can jist call me Ben," and then he blared out with laughter.

"Ben, do you live out at the colored allotment or are you from Cleveland?" I asked, knowing that those were the most likely possibilities.

"Yezz I do live at the allotment, been there for the best part of ten yeahs," said Ben.

Benjamin lived in Chagrin Falls Park, the poverty stricken black area that folks around town called the colored allotment, a small area south of town in rural Geauga County. Most of the blacks from the allotment lived in extreme poverty, much the same as they did in the southern towns and rural areas of their origin. They had either been brought to the allotment or came on their own accord during the migration boom, 1915-1940, when Negroes came north in large numbers to find factory jobs. They worked in factories for very low wages, especially those that came before 1930. The United States did not have a minimum wage law until 1930; at which time 25 cents an hour became the established minimum wage. Because of the social situation of Negroes during this time period, it is my belief that many of them were denied even the minimum wage.

The colored allotment and the village sat only a mile apart but the cultural and socio-economic differences between white Chagrin Falls and black Chagrin Falls Park were as different as the plantation house from its slave quarters.

At this particular time in my life, Ben was the only black person that I knew. The school districting boundaries were the reason for this provincial isolation from other cultures. The black kids from the allotment despite their close proximity to the village of Chagrin Falls, did not attend Chagrin Falls Schools. They were transported several miles further to the Kenston schools.

The small number of Negroes that lived in the allotment seldom frequented Chagrin Falls in the 1950s. I think they didn't feel wanted, and certainly didn't want to stir up any kind of trouble. And since they had their own grocery store, bar and gas station, they didn't need to come into town. Benjamin was one of the few exceptions. He worked in town for one of the merchants as a stock and cleanup man. I saw Ben quite often when I walked through town; I knew him from seventh grade into my early high school years. He always intrigued me whenever I talked to him.

"You're from the South aren't you, Ben?" I asked.

"I's from Mississippi," answered Ben.

"What was living in Mississippi like?" I asked.

"It was different than up heah. In Mississippi when us black folks walk down da street and white folks comin' the otha way we got out da way, sometimes off da sidewalk. Ya didn't wanna get in the white folks' bad graces. Up heah ya' don't havta do dat," Ben replied.

I didn't really understand the disrespectful treatment of people, just because their skin happened to be a different color. Discrimination didn't make any sense to me; I knew it wasn't right.

The fact that Ben came from the South also intrigued me. I fantasized a lot about the South because of books that I had read and songs that I had heard. I told Ben about some of my thoughts.

"I dream of far away places like Mississippi, where the sun always shines and I'm sittin' on the banks of the Mississippi River fishin' with my dog, kinda like Huck Finn did in a book I've been readin'," I enthusiastically commented and then continued.

"I ran away this summer, but if I do it again I'm goin' down to Suwanee or Mississippi or somewhere in the South, maybe way out west to Texas, where my grandma came from. You can get road maps free at the gas station. I don't know if I can read one, but I can try. When I get big I'm goin' down there for sure," I said.

Ben listened and smiled and shook his head up and down.

"Ben, do you know where Suwanee is, you know like in the song? *'Suwanee, how I love ya, how I love ya...my dear ol' Suwanee'*," I sang, trying to sound like Al Jolson, a white man that put black, greasy stuff on his skin and tried to imitate a Negro, while singing *Suwanee,* and other songs about the South.

"I don't know no Suwanee, but I know dat song. I only know where Mississippi is," said a laughing Ben.

"Ben, I got a job too. I started out makin' forty cents an hour, but now I make fifty cents. I do yard work for a lady on High Street. She gave me a ten cent raise the second week because she said I did real good," I proudly said.

"You makin' about what I makin'," commented Ben, as I prepared to ask him something that my foster mother had already told me.

It's interesting what Ben said because in 1952 the minimum wage was 75 cents an hour. Ben may or may not have known about the minimum wage law, and since it didn't apply to juveniles, I certainly didn't know anything about it either.

"Is it true that colored people make less money than white people for doin' the same job?" I asked.

"Ooh yeah, we all know dat. We don't like it, but dere's nothin' we can do," answered Ben.

"Ya know I don't think that's right; it isn't fair," I commented.

"Dere's lotsa things dat aren't right or fair in dis world," replied Ben.

I became so fascinated by Ben's openness and honesty, the more I knew him the more relaxed I felt about asking him questions.

"Did you ever know any slaves?" I asked Ben without knowing if he was old enough to have known slaves.

"My grandmama and granddaddy were slaves when my mama was a baby. Abe Lincoln freed 'em. Dey stayed on the plantation ta live and work afta dey free. Dey had nowhere ta go. Dey always said 'we is free,' but dey lived dare on da plantation until the Lord come and took em,'" answered Ben.

I talked to Ben about a variety of subjects; one day we talked politics.

"Ben, I learned in school that most of the people down South are democrats," I commented.

"Yezz, I think dey is," he responded.

"Because of all that stuff (discrimination) that went on down South, and since you're up here now, does that mean you'll be a republican?" I asked.

"I believe I will be, I'm up heah now," said Ben.

"I don't know what I'm gonna be, but my foster parents are democrats. They told me that just about everybody in Chagrin are republicans," I said.

"I think dey is," said Ben.

I knew that Ben could not vote in Mississippi because of his color, but I didn't know if he voted in Ohio. Blacks could not vote in the South until congress passed the Voting Rights Act and President Johnson signed it into law in 1965.

Despite our age, race and cultural differences, I considered Ben to be my friend. We had great conversations. He told me about pickin' cotton, playing a banjo that white folks gave him, and eatin' his mamma's fried chicken, and he taught me about life in the Old South. Ben also spoke about comin' north to try and get a fair shake. He said life is better up here, but still not good for "black folk."

Ben and I talked about many topics during our years of friendship. Unlike many adults in my life, he always listened to me and seemed to respect what I had to say; he said things that interested me; things that I never forgot. I didn't tell Stanley and Florence about my friendship with Ben because I wasn't sure how they would accept it, especially Stanley because he didn't like Negroes and often made fun of them.

Whenever I saw Ben I continued my conversations with him, "Maybe when I play for the Tigers you can come and watch me play. I'm going to help Chagrin win championships. I dream about playing football for Chagrin and I wanta play football in college some day. Football gets me worked up."

"I bet you izz gonna play!" agreed a smiling Ben. "I bet you iz!"

One late summer day in 1952 several weeks after I had met Ben I spotted him while riding my bike along the sidewalks of North Main Street.

"Ben, we won the Chagrin Valley Little League Baseball Championship! We beat out Solon, Bainbridge, Bedford Heights, and Twinsburg. Mr. Kermeen is our coach! He's great! He played in the minor leagues, almost made it up to the big leagues," I proudly told Ben.

"That's good! Oh boy, you is happy! You growin' like corn in da field. You goin' ta be a big boy. I can tell by dose feets." And then Ben said something that really made me feel good, "You's certainly a nice boy."

I'll never forget him saying that; I don't remember anybody else in Chagrin Falls ever telling me that. Some people might have felt it, but nobody else ever said it.

Benjamin, this elderly black gentleman back in the early 1950s, plenty old enough to be my grandfather, became friends with a young, white foster boy that passed through town. This may seem strange to some, but during my adolescent years Ben was the only elderly adult that I felt comfortable talking to, and I knew I could trust him.

Harry Truman was still President when I entered the seventh grade in September of 1952. Two months later in November, Dwight Eisenhower became our 34th President.

Entering seventh grade became both an exciting and stressful experience. With a K-12 enrollment of less than 700 students, one building housed the entire Chagrin Falls school system in 1952. The high school section of the building, grades 7-12 had an enrollment of 285 students. After being the kingpins in elementary school my classmates and I now walked the halls with 17 and 18 year old seniors.

My attire was typical and conservative. I wore khaki pants laced with a thin belt, shirts with narrow buttoned-downed collars, laced shoes with dark socks or sneakers with white socks. Florence made sure that my shirts and pants were always starched and neatly pressed. The girls would have looked good in anything, but they usually wore colored skirts, white blouses, saddle shoes or penny loafers with white socks.

In sharp contrast to the girls our own age, being around teenage girls made us younger boys fantasize, and did we ever. With shapely breasts and legs, luscious lips, sparkling silky hair, and a sense of maturity, some of the older girls were "knock-outs." One of my fantasies was lying on the beach of a deserted tropical island with the girl of my choosing, both of us wearing bathing suits and sun-tanned by the warm sun that was nestled in a clear blue sky and cooled by a soft ocean breeze–just like in the movies. My testosterone level would rise if one of my favorite beauties just made eye contact with me, but that was about as rare as the St. Louis Browns winning the World Series.

Another new friend emerged on the scene in seventh grade: Parks Odenweller, a tall, thin, athletic looking 12-year-old, who also happened to be bright and personable. Parks moved to Chagrin Falls from Westlake, a western suburb of Cleveland.

I looked forward to some of the classes that my new friend and I had together, particularly health and physical education. Our teacher, Coach Quesinberry, Chagrin's proud and successful football coach, always found time in health class to talk about Tiger football.

"Courage, dedication and hard work is what makes successful football teams; the same things that have made your parents successful. How many of you were at the game Friday?" asked Coach Quesinberry.

Parks and I and most of the students in our all-boys health class raised their hands. My new friend and I roamed the sidelines and end zones to see the Tigers methodically pound out a 12-0 victory over the Chardon Hilltoppers.

"Does anybody have any questions about the game?" asked Coach Quesinberry.

Parks raised his hand and Coach called on him.

"How come you don't kick your extra points?" asked Parks.

I whispered to Parks, "He'd rather kick ass instead."

"We don't have anybody that can kick," responded Coach.

After class, Parks, a future Yale graduate and star athlete, said to me, "I wonder why he doesn't train someone to kick. It may cost Chagrin a game some day."

Parks' insight into what might happen became reality. In 1954, our freshman year, the varsity lost to Orange, 7-6, on a missed extra point attempt. Star fullback Larry Wiley's PAT run came up inches short.

Some kids became jealous of Parks' athletic talents. I heard a few comments about him being cocky, but I knew that he wasn't. Parks exuded confidence, intelligence, enthusiasm and athleticism. He was one of the most talented and personable people that I ever knew.

When Parks and I attended Tiger football and basketball games together, at the end of each quarter, Parks' mathematical mind and enthusiasm for sports came to the surface. He would always say, "At this rate, the score will be ____." I couldn't wait until the next quarter so I could tell Parks before he told me, "At this rate, the score will be____."

During the early fall, springtime, and the dog days of summer, Parks always wore his black New York Giants baseball cap with the orange NY logo, blue jeans and a white t-shirt. A discolored, dark-brown Rawlings baseball glove swung from the handlebars of his racing bike. It's a mental snapshot of Parks that I have never forgotten.

Parks' brilliance never ceased to amaze me; I can't remember him getting less than an "A" in any subject. His mind stored and generated facts and statistics like a computer.

"What would you guess the Giants cumulative team batting average is, over the last five years?" asked a smiling Parks, knowing he had me stumped.

I didn't know what cumulative meant, but I pretended to know.

".269?" I answered.

"Actually .258," countered Parks.

"I'm gonna look up something to stump you on Parks, but you're so smart I probably can't do it. One thing I'm sure of; I'm glad you moved to Chagrin," I said, and Parks flashed his patented smile.

Stanley labeled my knowledge of baseball and football statistics as meaningless because it didn't help me in school.

"Herman, if you directed your brain toward your school work like you do sports you'd do a helluva lot better in school," said Stanley. Then he turned to Florence and continued.

"He knows every damn thing about ballplayers and teams, but not much about his school work; goddamn knucklehead!"

"But look at Parks! He's a straight 'A' student and he knows all that stuff," I countered.

"Herman's got an answer for every goddamn thing," commented Stanley.

Competing against Parks in sports helped me develop into a better player. Parks might have gained something from my competitiveness and refuse to lose attitude. When Parks and I played on the same team, most often we would win. One exception still lingers in my mind, the Riverside Park Grudge Match football games. Because we kept the teams balanced, the traditional gridiron battles took on a competitive flavor. We played about 50 Grudge Match games between 1952 and 1957, each team winning about half of the games. We referred to the games as Grudge Matches because the losers always challenged the winners to another game. Besides Parks, Bob "Searc" Searcy was usually my other teammate.

The games took on added importance because of bragging rights around school. Both teams practiced, developed game plans, and took the game seriously. We took turns calling plays backyard style, and it was my turn to call the next play.

"Searc, snap it to me. I'll tailback spin fake right to Parks and bootleg right. Searc, block and then go out to the left. Parks, after the fake, go out in the right flat and then go long. Let's go!" we yelled and clapped our hands simultaneously.

When we broke the huddle I felt like General Patton preparing to run Rommel off the North African desert. The last time we did the spinner, Parks got the ball and almost broke it for a touchdown. This time the defense waited for Parks, but he didn't have the ball. That gave me time to set up, and for Parks to get free from the entanglement at the line of scrimmage. He broke into the flat and when star halfback, Allan "Speed" Sindelar came up to defend, Parks went down the sideline. I threw the ball as far as I could; my buddy reached out with his huge hands and caught it for a touchdown.

"Gair, great pass!" yelled a deep breathing Parks.

"Parks, that was you! I just heaved it!" I yelled.

"Gair, next time we run that come back to me, I was wide open," said Searc.

The next day in school, Bill Stearns asked about the game.

"Who won the Grudge Match?" asked Bill.

"We did. We overpowered 'em. Did we win?" I asked making it sound like a silly question. "Does a bear shit in the woods?"

"What was the score?" asked Bill Stearns.

"33-31," I responded.

"Yeah you really rolled 'em! Jack said the score was 32-31," commented Bill Stearns.

"Jack always changes the score to make it sound like a close game. We gave them the last score so they wouldn't be discouraged; that way they will want to play us again. Did Jack tell you that we've won the last three games?" I asked, and didn't get an answer, just a blank stare; I continued.

"You know what, Billy Boy? If Jack Sprat keeps adding like that he's gonna get fat, Jack Sprat gonna get fat," I kept repeating the phrase because it fascinated me that I could make something rhyme.

"And if Jack Sprat keeps adding like that he's gonna be in Miss Neff's seventh grade math class again next year," I commented, just as the old fashioned big black bell high on the wall that resembled an inverted pregnant frying pan, began ringing.

Chapter VIII
Adventures, Sports and the Beginning of Adolescence

The ancient pathways where Tippy and I hiked might have been the same trails that were trampled across by the French fur trader, Francois Séguin. He began his exploits in the valley around 1742, and according to historians the name Chagrin is the Americanized version of his name.

All my life I have loved walking through and exploring the secluded woods, following the meandering creeks and rivers, snatching wiggly crayfish that laid under flat rocks in the creek beds, and discovering wild animal tracks embedded on the ground of the muddy and snowy trails of the backwoods. Catching a glimpse of deer gliding across snow-dusted fields or sun-bathed meadows and finding the tracks they have molded during their scavenger hunts became a thrilling pastime.

The enchantment of nature has always been magical: a choir of singing birds gathering around the gushing streams that ripple through the valleys; the surprise of delicate wild flowers bursting into bloom, blowing their perfume across my face; the sunlit leaves with colors of fire; a soft winter snowfall clinging to the branches of the sprawling white pines.

Tippy shared my closeness to nature. I watched him chase leaping red squirrels from tree to tree, scurrying rabbits into the briar patches, and ground hogs into their underground passageways. I learned some valuable lessons from my favorite companion: stay focused, chase your dreams, never give up, and always remain enthusiastic in the face of failure, there will be other chances. Ralph Waldo Emerson's thoughts about enthusiasm say it all, "Nothing great can be accomplished without enthusiasm."

Once Stanley proudly commented on Tippy's enthusiasm and hunting instincts: "Tipper tore a ground hog a new asshole right at the edge of the garden! That's the son-of-a-bitch that's been eatin' the corn! He was no match for Herman's hound, but he gave Tip a couple of nicks. Ground hogs can kill smaller dogs. Goddamn that birddog is tough and determined as hell!" Then he turned and looked at Tippy with a smile and prideful gleam in his eye. "Tipper's a tough birddog, aren't 'ya boy? Ha! Ha! Ha! He says 'Ya damn right I am! 'Ya just saw me in action didn't 'ya?' Ha! Ha! Ha! Ha! Ha."

Stanley's comment, "Herman's hound," put a smile on my face. It was a real acknowledgement from Stanley that he considered Tippy to be my dog too.

Despite the advantages of being close to nature, on three occasions grief resulted from my ventures into the woods. Back in June of 1951, I got poison ivy all over my body. For about a month I wasn't able to play baseball, go swimming or hiking, and I had to stay out of the sun. That summer turned out to be one of the worst of my growing-up years, but thanks to calamine lotion and Florence's insistence not to scratch, my poison ivy disappeared in time for our annual fishing trip to Long Lake.

Florence taught me about the shiny leaves of three that climb trees and fences and spread over the ground. But poison ivy did not enter my mind during my first experience kissing a young girl. Sandy, a girl slightly younger than me, lived at the Crawford's with her mother. One day she followed Tippy and me into the woods. At first I resisted her coming with us, but soon enjoyed the company. After our initial kiss we decided to lie down, and unknowingly got smothered in a bed of poison ivy. Grandma Davis' was right on when she commented about my poison ivy, "He looks like he was rollin' in it."

My second bad experience came on a spring day in 1952 when Tippy and I went on an all day hike with several of my 11 and 12-year-old friends. A few miles from home, we came across a water hole filled with large snakes and snapping turtles. We threw rocks at the larger snakes that we claimed to be water moccasins. I grabbed an armful of rocks and moved close to the ugly and scary snake pit. When I reached down to pick up a rock from my newly formed pile, Pete Racketan threw a rock over my head in the direction of the snake hole. At exactly the wrong time, I straightened up; the rock slammed into the back of my head causing me to see stars. With blood streaming from the wound, I staggered, but remained conscious. My friends saw a girl nearby on horseback and started yelling for help. The young teenager rode swiftly to my aid; she helped me take off my bloodstained t-shirt and then she wrapped it around my head. After she got my phone number she rode off to the nearest farmhouse repeating my number along the way. The girl returned several minutes later to tell me that "Mr. Davis is on his way, keep holding that t-shirt tightly." Tipper and I waited for Stanley in a field near River Road, and the Good Samaritan young lady sat in her saddle nearby until Stanley arrived. He took me to the medical clinic where I received several stitches. I still have a big knot on the back of my head from the misguided rock.

The following week on the way home from school anger got the best of me; I had to get even with Pete Racketan. I caught Pete walking home and reminded him of what he had done to the back of my head. When he started rationalizing that it wasn't his fault, I countered with a flurry of punches that sent him tumbling down the side of a hill next to Chuck's Beverages on Bell Street right to the edge of the Chagrin River. That same night, Mr. Racketan called Stanley and told him that I had beaten up his son. I listened at the top of the stairs to my foster father's conversation with Mr. Racketan.

"For what your son did he deserves a punch in the mouth! Did he tell 'ya what he did to the back of Herman's head?" asked Stanley. Several seconds of silence followed before Stanley spoke again.

"When you get the medical bill, you'll find out! Hells Bells! I would have done the same thing! Tell your son to watch where the hell he's throwin' rocks from now on!"

I never forgot Stanley's conversation with Mr. Racketan. It surprised me and it showed another side to my foster father. Besides toughness in his personality, from my point of view he had a sense of righteousness.

My third misfortune in the woods occurred one early spring day in 1953 when Tippy and I went hiking. I left early in the morning on a sunshiny April day, a couple of months prior to my thirteenth birthday. I brought my knapsack and canteen, but most importantly I brought Tippy, the dog that I truly loved.

A few minutes into our hike, a big, friendly, male German shepherd joined us. I tried to send our new friend home.

"Are you friendly, boy?" I asked. "I've seen you before but not out here in the woods; you live over on Falls Road," I said, as if the shepherd understood every word.

The name King was etched on a large metal tag hanging from the shepherd's collar.

"Go home, King! Go on boy, you can't stay with us. Your master is going to worry about you; now get home! Here, fetch this stick and keep on going; go on home, boy!" I insisted.

This stalwart of an animal stood and looked at me in typical shepherd fashion; ears standing on end, with bright, dark brown puzzled eyes looking right into mine waiting for my next move. King became the indisputable winner of this disagreement. When Tipper and I turned and headed for the river, we had company whether we liked it or not.

After the sniffing greeting, Tippy and King got along fine. Occasionally, when we took breaks along the river or under a big tree, my two friends stayed close to me, one on each side; I never felt safer.

Near the end of the day, on the last leg of our long hike and about a half-mile of woods from home the quiet and calm of this pleasant day came to an abrupt end.

King walked up to Tippy from behind and launched an unprovoked surprise attack. He jumped on Tippy's back and sunk his teeth into the back of his neck at the collar line; then he began dragging him along the ground like a rag doll.

I grabbed the nearest stick and whacked King over the head several times. Then I kicked the German shepherd in the ribs and threw rocks at his body. I purposely avoided throwing rocks at King's head because I feared hitting Tip.

"You son-of-a-bitch, let my dog go or I'll kill you! You fucker! You hear me, you bastard! I'll kill you! Let go or I'll bash your head in you fucker!" I yelled at the top of my lungs.

None of my counter attacks seemed to affect the German shepherd, and Tippy looked like he couldn't breath; I had to do something quickly or it would be too late.

I straddled King's back, swung my legs backwards, kicked him several times in the groin, and continued yelling for the Shepherd to let go. Then, out of rage and desperation I reached into King's mouth with both hands and attempted to lift and pry his jaws loose from Tippy's neck. King suddenly let go of Tip and when I tried freeing my hands from the shepherd's mouth my left index finger got ripped to shreds by King's strong teeth. With Tippy and I bleeding pretty badly, I went into a fit of rage. I picked up a large stick and several rocks and tried to overwhelm the shepherd to keep him from attacking again.

Tipper's injury and fatigue caused him to be too tired to run, but he walked toward home. Carrying a club in my hand and covered with blood, I turned King away from Tippy and chased the German shepherd until he disappeared into the woods. With my t-shirt rapped around my bleeding finger I ran to the nearest house.

The parents of classmate Patsy Brown called the Davises for help. Once again, Stanley immediately came to my rescue and drove me to the medical clinic about a mile away. With my finger, torn by teeth marks and wrapped in a bloodstained towel that the Browns had given me, I pleaded with Stanley.

"Tippy was bleeding pretty bad; will you call Florence to see if he made it home? He's hurt pretty bad, worse than I am and he had to cross Kenton Road to get home!" I said.

"That dog knows the woods better than the squirrels and deer. He knows his way home; he's probably home with Non right now. Don't worry, Herman; just be goddamn glad it happened near home and close to a house instead of out there in the boondocks, wherever the hell you go!" said Stanley reassuringly.

After getting my finger stitched, Stanley and I drove home. My foster father's prediction came true. Tippy got home safely, Florence treated his wounds and he rested peacefully in his box near the kitchen door.

"I think Tip's collar saved his life," commented Stanley.

The collar did save Tip, but I found it quite amusing that my warrior-type heroics did not seem to impress Stanley. Despite the collar, if I had not reacted with instinct, courage and outrage, Tippy would have been dragged along that blood soaked trail until he bled to death. And I could have been ripped to threads by King's mighty jaws.

A few days later Stanley spoke to Florence about the incident.

"I found out who owns that goddamned German shepherd; he lives on Falls Road. I called him, and the goddamn rummy thinks he shouldn't have to pay Herman's medical bills. He wants to split the bills with me. I'll be goddamned if I'm going to pay any of those medical bills! We'll see what my attorney has to say about this," said Stanley.

I learned some great lessons from that scary experience in the woods. The German shepherd attack caused me to realize that loyalty, love and an understanding of right from wrong gives the human spirit courage and determination during a time of crisis; and I also found out the true meaning of adrenalin. I learned about unpredictability to boot; there was no logical reason for King's attack, and it caught me completely off guard.

Stanley's feeling about the role I played saving Tippy's life changed somewhat a few weeks later.

"Both of 'em could have been killed out there. Damn that was something!" Stanley told Florence.

Stan may have gained respect for my courage, but the names he called me didn't change, "Herman, goddamn knucklehead, goddamn dummy and rummy." It came with the territory; I didn't like it, but I learned to cope just like I had learned to cope with all of my experiences.

The King incident changed my approach to hiking in the woods. I didn't feel safe anymore going in the woods without a weapon. Stanley did not allow me to use any of his firearms and for safety reasons Florence did not want me to have my own gun, but after that horrible experience with Tip and King, I needed some kind of weapon. Nobody suggested that I carry a weapon during my exploits in the woods, but after that battle with King I knew I was no longer safe out in the boondocks without a weapon. Being a foster child, caused me to be a lot more self-reliant and creative than I probably would have been.

I saved my money for a trip to the Army-Navy surplus store in Alpena, Michigan, during our summer fishing trip in 1953. I bought a World War II United States military combat knife and holster. Whenever I went hiking or camping I strapped the knife to my side. I never had to use the knife as a weapon, but I felt safe having it. In retrospect, it would have been a bloody mess if I had the knife during the shepherd assault. I'm not sure if more of King's blood or mine would have been spilled.

The German shepherd incident did not dampen my spirits about exploring the woods or camping out with my friends. Camping out represented excitement, adventure, and independence from our parents. My first experience camping out occurred in the summer of 1952. But the most memorable time happened in the summer of 1953 shortly after my friends and I discovered we had passed to the eighth grade.

Jack Richardson and I, along with two other school buddies, strategically camped in the woods near Whitesburg Pond, a short distance from the home of Congressman George Bender. The Ohio republican had weekend plans to entertain GOP dignitaries and campaign supporters in his drive for the U.S. Senate. Many prominent republicans on the national scene would be attending the party, including Ohio Senators Taft and Bricker.

We knew where George Harrison Bender stored the food and drinks because one of our camping buddies did yard work for the congressman. The future (1954-1957) U.S. Senator's Irish setter, left out to patrol the grounds at night, represented the major obstacle. Since a member of our camping party knew the family dog, he distracted the Irish setter while the rest of us participated in the raid. The plan went smoothly; we found the food stored in the unlocked garage exactly where we expected it to be and the congressman's friendly dog did not bark during the entire raid. The giant freezer had more steaks than a grocery store. We filled a burlap sack and a pillowcase with snacks, soft drinks, and some pretty healthy looking steaks.

We kindled the campfire before our raid, so it would be ready for the steaks. While feasting on fried steaks from our camping skillets, we told stories, sang, and bragged about our successful raid on Congressman Bender's party supplies.

"How are we going to eat all these steaks?" laughed Jack.

"You know what's really funny? How does Mr. Bender tell his friends that he ran out of steak?" I laughed so hard, as everyone did, I could hardly finish the sentence. The laughing and comments continued, "and he's sorry, but he's going to have to send someone out for hot dogs, or maybe Mrs. Bender could make some peanut butter and jelly sandwiches; or 'would you Senator care for a bologna sandwich instead'?"

We had some great times and fond memories from that fun-filled summer night, and fortunately, we didn't get into trouble.

Later that summer on July 27, 1953, with the signing of the armistice at Panmunjom, the Korean War ended. A short time later I found out my brothers had survived the war and would be coming home soon. I couldn't wait to see them and hear their war stories. Sometime in the early fall Kenny came to see me, then George a month or so later.

Their answers to my question, "Did you kill any communists?" surprised me. Kenny said, "I shot at 'em and they dropped–I probably did kill some of those gooks." George, who saw more action because he served in the front lines, withdrew more from my question, "I'm not sure how many I killed, I'm just glad it's over."

My brothers didn't talk much about their plans. Kenny said he might work with Uncle Harold on Merry's horse estate in Gates Mills until he could find something else. George said he planned to go to New York and work with horses again. He said he planned to see his father, but did not get into any specifics about his father's whereabouts. It had been five years since I had seen my dad. It caused me to believe that his parting words in 1948, "I'll probably never see you again," might come true. In retrospect, for some reason, my brothers made it a point to tell me little or nothing about our father or their plans for the future. My brothers' unwillingness to say much gave me more reason to feel like an outsider from the Palmers, and being a foster child, I also felt that way about every other family.

Kenny ended up getting married in 1953. He married a girl from Cleveland, and a year later, Laura was born; she was the first of five children. Kenny and his wife, Mary, didn't have the funds for a big wedding, but I remember attending their reception, held in the basement of Holy Name Church on the east side of Cleveland. On the other hand, I didn't know when George got married and for the next seven years I didn't hear from him or know anything about his whereabouts.

After a summer of camping out, baseball, hiking, and our annual fishing trip to northern Michigan, a new school year began. I would soon be entering the grade that most parents and teachers wished did not exist–the eighth grade.

Everybody in Chagrin Falls wanted their kids to be successful in all their endeavors, but a simpler and less sophisticated lifestyle existed back then, the athletic program not withstanding. Most of my classmates played football in one form or another in 1953, but we had to wait until our freshman year to be on a school team.

"We'll form our own team and challenge Orange or any school that will play us," said Bob Searcy.

Parks and I listened to Searc's ideas.

"If other schools can't form eighth grade teams, we'll challenge their freshman team to a game. We've got a helluva football class," said a confident Searc.

"Do you and Parks think ninth grade teams would play eighth grade teams?" I asked, in my usual naive way.

"They don't have anything to gain by playing us," answered Parks.

"I think our ninth graders would play us. There's no freshman football schedule; they just practice and get beat up scrimmaging against the varsity. They have to be dying to play a game. Besides, John Thomas wouldn't back down from any challenge; he would want to play us and like Coach Quesinberry says, stick our noses in it," said a convincing Bob Searcy.

"Searc, who would coach us?" asked Parks.

"Me!" responded Searc.

"You?" countered Parks, with a slight grin.

"Parks, you and Gair tell me what a great job of play calling I do in the Grudge Matches. We'll use a T-formation offense and a 5-3 defense just like the Tigers."

"You know something, people think because we're younger we can't compete with the older kids; that's bullshit! We have a better football class than them! I don't think they can beat us!" said an emotional Bob Searcy.

"Searc, put Gair at quarterback," suggested Parks.

"I will! Gair has a great arm; the best in our class."

"Seriously Searc, I've never handed off from a T-formation. I don't know how to do the handoffs and stuff. Besides, do you think I'm smart enough to be a quarterback?" I asked.

"Maybe we can use the single wing tailback spinner, Grudge Match offense. You've got those handoffs and fake handoffs down pat," laughed Parks.

"Gair we'll practice, so you'll learn on your own how to hand off! If we have to, we'll get Otto Graham to show you; and don't worry about thinking, I'll do it for you," laughed Searcy.

"I'm sure the great Otto Graham of the Cleveland Browns would show me how to play quarterback," I said.

Then we got back to strategizing for a possible game with the freshmen. Searcy pulled this game off by going right to John Thomas and asking him if the freshmen would play us.

"When do you want to play?" responded John.

"Give us three weeks to practice," answered Searc.

"Fine, I'll ask Coach if we can use the stadium field three weeks from Saturday. Searcy, who's coaching you guys?" asked John Thomas with his characteristic partial smile.

"It's a secret," responded Bob.

The unofficial game against the ninth graders became the first real football game that any of us had played in. Less than 100 parents and fellow students showed up for the game and they all stood along the sidelines. Just before the game started the butterflies in my stomach churned so hard that if I opened my mouth too wide, they would have flown out.

Parks' kickoff bounced so sporadically down the field that the ninth graders started out in a hole. We forced them to kick and immediately had good field position. But our offense sputtered, mainly because of middle linebacker John Thomas.

After a scoreless first quarter the freshmen got rolling. John Thomas scored in the second quarter and ran for the point after touchdown to give the ninth graders a 7-0, halftime lead. We moved the ball well in the third quarter but couldn't score, mainly because of the competitiveness of John Thomas. In the fourth quarter the momentum swung in our favor; spearheaded by the running of Steve Van Nort and Keith Foster and my only completed pass, a 15-yarder to Parks, we mounted a long drive and scored. Searc called the play for the one-point conversion, a quick look-in pass to either one of our lanky ends, Parks or Bruce Bird. When I took a step back to look for Parks or Bruce, Thomas blitzed and my desperation heave fell incomplete. Final score: Chagrin Falls Freshmen 7, Chagrin Falls Eighth-Graders 6. This unprecedented football game might have been the only Eighth-Grade versus

Ninth-Grade game in school history.

Eighth grade did not surface as one of my better years in school. I had the dubious distinction of being number one in my class for getting into trouble. I led my class in detentions with my buddy Jack Richardson close behind. Tardiness and the playful activities that we engaged in during study hall caused most of our detentions.

Almost daily during eighth period study hall, Jack and I had paper airplane wars. Landing your plane on the enemy's table counted as one kill and hitting each other with our paper airplanes counted as two kills. We kept score of our battles and every couple of weeks a new war began; whoever won the most battles won the war. Jack called his paper war machine Reggie and I called mine Puma. Because of the Reggie-Puma War, Jack and I had nicknames that stuck with us throughout our school years and beyond.

The Reggie-Puma War became so popular around school that I wrote a small piece about the classic study hall battles in the school newspaper, *The Grapevine*.

The trouble that Jack and I got into in school didn't compare to what we did outside the walls. Halloween should have been outlawed in Chagrin Falls during the 1950s because of the level of mischievous behavior that some of us engaged in. One of our favorite activities involved rolling tires and pumpkins down Grove Hill, the steep hill at the north edge of town that led directly into the center of Chagrin. I lived near the top of Grove Hill and Jack lived nearby on Cottage Street.

Rolling pumpkins down Grove Hill continues to this day as a Halloween tradition, but in much larger numbers. We used to roll two or three pumpkins at a time down Grove Hill, now they roll truckloads down the hill, a tradition that began after my childhood days in Chagrin Falls.

Besides our Grove Hill pranks, we set up roadblocks, filled unlocked parked cars with leaves; an easy task because everybody left their cars unlocked. We let the air out of tires; it was usually teachers' cars or other people that for some reason we just didn't like. Once we ordered groceries by phone, and then watched the delivery truck pull into someone's North Main Street driveway with the fake order. One of our disturbances made the front page of the local newspaper. The article headlines read, VANDALS DESTROY PARKING METERS. A police investigation and an assembly for Grades 7-12 resulted from the vandalism. The citizenry didn't like the parking meters because they saw them as a way for city hall to drain more money from the people. But it took a couple of adolescents with a "Spirit of

1776" mentality to do something about it. Jack and I dug up the new parking meters and threw them in Mayor Gresham's front lawn.

Superintendent of schools Lewis Sands presided over the assembly to denounce the vandalism. Mr. Sands, with bushy eyebrows and his usual serious demeanor, stood in front of the assembly and began speaking.

"The reason for this assembly is the recent vandalism that has struck our community. Just last night, the new parking meters were dug up and thrown in the mayor's front yard. I'm mad about this, I'm really mad, I'm mad," repeated the monotone voiced Lewis Sands.

The thing that I remember most about Superintendent Sands' speech is that he said he was mad, but showed no emotions. He was a very levelheaded man and a very good superintendent for Chagrin Falls' schools. But like most adults, Mr. Sands was somewhat naïve. Knowing that we caused the assembly, and in turn got a break from the rigors of the classroom, motivated us to plan future adventurous stunts that we could hopefully get away with. And being adolescents, we found humor in just about anything. Periodically, throughout our school years we imitated the popular and successful superintendent by going around saying, "I'm mad, now I'm mad," and ala Mr. Sands, showing absolutely no emotion or inflection in our voices.

Camping out, Halloween pranks, and the eighth grade-ninth grade football games stand out in my memory, but I also remember outdoor basketball pick-up games, playing basketball at the Federated Church gym and Coach Quesinberry's Saturday morning basketball leagues at the high school.

Coach's organizational skills and service to the youth of Chagrin Falls made Saturday morning basketball a fun and competitive experience. A curtain at mid-court separated the gym so that simultaneously two cross-court games could be played at the side baskets. We rushed to school every Monday morning to see the schedules, standings, court numbers, game times and scores that Coach posted on the gym bulletin board.

Parks and I always went to the high school home games on Friday night. We got psyched for Saturday morning round ball watching the color and excitement of the Tiger games and talked about the days when we would be Chagrin Falls Tigers. We also predicted the winners of Saturday's games and bet a pack of baseball or football cards whenever we disagreed on who would win. Since sports cards were not sold year around, our debts were sometimes paid the following spring, or just forgotten.

Winning on the field of play mattered more to me than anything else. I used to lie awake at night thinking about the games and yearning for the next competitive experience. Stanley or no one else encouraged me to play sports; it was something that I just loved to do. Stanley did play catch with me on one occasion. But my foster father always felt that I put too much emphasis on sports, and that detracted from my schoolwork and chores that needed to be done around the Davises. Florence wanted me to do well in school, but was more accepting of my fascination with sports.

The competitive nature of sports is what inspired me. I wanted to be successful at everything that I did. Even though the classroom as a whole was a struggle for me I did excel in certain subjects, mainly geography, history and geometry, and I loved writing themes. But the real proving grounds for me were the playing fields of Chagrin Falls.

On a couple occasions I hinted about how nice it would be to have a basketball hoop, but Stanley would have no part of that. The old barn, converted into a two-car garage would have been a perfect place for a hoop. I often fantasized about having a basket and a concrete court where the scattered pebbles of gravel laid; it might have become the best outdoor basketball court in Chagrin Falls. I would have practiced religiously if I had my own hoop. Knowing the disappointment of not having a basket at home when I was a child, I decided early in life that my children would always have a hoop.

Since the only animals that we had to feed were chickens, the mice infested haymow was used as a storage area for old farm equipment: horse harnesses, reins, bridle bits, hand plows, cow bells, butcher blocks, trunks and many other things that got lost in the clutter.

Besides hiking in the woods with Tippy and the fishing trips to Michigan, playing football, basketball and baseball were the themes of my life. I had the calendar year divided into four seasons: August through November–football season; December through March–basketball season; April through July–baseball season; June through August–fishing season. The entire year, January through December, was Tippy season.

I improved my baseball skills through pick-up games, playing catch and throwing tennis balls at the side of the barn. Parks and I made a makeshift diamond on a slope in Davises' 15-acre field. We cut the weeds with sickles and scythes and used flat rocks from the creek for bases. The weeds offered somewhat of a natural backstop and kept the ball from rolling very far.

"Be careful, Herman, that goddamn scythe'll take your leg off or your friend Parks' leg!" warned Stanley.

Parks and I learned to pitch without a catcher, play defense alone, and run uphill from second to home. We had fun no matter where we played, but it was a lot more fun playing on the level fields at Riverside Park and behind Parks' house.

My favorite solo baseball game was throwing tennis balls at a target on the front of the barn. I called the balls and strikes and made it challenging by decreasing the size of the strike zone and moving the pitcher's mound further from the target. Sometimes I pretended the games to be the World Series, other times it was two teams that had names I liked: the Cardinals, Braves, Dodgers, Giants, and especially the Indians and their archrival, the New York Yankees.

"Here we are at Lakefront Stadium along the shores of Lake Erie for the first game of a four-game series matching the American League's top two teams, the Cleveland Indians and New York Yankees, in one of baseball's hottest rivalries," became my typical opening remark before announcing the starting line-ups and firing the first pitch.

From reading the paper and listening to the games I knew the names of the players and their positions, the batting order and the approximate batting average of every player. I also knew the record of each team and the pitcher's earned run average, and when I didn't exactly know some of these details, I took an educated guess. When the games ended, I announced the final score followed by broadcaster Jimmy Dudley's patented farewell, "So long and lots of good luck, ya' heah!"

Hitting stones and gravel from the driveway in front of the barn became another solo game that I often played. I used an old dented, discolored Louisville Slugger. I loved the sound of the wooden bat hitting the pebbles as I smashed them into the open field. I didn't play this game when Grandma Davis watched, because she had no sense of humor; she didn't like the gravel disappearing from her driveway.

I played another creative game, ping-pong baseball, especially with Rick Thomas, another good friend of mine and the younger brother of John. Rick was a year behind me in school and John a year ahead of me. Their father was the honorable Federal Judge William K. Thomas, one of the judges who presided over the Kent State shootings in 1970. The game of ping-pong baseball that Rick and I had such loyalty to, was played at close range and required two players, a pitcher and a batter. The distance the ball traveled in fair territory determined one of five outcomes: single, double, triple, home run or out. Both players kept track of base runners, outs, the count on the hitter, and of course the score.

Ping-pong baseball had a challenge to it that I loved: The small ball, even though it moved slowly, could not be hit very far, and the pitcher could throw curveballs and sinkers. A sinker-curve, thrown like a knuckle ball in baseball became the toughest pitch to hit. Rick and I, in our minds, were the kingpins of ping-pong baseball in Chagrin Falls.

In the spring of 1954, around the beginning of baseball season, I was delighted when Florence told me Stanley decided to purchase a new Plymouth Station Wagon. Up until 1954, Stanley drove a faded sky-blue 1949 Plymouth and unpretentious Florence drove a 1929 Model A Ford. It was a coupe with a rumble seat and blacker than coal, the only color that cars were painted in 1929. When I rode in the Model A, it made me cringe. Florence's car was built 25 years earlier and when it was new it sold for around $450. By the 1950s it was a collector's item. But I didn't care about the antique value or the nostalgia that the old Model A Ford created in the minds of some. I was worried about, of all things, my image. Nobody else in town had a jalopy like that, so it never went unnoticed puttering down Main Street in Chagrin Falls. When I rode with Florence I tried to hide when I saw my friends, but a car so outmoded always made people stop and look, so all my friends knew who had the old black Model A Ford from the 1920s. In retrospect, it seems rather odd that an old car would embarrass me, considering my background, but I was immature and desperately wanted to be just like my friends and their normal families. But today, I wish I had that car.

Chapter IX
My First Year of High School

My freshman year in high school (1954-55) I grew to be over six feet tall. For the first time in my life, I became acutely aware of the differences between my family and me. The growth spurts that I experienced caused a big separation in height between my biological family and me. But since I hadn't seen my father in six years, and hardly thought about him, the physical differences seemed irrelevant. It might have seemed unlikely from a physical standpoint that Kenneth Palmer could have been my father, but he was the only father that I knew.

However, the awareness that resulted from the physical differences and his departing words in 1948, "I'll probably never see you again," had me thinking that he might not be my father. But there was much confusion; his words in Juvenile Court certainly seemed fatherly, "My mother in New Jersey can take Gary and raise him," making the issue of my identity, cloudy at best.

My confusion caused me to rationalize. Seldom did I notice family resemblances in other people. I considered people to be genetically unique, not necessarily having any resemblance to their parents. It was the same way I viewed myself. This philosophy and the fact that no one told me any differently, made the Palmers appear to be my biological parents.

Growing up, my mother and father had been a source of shame and embarrassment for me. I tried to repress my memories of alcoholism, domestic violence, abandonment, poverty, and the Detention Home. I didn't want anyone to know about my past. But on rare occasions, unpleasant reminders would surface. Two of them occurred during my freshman year in high school. Mechanical drawing class became the setting for one emotional incident.

"Close the door! Were you born in a barn?" said Mr. Fry in his usual non-insulting way.

I came in to his mechanical drawing class from the shop area to ask a question about my Industrial Arts project, and in doing so I left the door partially open. Bob Lambert, an upperclassman, was doing some make-up work at one of the mechanical drawing desks and couldn't refrain from commenting on my teacher's remark.

"Speaking of barns, remember that shack you lived in up on North Main? You remember," said Lambert looking directly at me with a smile that had insult written all over it.

The comment took me by surprise; seven years had passed and until now no one had brought up the sensitive issues of my past. Simultaneously, feelings of hurt, embarrassment, speechlessness, nervousness and anger jostled in my mind. I had the urge to fight, but a freshman punching a junior did not seem like the smartest thing to do, and Bob Lambert didn't appear as a pushover. I remember a few years ago seeing Lambert in a fistfight at Riverside Park and he bloodied his opponents' nose pretty badly. Knowing this, I still approached the not-so-good football player and self-proclaimed tough guy with my teeth locked firmly together and my fists clenched. I had never backed down from anybody that wanted to fight and I didn't plan to start now. Lambert, sensing my anger, stared at me momentarily and then glanced over at Mr. Fry.

"Palmer, get your butt back in the shop and get to work! Your project's due Friday!" Mr. Fry yelled.

The second ninth grade incident involved some unfavorable comments about my grandmother's second husband, Bill Kelley. It happened in science class; we had some free time at the end of class and our teacher left the room to speak with someone in the hall. Jerry Richardson, no relation to my buddy Jack, sat directly in front of me. He turned around, cracked a smile and said, "Do you ever drink beer?"

I responded, "Only once; my brother gave me a couple of bottles last summer when I cut his lawn. I had to stay over at his house that night because of those beers. Why, have you ever drank beer?"

Jerry, with teeth that always appeared to be yellow and uncared for prominently showing, laughed and said, "We get drunk every weekend."

"Who's we?" I asked.

"Me and my friends," responded Jerry.

I may have been naïve, but a 15-year-old getting drunk every weekend seemed unbelievable.

"Where do you get the beer from?" I asked.

"I don't know if I should tell you," he said.

"Why not?" I asked.

"Isn't Bill Kelley your grandfather?" said Jerry.

"He was when my grandmother was alive. What I mean is that he was married to my grandmother," I responded.

"Then he was your grandfather, right?" continued Jerry.

"Kind of, I guess. He was my grandma's second husband. I haven't had much to do with him since my grandma died. He's always drunk!" I answered.

"Don't get mad when I tell you this. Bill Kelley buys us all the booze we want; we pay him for doing it," said Jerry.

I jumped up and grabbed my beer-drinking classmate by his shirt, twisting it so hard his face got red.

"Are you bull shitting me?" I asked.

"Hell no! I didn't have to tell you!" he responded.

I continued talking and let go of Richardson's shirt, "I can't believe this! Why didn't you tell me this before?" I asked.

"I didn't know how to tell you. I thought he was your real grandpa. Besides, me and you don't hang out together anyway."

I felt lucky that I played sports and didn't hang out with Jerry Richardson or fall prey to the same temptations. I also felt fortunate that Bill Kelley decided not to keep me after Grandma died. Stunned by my findings, I continued to question Richardson.

"Why does he do this? Couldn't he go to jail for this?"

Richardson responded, "We give him money; he'll do anything for money so he can buy more booze. He can get in trouble and be arrested for contributing to the delinquency of a minor."

"You better be telling me the truth!" I said.

"I am," was Jerry Richardson's final response.

This incident became one of the most embarrassing moments of my life and made me realize that despite the problems I had at the Davises', I was lucky to be there. The two ninth grade incidents also made me aware that nothing remains a secret for very long in Chagrin Falls.

Fortunately, I had developed the ability to push things aside, store them in a separate box in my mind and continue on without allowing them to affect my life. The normal things that happen to an adolescent growing up in a small town during the 1950s took center stage. The excitement of sports, television, my first girlfriend, hiking with my dog, getting into mischief with friends, and listening to music and sports on the radio dominated my first year in high school. I loved pop, country, and especially old time songs about the South. In my imagination, the sun always shone on happy and friendly people down South. My image of the South changed somewhat after knowing Ben, but I still had fantasies about life below the Mason-Dixon line. I imagined endless acres of rivers, lakes, and woods. I envisioned every boy having a dog and looking like Huckleberry Finn. By age 14, Virginia was the furthest south I had been. That didn't stop me from singing my favorite songs of the South while hiking in the woods and walking to school. A couple of them I especially liked singing:

Suwanee, how I love ya, how I love ya,
My dear ole' Suwanee.
The folks up North will see me no more,
when I get to that Suwanee shore.

Oh, the yellow rose of Texas is mine forever more,
nobody else has missed her, not half as much as me.
You can talk about your Clementine and sing of Rosalee,
but the yellow rose of Texas is the only girl for me.

Despite liking songs about the South, my favorite songs were college fight songs. The only record I had during my growing up years were a *Medley of College Fight Songs.* Singing the fight songs on the way to freshman football practice in 1954 got me psyched-up for practice.

We practiced every day with no ninth grade games to look forward to. Our coach, Tom Mattern, a senior basketball player and future director of the Chagrin Falls Schools' Alumni Association, made the practices as challenging as he could under the circumstances. Freshmen didn't dress for varsity games, but we never missed attending the games and supporting our upper class heroes.

The biggest game of the year loomed on the horizon for the unbeaten Tigers. The game against the largest school in our conference, the Mayfield Wildcats, decided the conference championship all four years that I played high school football.

The Wildcats avenged last season's 13-0 Tiger victory by destroying our hopes for an undisputed championship, 13-7.

I hated losing even if I wasn't playing in the game, so I led a small group of angry freshmen on a mission to get even. We ambushed the Mayfield school buses as they jubilantly headed down East Washington Street on their way home. We threw grapefruit-size green hedge oranges (monkey balls) at their buses. The monkey balls made loud thudding noises when they hit the sides of the buses. I unleashed one that went crashing through a window of the band bus. I had carried my anger and distaste for losing way too far.

After being notified about what I had done, Stanley gave me a good tongue-lashing. "How the hell do you expect to play varsity football next year? What are you gonna do, kill your opponent if they beat you, or just try to beat 'em up? Maybe you could throw hand grenades at the ball carrier; that would sure as hell stop 'em. Goddamnit Herman, I don't know about you!"

I saved myself from expulsion by admitting what I had done. The fit of anger, a low point in my high school career, could have resulted in serious injury, but amazingly and fortunately no one got hurt. I apologized by phone to an administrator at Mayfield High School. They accepted my apology and did not pursue delinquent charges–I didn't even have to pay for the broken window. One thing I learned from this incident that holds true more often than not–it pays to be honest.

On the political front in 1954, the United States Supreme Court ruled that segregation by color in public schools violated the Fourteenth Amendment to the Constitution. In my conversations with Ben, I don't remember the Supreme Court decision being brought up, probably because in Ohio the Fourteenth Amendment never became an issue.

I remember a colored boy in our school my freshman year. A senior named Charlie Jenkins moved from Cleveland to Chagrin Falls in 1953 or 1954. He lived in a rural area south of town and played as a reserve guard on the basketball team. Charlie, rather short and a little on the chunky side, had a good two handed set-shot. I remember him being the only Negro in our school and coming to a high school dance with his Cleveland girl friend, a pleasant colored girl from Glenville High School. Their personalities kicked in and they became very accepted and well liked at the dance.

Besides Charlie Jenkins, another colored boy emerged on the scene in the ninth grade. Johnny Sapp, a Kenston High School student, lived at the colored allotment. Like other colored people that I knew in my life, namely Bailey and Ben, Johnny had a good sense of humor. He hung around Chagrin and became friends with several of us provincial white lads from the village. Johnny, small in stature, but strong and a fast runner, liked to bowl, run races and play basketball with us at the Federated Church gym. Whenever we didn't have enough players for a pick up game, Sapp and I always played one-on-one or we played the shooting game of elimination that the world refers to as H-O-R-S-E.

It always bugged Johnny that he was quicker and faster than me, but could never beat me playing basketball. I had a height advantage and my shooting skills were superior because I played all the time.

One day Johnny and I started betting two bits on each game of H-O-R-S-E. The game, of course (a horse is a horse of course) gives you a letter each time a shot is missed that your opponent makes, until someone gets H-O-R-S-E on them, causing elimination. We also bet two bits on each one-on-one game. He kept losing and losing and losing, but never wanted to stop betting.

"Johnny 'Maplesapp,' I know why you think you can beat me, cuzz I'm white and you're colored. You think that colored boys can always beat white boys in basketball. Well Johnny Appleseed, I got news for y'all," I said.

"I can beat your ass if I keep playing you. My shots goin' down baby! Johnny ain't takin' no more shit from y'all! Let's go double or nothin' again," he said.

Since we were in a church gym I didn't like it when Johnny swore and I told him so. He just laughed but I don't remember him doing it again. I had my own set of rules about swearing: You could swear outside, in school or just about anywhere, but never in church or in front of a girl. Despite getting into a lot of trouble and being anything but a model student, I considered both to be disrespectful.

Anyway, back to basketball: Johnny and I kept playing double or nothing; he kept hoping to spring an upset so that he would not owe me anything. He never won, and over the course of several visits to the Federated Church gym, Johnny owed me 100 dollars. Every time I saw him I always kidded him about owing me the money, "OK Johnny 'Maplesapp,' or is it 'Appleseed'? Where's my hundred dollars?" I used to say. Of course, where would any young law abiding boy, colored or white, get 100 dollars in 1954, or any year for that matter?

I always wanted Johnny to go to school in Chagrin so he could be a fast colored boy on our football team, but he had the misfortune of being a Kenston Bomber. I felt sorry for Johnny if he ever played football for the Bombers because Kenston got steamrolled by the Tigers in the 1950s. They were Tiger meat for us "boys from the valley" or like the Solon Comets used to call us, "The boys from across the river." Solon, a team that considered us their archrival also called us "The boys from Chaggy Balls."

But wasn't I talking about Johnny Sapp, the fast, wiry colored boy from the allotment that I befriended during this time period of my life? You know the kid with a great sense of humor who liked to gamble and always thought he could beat his buddy "Pume" playing basketball. The same Johnny Maplesapp that jumped back into my life years later when he was parking cars at a football game while serving as a deputy with the Geauga County

Sheriff's Department. I'm getting' off the beaten path again; there's another story about Johnny Appleseed and my days growing up in Chagrin Falls that I wanted to tell you about. It was the time he got into a fight with his friend and mine, Jack Richardson. It happened outside the bowling alley and it may have been over money that Johnny owed Jack from bowling bets. Apparently, Johnny also made bets with Jack that he couldn't pay. Jack and Johnny matched up well in height, but Johnny appeared to be a little quicker and stronger than Jack. I knew from the welfare home that colored boys had hard heads and were good fighters. I showed up because I didn't want to see either of my friends get hurt, but I wanted Jack to win because he had been my friend a lot longer than Johnny had and also because I saw Jack as the underdog in the fight. Race may have been another reason why I wanted Jack to win. Especially back then, black and white people alike rooted for people of their own race. To root for people of your own race, nationality, hometown, state and country was something that everybody did. Anyway, the fight between "Johnny and Jackie" did not turn out to be brutal or I would have stepped in, but if I had been refereeing, Johnny would have been declared the winner. Jack had a few cuts after the scuffle, but nothing serious. They shook hands after the fight and soon were friends again. Even though Johnny played basketball with us at the church gym, I don't remember him playing high school basketball for Kenston or football for that matter. He would have taken quite a ribbing if he had.

During the same school year, 1954-55, Chagrin's varsity basketball team had two future service academy athletes leading them: Pete Van Nort, a future football and basketball player at the Naval Academy and Larry Wiley, a future lacrosse player at West Point.

But the Tiger freshman team, mainly because of Parks, became the most dominant athletic team that I ever played on. Our undefeated season included winning seven of eight games by 19 points or more and averaging almost 30 points a game more than our opponents. Parks averaged 20 points a game, and if it weren't for Coach Quesinberry substituting freely when the 24-minute games started getting out of hand, my talented friend would have averaged 30 points a game.

One of many unforgettable Coach Quesinberry moments occurred in the fourth quarter of one of our lopsided ninth grade games. A teammate and friend of mine, Bill Reitz, grabbed a defensive rebound and scored...for the other team! Coach seemingly took Bill's mistake in stride by acting as if nothing happened. Since we had the game easily won, I figured that Coach must have felt that scoring for the other team really didn't matter. But when Bill came off the court, most people would have paid the price of admission just to hear Coach's comment.

"Reitz! Don't you know which basket is ours? It's a good thing it's not a close game or they'd run you out of town! They'd send you over to Solon on one of those freight trains that comes through town!" said the incomparable Coach Quesinberry, without cracking a smile.

Having Coach Quesinberry as a role model and growing up in Ohio during the glory days of sports had a big impact on my life. Participating in sports surfaced as the most important experience in my life. Because I didn't have much going for me, life would have been pretty meaningless without sports, especially football.

Although I don't remember, the Cleveland Rams won the NFL Championship in 1945. The following year the Rams moved to Los Angeles, and the Cleveland Browns, led by Massillon, Ohio native and Hall of Fame coaching genius, Paul Brown, became a new professional football franchise. The Browns spent four seasons, 1946-1949, in the All-American Football Conference and won four consecutive titles. In 1950 they entered the National Football League and rocked the football world by winning the prestigious National Football League title; they defeated the former Cleveland NFL team, the Los Angeles Rams, 30-28. The new kids on the block played in the Super Bowl equivalent, NFL title game, seven times the first eight years in the league. Besides 1950, the Browns became NFL champions in 1954 and 1955. The 13 professional football seasons from 1945 through 1957 saw Cleveland professional football teams play in an unprecedented twelve championship games, winning eight titles. Except for the 1945 Cleveland Rams, Paul Brown coached every team.

One of the highlights of my growing up years occurred when Parks and his father and I attended the 1954 NFL title game against the Detroit Lions. Thanks to Parks' dad we had great seats–30-yard line, upper deck on the southeast side of Municipal Stadium. The game, played in a snowstorm, resulted in some no-shows allowing Parks and I to move into two empty seats by the railing. The heavy snowfall throughout the game created poor visibility but enabled us to make snowballs and blast the Lions fans that were seated in the lower deck directly below us. Parks and I wanted to get even for last weeks 14-10 loss in Detroit.

Not only did the Detroit fans take a beating from our snowballs, so did their team. Cleveland's defense forced eight turnovers, and Otto Graham had a field day passing to halfback Ray Renfro. In the Super Bowl of our time, our beloved Browns romped to victory, 56-10.

That same year, 1954, the Cleveland Indians won the American League Pennant and set a major league record for most victories in a season. Also in 1954, thanks again to Mr. Odenweller, Parks and I attended the Major League All-Star game in Cleveland. The tribe's Al Rosen hit two home runs to lead the American League to an 11-9 victory.

Two of Ohio State's National Championship football teams were crowned in the 1950s; Woody Hayes' Buckeyes won National Championships in 1954 and 1957.

After the freshman basketball season ended I wanted to transform my skinny 160-pound body into a mass of muscles, mainly because I wanted to be a good football player. But in the mid-1950s a misconception existed about strength development. Weight training was taboo; it scared coaches because they thought it would make their athletes muscle bound and uncoordinated. This viewpoint resulted from body builders who religiously lifted weights for contests, to be photographed for magazines, or just to admire themselves. They looked as though they could not catch a pass, shoot a basketball, or swing a bat. This was an era when there was a definite lack of knowledge and understanding about the advantages and techniques of weight training to enhance athletic performance. The lack of knowledge resulted in a generation of weak athletes, compared to today's standards.

I answered the objection to weight training by sending away for the Joe Louis Physical Fitness Program. The fitness development plan emphasized many variations of push-ups to build strength in the upper body. In so far as I had just started the fitness program, I hadn't developed any muscles yet, but that didn't stop me from one bizarre confrontation. It involved my buddy Jack "Reggie" Richardson, and the owner of the Kitchen, a small eatery in town.

"Redge, what do you think about DeLorian?" I asked.

"I heard he's a communist," responded Jack.

"I heard he's a card carrying communist. Florence and Stanley told me that means he's a real communist. I wonder why people keep going to the Kitchen if they know that."

"I don't think too many people go there anymore, Pume," replied Reggie.

I didn't completely understand Communism, but I knew it to be an evil form of government. I knew that communists wanted to destroy our democracy and take away our freedom, like they had done in some parts of Europe.

"Let's go see DeLorian and tell him if he likes being a Communist to get the hell out of our country and go to Russia or China or one of those screwed up places!" I proclaimed.

"Ha! Ha! OK Pume, if you want to, but we might get into trouble," answered Jack.

"What's new?" I responded.

In the dead of winter, early in 1955, we arrived at the Kitchen. Only a few customers sat in the restaurant and DeLorian lingered in the Kitchen's kitchen preparing orders. I asked the waitress if we could see him. When several minutes passed and he did not respond, I became impatient.

"DeLorian, come out here!" I yelled. When he didn't respond I got a little braver, "DeLorian, you fat ass come out here!"

I knew that would get his attention but I was scared to death after saying it. DeLorian, a rather stocky, overweight man, about 5'10" and well over 200 pounds wearing an apron tied around his waist, came out of the kitchen and walked slowly toward our table.

"I'm going to have to ask you to leave, Palmer!" said DeLorian, then he paused for several seconds and continued, "I know your brother Kenny."

It always bothered me that my brother knew DeLorian and had dated his daughter, Violet. It puzzled me why Kenny would date a communist after fighting them in Korea. I hated communists, and I wondered why my brother didn't hate them too, after all, they tried to kill him. I wondered what his reasoning was for dating a communist. I would puke if I ever kissed a communist girl and I'd probably puke right in her face. I became embarrassed and angry knowing that other people heard DeLorian say that he knew my brother. Out of the clear blue sky, I pushed back the chair and sprung to my feet like I did later in my life when reveille sounded in boot camp. I was too mad to be nervous any longer.

"We don't have to leave, DeLorian! This is the United States not Russia. I don't care if you know my brother; he fought you communist bastards in Korea," I proclaimed.

"That's it, Palmer, get out of here right now or I'm calling the police!" yelled DeLorian.

"DeLorian, you're nothing but a fat-assed fuckin' communist!" I yelled back.

I grabbed the tablecloth and ripped it off the table; a salt and peppershaker, napkin holder and ashtray went flying across the floor of the small restaurant. I pushed the table over directly at DeLorian; then Jack and I ran for the door and DeLorian began chasing us. We ran outside and sprinted toward the rear of the Kitchen. With DeLorian in hot pursuit, Jack and I grabbed several giant icicles hanging from the Kitchen's gutters and began firing them at the out-of-shape restaurant owner. One of my flying icicles hit DeLorian directly in the chest at the same time that he lost his footing and fell down in the snow. We followed up with a flurry of icicles; most of them missed but a couple more grazed him as he continued to chase us.

"You Goddamn young shitheads! Palmer, your ass is in a lot of trouble!" yelled DeLorian.

"Better dead than red, your commie asshole!" I yelled.

"Redge, he's after me not you!" I hollered.

"I wonder why," cracked Jack.

"We'll split at Cottage Street, here he comes!" I yelled.

"He's getting into his car!" hollered Jack.

I headed home by running to the top of Grove Hill. A few hundred feet from where I lived I spotted my friend, Steve Van Nort, walking home from school.

"Steve! DeLorian is after me! I'm going to hide in the field! Tell him you didn't see me!" I yelled.

I could hear them talking when DeLorian pulled up to ask Steve if he had seen me.

"Did you see the Palmer kid?" DeLorian asked Steve.

"No, I didn't see him," answered Steve.

While hiding in the field, I watched DeLorian go right to Davises' front door. Grandma Davis answered the door and according to her, this is how the conversation went.

"The Palmer kid lives here, doesn't he?" asked DeLorian.

"Yeah, but he's not here; what do you want?" responded Grandma Davis.

"I own the Kitchen and he came in my restaurant and yelled insults at me that I can't repeat, knocked over a table, and hit me with icicles, I'm filing a police report," said DeLorian.

"We'll have a talk with him about that because he's not supposed to be in your place anyway; now you better leave," announced Grandma Davis.

This is the only time that Agnes didn't get mad at me when I got into trouble.

"Herman, goddamn it! Don't ever go in the Kitchen again. He might be a communist, but leave the son-of-a-bitch alone!" said Stanley.

Going into the Kitchen and starting trouble may have satisfied a need for violence, but more likely it was an indication of both immaturity and insecurity, causing me to feel that I had something to prove. I didn't have the confidence or courage to challenge DeLorian alone, so I dragged Jack into my spontaneous scheme. On the surface, my hatred of communists stemming from the Korean War was the reason for the violence at the Kitchen. But a big reason was a chip I had on my shoulder that sometimes came tumbling off. In retrospect, I wonder if I had lived in a Russian Communist neighborhood, if I would have felt the same way about communists.

Late in the school year in ninth grade, I noticed that I hadn't seen Benjamin around the hardware store in quite a while. One day I went in the store, looking for him. Knowing that he only worked in the back storage rooms or outside, I snooped around hoping to see him. Someone in the store told me Ben didn't work there anymore and they didn't know what happened to him. Johnny Sapp, who knew Ben from the allotment, hadn't seen him either.

I missed the conversations with Ben and I hoped that nothing bad had happened to him. I remember thinking that maybe he had moved back to Mississippi or somewhere else. Since I didn't have parents or grandparents Ben kind of took the place of a grandfather for a brief time in my life. He had a cheerful, positive attitude and a great sense of humor. The things he taught me inverted the stereotype that many people believed about colored people. Bailey, Johnny Sapp and Charlie Jenkins also contradicted those stereotypes.

When I read the papers or heard Stanley and Florence talking about the white gangs and black gangs fighting with knifes, razor blades, clubs and guns in Cleveland and other big cities, I thought about how different my experiences with colored people were. But, if I had lived in the city, my perception of colored people probably would have been totally different. Maybe I would have hated blacks, been scared and insecure around them and joined a gang for protection or revenge. Maybe I would have been killed, seriously injured, or gone to prison for killing or injuring someone else. It made me appreciate more than ever the placidity of my hometown.

The spring of my freshman year brought a new twist to my life. Cindy Hurst, a mature seventh grade girl, became my first steady girlfriend. Alas, the puppy love and infatuation relationship ended a few months after it began. What I missed most about Cindy was sitting out on the brick patio behind her house on a wooden bench and necking. Since I wasn't used to kissing before I dated Cindy, whenever our lips touched it was a heavenly experience, something I yearned for whenever we were apart.

I'll never forget Florence's reaction when I told her Cindy and I had broken up, "Why did you and Cindy break up? Did you try to get something off of her?" asked Florence.

It caught me by surprise because Florence never talked like that. I also wondered how she could have such insight into problems that young people sometimes faced. My naivety made me rationalize that things had to be different during her younger days in the 1920s; this was the modern era–the 1950s. So, I responded to Florence's question reluctantly, "No Florence, we just had some disagreements."

Later in life someone commented about Cindy's mother's attitude concerning our brief relationship by saying to me, "You weren't good enough for her." After all those years, it made me realize that her mother may have been the reason for our breakup. In defense of Cindy's mother, she wasn't the only mom in Chagrin Falls that felt that I wasn't good enough for their daughter. Quite frankly, I couldn't blame anybody for feeling that way. If I had a daughter, I would have been particular about her choice of mates also.

The breakup with Cindy certainly had an impact on future relationships. It made me aware that most of the popular and pretty girls were not interested in me. Maybe things would have been different if I had been good in school and didn't get into so much trouble.

But in reality, I was one of those Chagrin Falls kids that just didn't measure up, a misfit so to speak. Unfortunately, since I took things so personally, the breakup with Cindy did leave some scars. I didn't have a steady girlfriend again until the spring of my senior year. That was unfortunate and often painful because there were so many girls whose companionship I would have enjoyed, especially the romantic part.

Resultantly, I spent much of my spare time listening to pop music on the radio and dreaming about some of those gorgeous Chagrin girls.

Chapter X
My Sophomore Year and Coach Quesinberry

The strongest male role model in my life, Coach Quesinberry, didn't mind me not having a girlfriend. Coach was a stalwart of a man with a passion for toughness, especially gridiron toughness. He believed that football played a major role in the total development of young men and that girls had the potential to interfere with the football maturation process. Girls interfering with football must have been a theme of high school coaches back then. When I read former Solon star Dave Meggyesy's controversial book about football, *Out Of Their League*, he mentioned that his high school coach, Bob Vogt, also lectured about the pitfalls of dating young girls, especially girls with reputations.

But wasn't I talking about my staunch and respected coach, Ralph Quesinberry? "Quiz" as he is affectionately referred by many of his former players, began teaching and coaching in the Chagrin Falls school system in 1946, and soon became a Chagrin Falls icon. He was a big influence in my life, and the lives of many other young boys growing up in Chagrin Falls.

Orphaned at an early age, Coach grew up in Tiffin, Ohio and spent much of his youth in a children's home. He attended Bowling Green State University on a football scholarship, completing his education in 1946 after a World War II stint in the Army.

Ralph Quesinberry had been a co-captain at Bowling Green where he played center and linebacker in spite of weighing only 170 pounds. During the 1950s Coach earned a master's degree from Kent State while teaching and coaching full time at Chagrin Falls High School. Success came quickly for Coach Quesinberry. In 1947, his first year as head football coach at Chagrin Falls High School, he finished the season unbeaten.

Coach Quesinberry had a strong family bond with his wife, Peg, his two sons, Dave and Tom and a daughter Sue, who was not yet born when I was a sophomore in high school. Coach stood less than six feet tall and had put on quite a few pounds since his college football playing days and his stint in the Army, but he was a warrior in every sense of the word. He served as a medic in one of our nation's biggest battles during World War II, The Battle of The Bulge. The month long engagement (December 16, 1944-January 16, 1945) fought in the wooded Ardennes region of south Belgium became the last German offensive on the Western Front. The Germans were initially successful in their plans to divide the allied forces and prevent an invasion of Germany, but Allied resistance and reinforcements led by General Patton caused the Germans to withdraw. Both sides suffered heavy losses at the historical battle, named after the "bulge" that the Germans drove into the allied lines.

Coach's gym classes reflected his military background. He emphasized silent military drills, physical fitness, tumbling, gymnastics, and team sports. High on Coach's gym class priority list were rope climbing and springboard activities that tested a student's nerve, strength and will to succeed.

In the spring near the end of the school year, Coach proudly put on his patented gym shows that showcased to the community the benefits of a good physical education program. The final act of every gym show saw the senior boys displaying their military splendor by partaking in silent marching routines with precision turns memorized and executed without commands. The maneuvers were practiced over and over so they would be performed flawlessly in front of an appreciative audience. The Army veteran's militaristic themes became beneficial to the body, mind and spirit. With memories of World War II and the Korean War fresh in mind, Coach's gym shows were understood and appreciated by most people. It reminded them of the importance of physical conditioning and military discipline.

Besides coaching freshman basketball, varsity football and track, organizing and running Saturday morning basketball leagues, and putting on gym shows, Coach volunteered his services to the kids of Chagrin Falls in other ways. To meet the educational, athletic and recreational needs of the kids of Chagrin Falls, he helped organize summer programs at the recreation center, and always extended himself beyond the call of duty whenever there was need for his assistance and leadership.

The services that he rendered made him a special person. But Ralph Quesinberry the man and the hard-nosed football coach are my fondest memories of the person who became the role model that I desperately needed.

The things that Coach did and especially the things that he said have lived with me forever. There were a few clichés among Coach's vocabulary of quotes, but most of the things that he said over and over were vintage Coach Quesinberry.

Before football games against teams not particularly strong, in an effort to condition us not to under-estimate an opponent, Coach would say, "They'll be over here with the band and cheerleaders and they'll have flags and banners up and down the field. They would like nothing better than to beat you. They'll be after you with both barrels. You better be ready for the fight of your lives."

At the expense of a 15-yard penalty, he believed in intimidating the quarterback on the first defensive play of the game, especially a young signal caller. He had an uncanny way of suggesting his intent.

"If your momentum carries you on the first play, let the quarterback have both barrels. We'll take the fifteen yards."

There are other unforgettable quotes that became trademarks of Coach Ralph Quesinberry:

"I've seen better heads on beers!"

"Run it again!"

"You're going to get our quarterback killed!"

"Bout through!"

"You're the worst (player's position) that I ever coached."

"It's running down your leg."

"Walk it off." Coach never wanted to believe that one of his players could be injured.

"I don't care if he goes in the grandstands." This means if the player that you are assigned to block is 100 yards removed from the play, block him anyway.

"If it's not raining at 28 South Street (Coach's home address), we'll practice."

"You'd be the first to run if I got the (boxing) gloves out." He said this when he thought two antagonists did not really have the courage or will to fight.

"Everybody'll be after us." This statement characterized the emphasis our opponents put on the Chagrin game. It meant that we had to be ready for a battle every time we stepped on the field.

"We're in this together."

"If you can't do the job I'll find somebody who can."

"My wife can run faster than that."

Because of Coach, football became more than just a game to me. It was a builder of character, a way to become a man, a rallying point for spirit, pride, honor, and most importantly, a way of life. And because Coach had such high expectations on the gridiron, I never wanted to let him down. More than anything, I wanted to win and receive the recognition from Coach.

Coach touched many peoples lives, among them former football star, Don

Evans, a 1951 graduate. Don, a member of the Chagrin Falls High School Athletic Hall of Fame is writing a book entitled *The Q Factor*. The book is a tribute to the legendary Coach Quesinberry.

I have many early memories of Coach going back to when he taught physical education during my elementary school days. At first I was scared to death of him, but I quickly learned that I just had to do what I was told and do it with enthusiasm and everything would be all right.

One incident has remained embedded in my mind as if it happened yesterday. It occurred on a hot, August day in 1951, as I watched a Chagrin Falls Tiger football practice. My skinny 11-year-old body stood on the sidelines of the football field near the west end zone. Barefoot and wearing a bathing suit with a towel draped around my neck, I waited for the "rec" center swimming pool to open. Coach Quesinberry, not happy with one of his player's blocking efforts got everybody's attention within shouting distance. The player was Tom Conway, better known as Tim Conway, the Hollywood actor that starred in several movies, but is most famous for his part in two television shows, McHale's Navy and the Carol Burnett Show. Coach got into Conway's face, "You're going to get our quarterback killed! If you don't start doin' the job, I'll find somebody who can! We're gonna run this play until you get it right! Run it again!"

Then Coach booted Conway in the rear end with the inside of his right foot. I remember the incident as if it happened yesterday. I recall thinking how tough, exciting and important football really is. Then something flashed through my mind that I still remember; "If all that can happen to me playing football is to get kicked and yelled at, that ain't nothin'."

A few years after the Conway incident, my ability to withstand criticism and humiliation from Coach got put to the test. One October evening in 1955 I received a verbal blasting that would either make or break me as an athlete, and quite possibly, as a person.

It was my sophomore year and we were playing Brooklyn, a school located on the near west side of Cleveland. Chagrin scored in the fourth quarter and took the lead for the first time in the game, 6-2. As a newly appointed member of the kickoff team, I sweated to make the tackle and contribute to the Tiger's fifth consecutive victory. Cantwell, Brooklyn's star halfback, fielded the kickoff and headed toward the west end zone directly in my lane of responsibility. I sprinted up field with the hope that I would not get into an agility contest with the elusive star player. I wanted the Brooklyn ball carrier to appear like magic in front of me so my long and skinny 170-pound body could hit him with a full head of steam. My anxiousness and lack of experience caused me to get too deep in my running lane. Cantwell cut diagonally behind me and headed for the goal line. He got tackled inside the Tiger 10-yard line and the Hurricanes had first and goal with the clock ticking down in the fourth quarter. When I came to the sidelines, upset because I did not make the tackle, I stayed away from Coach Quesinberry, but he didn't stay away from me.

"You goddamn dumb sophomore, you'll never play for me again! That was a stupid and gutless play! What are you going to tell these seniors if they lose because of you? You better hope they don't score! If you cost us this game!" Coach hesitated and then continued, "Get out of my goddamn sight!"

"Gutless" surfaced as the most humiliating name that I had ever been called. I wasn't gutless saving my dog's life by engaging in hand-to-hand combat with a German shepherd, or vowing that I would fight to the death for my country if called upon. My dad and Stanley had cursed me down, but prior to this October Friday night in 1955 I had never been called a coward. It would be bad enough to win and be called gutless, but if we lost I might as well really run away from home this time.

Standing on the sidelines with tears streaming down my cheeks and no one talking to me or offering sympathy, I realized more than anything the importance of the game of football: to my coach, my school, my teammates, and especially myself. Football helped me vent my frustrations and it gave me a purpose in life. But once again I had failed to succeed. I felt I had begun a trend of failure that started in the classroom, continued at the Davises', and now had spilled over to the athletic field. If sports didn't work out for me, I was in deep shit because there was nothing left.

The Tiger cheering section continuously pleaded, "Hold that line!" I prayed to God that Brooklyn would not score. At this juncture in my life, it had to be the strongest prayer that I can remember delivering to our savior, Jesus Christ. Maybe somebody up there would listen, and like Woody Hayes used to say, "by golly" they did. The Tiger defense kept the Hurricanes from scoring and we posted a 6-2 win to remain unbeaten.

I blamed myself for the embarrassing humiliation. After all, Coach Quesinberry had emerged as the strongest male role model in my life. I wanted to be a coach and physical education teacher and military man just like him.

Coach's words after one football play my sophomore year became a turning point in my life. The humiliating incident would have caused some to lose confidence in their ability to play football, and also lose respect for their coach. Conversely, it motivated me to prove myself, and I never lost respect for my coach.

My favorite president, Theodore Roosevelt echoed my feelings:

> *Far better it is to dare mighty things, to win glorious*
> *triumphs, even though checkered by failure, than to*
> *take rank with poor spirits who neither enjoy much*
> *nor suffer much, because they live in the gray twilight*
> *that knows not victory nor defeat.*

In retrospect, there is one astonishing thing about high school football in the 1950s that remains scary and is quite unbelievable. We did not drink water during practices and games because most coaches, including Coach Quesinberry, thought it to be a weakness, something that would make an athlete sluggish and prevent him from performing well. Many times my teammates and I felt sick and dizzy, a sign of heat exhaustion, due to dehydration. It's a miracle that there were no serious problems like heat stroke, at least none that I knew of, especially on the practice fields at Chagrin because of the ferocity of our physical conditioning program. Practices sometimes lasted two and a half hours in the hot summer sun and then we ran wind sprints until we teetered on the verge of collapsing.

I remember teams coming to Chagrin with big containers of water and because I had been unintentionally brainwashed I thought that any team that drinks water while playing the Chagrin Falls Tigers were weak and undisciplined and couldn't possibly beat us. Confidence, whether derived from something positive or negative, is a powerful tool. We never lost to any of those teams that brought big containers of water and that reinforced the message; our training rules had a reflection of superiority over our water-guzzling opponents. The astonishing thing is that the majority of our opponents weren't permitted to drink water during practices or games either.

We took salt tablets when we came off the field to restore sodium in the blood lost from perspiration. It was the only time that we were permitted to drink water. Players are now required to take water every 15 to 20 minutes during practices and games or whenever they are overheated and need to be hydrated.

It wasn't Coach's fault that he subscribed to the no-water philosophy. It was a sign of the times that resulted from lack of knowledge. Coach was a product of what he had learned playing high school and college football.

Chagrin Falls, like most schools in those days, had no trainers. Resultantly, there was nobody to insist that players stay hydrated during practices and games, especially during conditions of extreme heat. Of course, we now know that Coach's no-water policy was risky and ill advised, and bordered on insanity.

On the world front in 1955, Germany became a NATO member; Winston Churchill resigned after serving as Britain's Prime Minister for 15 years; the United States Air Force Academy opened; and blacks in Montgomery, Alabama, boycotted segregated city bus lines.

Everything that happened away from Chagrin Falls seemed so distant to me, almost as if it happened in another world. My biggest concern centered on getting through school and being successful in sports.

Basketball, my sophomore year, was a positive experience and helped boost my confidence. The junior varsity team that I played on won the conference championship, and the varsity led by outstanding second year coach, Dale Bruce, advanced to the state Class "B" final four in 1956.

Chagrin's quest for a state championship ended when Columbus St. Mary's smacked a 20-point rout on the Tigers in the state semifinal game. Parks made the state Class "B" all-tournament team. He and Class "A" standout, Jerry Lucas of Middletown High School, Ohio State and New York Knicks fame, were the only sophomores to make the all-tournament teams.

I continued to struggle academically in some subjects my sophomore year, but I performed above average in a couple of subjects. I became a good geometry student and Mrs. Hensley's English class may have unlocked a hidden talent.

"At the end of every six weeks grading period a book report is due. You may do an oral or a written report. You should read daily and outline each chapter," instructed Mrs. Hensley.

Petrified by the thought of speaking in front of my peers, I always chose to write my book reports. But nevertheless, book reports presented a major obstacle in my life. My obsession with sports and the outdoors combined with poor reading skills caused me to shy away from reading books. My immaturity and lack of self-discipline prompted my belief that reading was for girls and sissies, not for Davy Crockett-Babe Ruth types like me. I wondered how I could possibly read six books during the school year and report on them.

I attemped to trick Mrs. Hensley by making up sports and adventure stories. I usually did it a few days or even the night before the due date of the book report. I also made up the names of the authors, gambling that my teacher would not check out the authenticity of my book reports. I turned in my fantasy stories as if they had been real books that I read. My book report grades fell between a C minus and a B plus. At the time, I figured Mrs. Hensley didn't know about my imaginary books, but in retrospect maybe she played along and tried to encourage rather than discourage my creativity. I probably will never know the answer for sure, but my tenth grade English teacher might have played a major role in my creative development.

Florence, Stanley and my teachers encouraged me to focus more on academics, but my thoughts, plans and actions had a one-dimensional flare. Sports, the major part of my world, kept my dreams alive, enabled me to stay in school, and laid the foundation for my life.

I made the varsity baseball team my sophomore year, but sometimes I participated in track meets on the same day that I had a baseball game. I'll never forget one sunshiny spring afternoon when I was warming up for a baseball game. When I saw track coach Ralph Quesinberry walking toward the baseball field I knew something was up. He came over to the field, stood in front of me and began talking.

"Palmer, go down and high jump for us—we need some help there today. You and Fletcher can help us get some points in the high jump. You'll be back in time for the baseball game. I already signed you and Fletcher in. He's already down there."

In my full dress game baseball uniform I jogged down to the far end of the football field to the high jump pit. I did a few stretches and ended up placing somewhere behind teammate Jim Fletcher, a junior, who finished second in the event. My long skinny legs and 6'2" body enabled me to scissor kick over five feet at a time when the school record was only 5'7". Participation in two sports on the same day could only happen at a small school like Chagrin Falls High School. But I still liked baseball better than track; I pitched, played first base and the outfield.

Irony filled the air that same spring, a few weeks after the high jumping episode, and six or seven months after the sideline humiliation when Coach told me I would never play for him again. This time he called me into his office; I immediately figured I must have done something wrong and might be getting a swat, "The board of education applied to the seat of learning," like we used to say. Surprisingly, Coach wanted to talk to me about next football season.

"We're going to move you to center next season. We need strength in the middle of our line. Center is a key position. You better do the job; we're not going anywhere without a good center! You'll still play end on defense," remarked Coach before continuing. "The toughest defensive player is usually the guy that lines up over the center. You better be ready to do the job!"

Coach seemed definitive about his plans for me. He didn't ask for a response about his decision, and thanks to God he never mentioned the sideline incident last football season. What inspired me most about playing center was that Coach was a center himself during his playing days at Bowling Green—he knew that good center play was important to the success of a football team. He called the center "The leader of the offensive line." Because of that philosophy, he always seemed to have good centers at Chagrin, so there was a standard that I had to live up to, skinny legs and all.

One of my favorite pro players, Chuck Bednarik of the Philadelphia Eagles played center and linebacker. Revered by the entire football world, Bednarik became one of the greatest players that ever played professional football.

It must have taken a lot of swallowing of pride for Coach to talk to me like he did, especially, after what happened last year. I didn't even earn a varsity letter my sophomore year and Coach had reason to think that I would be an important player on next year's team.

I could hardly wait for next football season. I wanted to work hard and eat plenty so I could get bigger, stronger and faster, to help my team win. Thoughts about success on the gridiron raced continuously through my mind. As crazy as it seemed after I almost cost Chagrin a victory last season, it looked as though Coach Quesinberry thought that I would become a football player after all. I wonder what changed his mind? Maybe because I got bigger and he knew that I loved football. Possibly, he saw a willingness and determination to help my school win, like the time I high jumped before the baseball game. Regardless of his reasons for counting on me next football season, it made a real difference in my life. I could now be somebody important, somebody that others looked up to, and most importantly, I could help my team win.

My sophomore year came to a close at the senior assembly in 1956. Something said at the assembly indicated the way many people viewed me. The last will and testament of senior Barbara Bauman, whose swimming pool and pool table became gathering places for friends and classmates, said it all; it was something that I have never forgotten.

"I, Barbara Bauman, be will and bequeath my eight ball to Gary Palmer, in hopes that he will come out from behind it."

Chapter XI
The Agony of Death and Defeat

My last two years of high school were dominated by sports and tragedy. It all began during the summer of 1956, a few months before President Eisenhower got elected to his second term in office. I had just turned 16 and there was excitement in the air about the upcoming football season, but some other things went awry in my life. Tippy, the joy of my life developed a limp that made walking painful and running impossible.

"Either Tipper got hit by a car or somebody threw something at him," commented Stanley.

"He's been straying a lot at night lately," responded Florence.

"I think he's got a girlfriend. John (Crawford) told me he saw a dog that looked like Tip on Cottage Street the other night," said Stanley.

"Is Tip going to be okay?" I asked.

"His hip is causing a lot of pain. I took him to the vet today. He won't be taking hikes or chasing rabbits for a while," said Florence.

Unfortunately, Tippy's condition worsened. He would whimper at night with pain. I prayed that Tip would get better so we could continue doing the things that had bonded us over the past seven years. I spent a couple of restless nights reminiscing about the past and my special relationship with Tippy. Then Florence brought the inevitable news.

"Gary, Tippy is in too much pain. We're going to have him put him to rest. It's going to be difficult for you because of your closeness to him, but it's not fair for Tip to suffer like this."

I knew this day would come but I hadn't expected it to be so soon. Tippy, at age 13, might have been old by some people's standards, but not by mine.

"Florence, he might get better," I tearfully said.

"Gary," Florence said, then she looked at me, turned away and went upstairs.

I went to Tippy's wooden box by the back door, threw my arms around him and cried like a baby. I don't know how many times I told Tip that I loved him and that God would take care of him. I stayed with him a long time knowing it would be his last night.

We buried my beloved dog behind the cherry tree in a wooded area near the chicken yard. I marked his burial spot with a cross, made from tied together tree branches. I remember that summer day in 1956 very vividly. We all stood around Tippy's grave and I said a silent prayer for him. It hurt to say goodbye to my companion and to come to the realization that I would never see him again.

Besides missing "Tipper," I hadn't seen Ben for several months, but I thought about him every time I walked past the hardware store on North Main Street in 1956. I heard on the news and read in the paper that Martin Luther King had emerged as the leader of a campaign for desegregation and human rights. I wondered if Ben knew about the Reverend King. I had this awful feeling that Ben might have passed on. Otherwise he would have told me about leaving his job or I would have seen him around town.

Something else happened in the summer of 1956–my buddy, Parks, transferred to University School. His family, especially Parks' father, felt that the upscale private prep school would be more challenging and open the door for admission to an Ivy League university. His transfer took me by surprise because he never talked about transferring. Besides Parks being my close friend, I knew our athletic teams, particularly basketball, would suffer without him.

Initially, many people seemed angry and resentful over Parks' departure, almost as if Chagrin Falls owned him and he should not be allowed other options. Nobody, not even me, seemed to be concerned about Parks and his family's freedom to choose. Everybody wanted him to stay at Chagrin Falls High School because of his athletic talents and the ensuing glory that would result if he remained a Tiger.

Parks had displayed his basketball prowess in ninth and tenth grades. Another final four appearance in basketball would be a realistic goal with Parks, but not likely without him. But life goes on and I would soon get over Parks' departure from our school.

I entered my junior year hoping for higher levels of achievement in academics and athletics. I wanted to get better grades because I knew that Florence wanted me to go to college, and since the days when I was a little boy I always wanted to play college football. But at this stage of my life, only Florence had enough confidence in me to consider college an option. And probably no one other than Florence and me thought that I would ever be a college athlete.

Even though I wanted to get better grades, my major concern centered on achieving success in sports. On August 20, 1956, when football practice began, just as coach had promised, he switched me from end to center.

Despite getting a couple of cracked ribs in a preseason scrimmage, I did not miss a practice. With taped ribs and a special pad to protect them, I prepared for the County League Preview game, an abbreviated game that showcased all the teams in the league. I had dreamed about playing for the Tigers ever since I was a little boy, and now my dreams would soon come true. I polished my black helmet and shined my shoes like Coach told us to do so that they would sparkle under the stadium lights. I laced my shoes with new white laces that I had been saving for this occasion. The thoughts of football glory and victory on the gridiron were all the motivation that I needed.

When I saw the Brecksville Bees' managers enter our stadium carrying large containers of drinking water, it gave me confidence that we would win. It was an electrifying feeling when we ran onto the field, heard the cheering crowd and breathed the fresh autumn air. The football atmosphere on that September evening in 1956 stands to this day as one of the most treasured moments of my life. It was such a high I could have played a football game every single night of my high school life. The heck with books and girls, television, foster parents and everything else, nothing could compare to Friday night football. In an abbreviated game, we scored more points that evening than any of the County League teams and whipped the Bees, 13-0.

Our season opener the following Friday night would be even more exciting. I continued wearing my protective rib pads because of the soreness and my inability to take a deep breath. Seven players scored and everyone got a chance to play in a 46-0 romp over neighborhood rival, Kenston. The 46 points that we scored turned out to be more than our opponents scored the entire season. We outscored the opposition 209-34 in 1956 with 45 players on the roster, one-half of the male enrollments in the upper three grades at Chagrin Falls High School.

Our defensive team led by an all-junior line, including Steve Van Nort and myself at ends and senior co-captain John Thomas at middle linebacker, became one of the best in the Cleveland area. We registered six shutouts and held our opponents to an average of three points a game.

There were some big games against some worthy opponents in 1956, but the Mayfield game loomed as the biggest. The week of the Mayfield game I wrote two sayings in one of my school notebooks.

"When the going gets tough the tough get going" and Coach's words of wisdom, "Whatever you do Friday night you will live with for the rest of your life."

The Mayfield game, played on a brisk October Friday night proved to be an experience I never forgot. First year assistant Coach Lucio Martin, affectionately called Luish by Coach Quesinberry, talked to us before the game, "They put their pants on just like we do, one leg at a time."

I respected Coach Martin, a big, tough, but gentle person of Italian descent, the same nationality as several of Mayfield's players.

Early in the fourth quarter I got kicked in the head on a cross body block and sustained a mild concussion. Dazed from the blow, I did not let anybody know how I felt for fear of being taken out of the game.

With less than seven minutes left in the fourth quarter, Mayfield clung to a 6-0 lead, and we had the ball about 60-yards from their goal line. Even though I suffered some memory loss, I'll never forget John Thomas' words as we gathered in the huddle preparing for a victory drive. He looked into our faces conveying a sense of determination, pride and urgency, and then he spoke.

"Everyone on the line, we're takin' it in! We have to do it now! Like Coach says, we're in this together. I guarantee I'll kick the extra point!"

Quarterback Dave Banning chipped in, "Their asses are dragging, let's put it to em' now!"

Inspired by a sense of urgency, we started moving the ball. Even though Mayfield, a school twice our size, had a big depth advantage, they seemed to be more tired than us. Coach Quesinberry's conditioning emphasis once again paid dividends. Behind the field leadership of Banning, the running of Van Nort and Thomas, and a completed pass to "Nort," we drove the ball right to Mayfield's goal line. Victory loomed only a heartbeat away as we registered a first down on Mayfield's 3-yard line. Our worst enemy now did not appear to be the exhausted Mayfield defense, but rather the game clock–there were only a few ticks left.

We quickly lined up for the final play. My teammates and I were ready to burst into the end zone and write another chapter of Chagrin football history. One play away from victory, the adrenalin poured through my veins like never before. We just needed one more play to win this game, the most important football game that I had ever played. Pleasant thoughts of obliterating the defender across the line from me raced through my mind. This night would soon become the happiest night of my life; I felt it in my veins. Then reality set in, before getting a play off, the clock read zeros. The referee picked up the ball, fired his blank pistol into the air and kept repeating that the game had ended. I don't remember if we had used our timeouts or just didn't call one at a critical time in the game. But I do remember being numb, disappointed and stunned, like all proud and successful athletes are when they experience defeat. Some of my teammates stood disbelievingly with their heads facing the grassy turf behind Mayfield High School while others lay lifeless on the field. The feeling surfaced as a much worse one than what ran through my bones at last year's sideline incident because we lost this game and with it probably the championship. I felt as though my world had just come to an abrupt end.

Coach spoke briefly and meaningfully and it left a lasting impression, "If you can look in the mirror and say to yourself 'I gave a hundred percent,' there's nothing more anyone can ask, but if you can't," there was a pause, "you better seriously consider what you're made of."

Knowing that we had to beat Mayfield to be champions and that this had been the first losing high school football game that I played in, Florence waited up for me that night. My foster mother knew that my hopes and dreams centered on sports, especially football. She also knew how personally I took things. Florence always seemed to say the right thing during times like these, almost as if God himself had helped her with the words.

"Gary, this may sound silly to you right now but you can benefit from the lessons of this experience; it can help you in life. Because of your dedication and determination and because you take things that you believe in so seriously, you are destined to be successful. You think that others don't see these things in you, but I'm closer to you than anybody, even Coach Quesinberry. I am proud of you," then she paused before continuing, "Am I ever proud of you!"

I buried my head in my arms face down at the kitchen table. Florence came over, put her arm around my shoulder and gave me a squeeze, then went upstairs. The tears continued to flow after Florence left. I knew if I had played better the Mayfield game would not have come down to the last drive. There's no worse feeling in the world than the feeling that you have let people down.

The 9-1 Tiger football record included a 14-0 victory over archrival Orange, a team that the Tigers had lost to eight consecutive times, and a season ending 23-7 victory over Bedford, a school about six times the size of Chagrin Falls High School. Between the Mayfield and Orange games, we defeated another neighborhood rival, Solon, 6-0. I made Tiger of the Week for the Solon game, but Pete Southmayd made the two biggest plays of the game. Pete scored the game's only touchdown, a 30-yard run on a dive play between right guard and tackle. Then, just before halftime, Southmayd turned in another key play. Solon tried a fake punt and Pete made an open field tackle on halfback Russ Davis, saving the game for the Tigers. Pete joined the Marine Corps in 1962 after graduating from the University of Virginia. He served two tours of duty in Vietnam and spent 27 years in the Marine Corps before retiring as a Colonel in 1989.

Being one play away from both a perfect season and a championship in 1956 managed to rank as a major disappointment, even though it was the best football season in nine years for Chagrin. There weren't too many teams anywhere that duplicated our football success in 1956. But, now that football had ended, I took my competitiveness into basketball.

With a combined total of 52 boys in the junior and senior class, the 1956-57 Tiger basketball team won the league title and finished with a 16-5 record. Under first year Coach Bill Gallagher, we finished 4-1 in the state tournament, only two victories away from another final four berth. Steve Van Nort, Jack Osman and I became the leading juniors on a senior dominated team.

On the world front the Russians took a giant step in the space race in 1957 when they launched Sputnik I and II, the first earth satellites. President Eisenhower sent paratroopers to Little Rock, Arkansas to enforce the federal court order to desegregate public schools and a tidal wave struck the Texas and Louisiana coasts following hurricane Audrey, leaving 530 people dead and missing. Also in 1957: Parks' beloved New York Giants baseball club moved to San Francisco; the Dodgers relocated from Brooklyn to Los Angeles; and the Ohio State Buckeyes won their second national football championship in four years.

While all these national and international events happened in 1957 at the end of my junior year and the beginning of my senior year, I hung on to a very provincial focus. I wanted our football team to be unbeaten league champions and despite not achieving very well academically, I wanted to earn a college football scholarship. I also wanted the Tigers to win basketball and baseball championships, and I wanted to do something that no one in my family had ever done–graduate from high school.

Coach got me a job during the summer of 1957 at George Arthur Coal and Supply Company. My duties were loading and unloading 94-pound bags of ready-mix concrete, shoveling coal, and bailing hay at the bosses' farm. The $1.25 cents an hour job enabled me to save almost my entire earnings, but more importantly it helped build muscles for the upcoming football season.

I keep coming back to football; even though I was not a great player, football was a major part of my life. With several key players returning, our goals for the 1957 football season remained the same as last year, an unbeaten record and league championship.

Keith Foster, a 6 foot, 250-pound stalwart tackle, did not return his senior season. Foster moved to Georgia and became an all-state performer before playing college football at Wake Forest. Unfortunately, Keith had a very short life–my former teammate died of a heart attack at a young age.

We had a new assistant coach in 1957. John Piai, fresh out of college, began his coaching career at Chagrin in 1957. Coach Piai, proud of his roots in Greenville, Pennsylvania and his football playing days at Thiel College, became a successful head coach when he replaced Ralph Quesinberry in 1962.

Motivating words from the enthusiastic Coach Piai furthered my desire to attend college and play football. "The best four years of your life are the four years you spend in college." Coach Piai invited my buddy Bill Cutshaw and me to a Thiel game during the fall of 1957. We went in the locker room before the game, met the players and coaches and sat on the sidelines during the game. Bill and I became acutely aware of the intensity of the hitting that takes place in college football–it was like night and day from our high school experiences on the gridiron.

Being a small public school we didn't play any of the big powers in Ohio High School football, and since the state playoffs did not begin in Ohio until 1972, Mayfield and Orange loomed as the ultimate football experiences. For the fourth consecutive year, the winner of the Chagrin-Mayfield game would get at least a share of the conference championship. Beating Mayfield and Orange were the top priorities in my life. To me, there was nothing that could rival success on the gridiron, not getting straight A's or having sex with the girls of my choice, not even having a date with movie stars like Marilyn Monroe or Rita Hayworth.

Mayfield did not get its reputation just because they outgrew us and became a much bigger school. They had several major college (presently Division 1-A) players. Most notably, future Ohio State All-American and Detroit Lion tackle Daryl Sanders. From my defensive left tackle position, I played directly over Sanders in the 1957 Mayfield game.

My teammates and I waited and prepared twelve months for the opportunity to play Mayfield again, knowing that more than likely it would be the championship game. Players like all-state fullback and future Chagrin Falls High School Sports Hall of Fame inductee Steve Van Nort, big Bill

Cutshaw, Gary Schwerzler, Bill Reitz, Rick Thomas, Pete Southmayd and Ronny Rood. Al Sindelar, a key player who missed the second half of the season with a knee injury, remained with us in spirit.

In the locker room before the Mayfield game the tears started flowing during Coach Quesinberry's pre-game speech, and especially during and after his familiar pre-game prayer.

"Dear Lord, give us the strength and courage to perform to the best of our abilities. We pray that no player on either team is seriously injured, Amen." I added my own prayer, "Please God Almighty, give us more strength and courage than ever before. Please God, may we win this game. Please! Please! Please God! Amen." I prayed, realizing that it might not be religiously correct to pray for victories, but I knew that God would understand. My powers of rationalization told me that if the green and white in the other locker room weren't praying as hard as us, maybe my prayer would give us an edge.

Unfortunately, the request to God for no serious injuries did not get answered. Mayfield junior halfback Bill Spetrino received a broken neck in a collision with my good friend, Bill Cutshaw. Amazingly, Spetrino recovered from his life-threatening injury. He made a marvelous comeback and not only played football his senior year, but he also earned a football scholarship to Bowling Green.

Mayfield halfback and future Purdue Boilermaker Dave Hoehnen came out to greet Steve Van Nort, Bill Cutshaw and myself for the coin toss. Mayfield won the toss and elected to receive. I knew we would win when I looked into Hoehnen's eyes. On the way back to the team, I began thinking how nervous Hoehnen looked. It made me realize how nervous I must have looked to him. Going into a game nervous was the norm for me, but I never went into a game scared–it's the kiss of death for a football player. My ritual of throwing up on the field just before kick-off, confirmed the anxiety that I experienced before every game, especially this one. Other players were able to contain their emotions without throwing up, but I couldn't, no matter how hard I tried.

Coach Quesinberry named me tri-captain for the biggest high school football game that I have ever played in. Being named tri-captain for the Mayfield game, along with finishing second to Steve Van Nort in the balloting for team captain, were among my greatest honors. The feelings of emotion from the ready to explode adrenalin pumping through my veins are impossible to put into words. I stood proudly next to two outstanding football players and good friends, Bill Cutshaw and Steve Van Nort.

During our nation's fight for independence from Great Britain, when Thomas Paine wrote the second of his inspirational papers, *The American Crisis*, one passage became especially meaningful on this warm, October Friday night in 1957. Paine wrote, "The harder the conflict, the more glorious the triumph."

The spirit and excitement of this Friday evening reverberated in the air. It made me think of warriors going to battle for a just cause with throngs of people cheering them on. The rhythmic chants still echo in my ears.

Hooray for Tigers! Hooray for Tigers!
Someone in the crowd yells hooray for Tigers!
One! Two! Three! Four! Who ya' gonna yell for,
Tiiigersss that's us! Rah! Rah! Rah!

This cheer, repeated several times by the loyal, spirited people who supported the Tigers, became a Chagrin tradition. But on this night the cheers grew louder and lasted longer, because the game surfaced as something much more than just another football game.

Right from the beginning, the hitting reflected more intensity than in other games. When I ran down the field on the kickoff team, Mayfield's Bill Robechek knocked me out of bounds with the hardest block I had laid on me all season, even though I managed to get back in bounds and make the tackle on Dave Hoehnen. These kinds of games had always been to my liking. Tough opponents inspired me to perform at a higher level. It made me realize that tough competition helps an athlete rise to greater heights, allowing them the opportunity to reach their full potential.

Being a key player at a small school in a big game, I knew there wouldn't be any chances to rest. I did not leave the playing field for one single offensive, defensive or special teams play. Physically exhausted and nearly dehydrated, I gasped for breath, as I looked up at the scoreboard in the fourth quarter. It read: HOME-13, VISITOR-13, with three minutes to play. I didn't know this at the time, but the dehydration factor may have been taking its toll on my teammates and me. The plays that I had been making earlier in the game trickled from reality. Tears were streaming down my face because I wanted to play better, but I was so physically zapped I couldn't muster the energy level that I had earlier in the game. There had never been a time in my life when I wanted to perform better, but in reality mental and physical fatigue had pretty much drained my mind and body.

The Wildcats had the ball on our 40-yard line; with Schwerzler, Cutshaw, Van Nort and myself in the middle of the Tiger defense and three minutes remaining, Mayfield knew the route to victory had to be on the outside. Dick Maynard's 40-yard run on a pitch sweep gave Mayfield the go ahead touchdown and a 20-13 victory. An assignment and mechanical breakdown occurred on Maynard's run, but fatigue and probably dehydration surfaced as the real villains.

The loss became more devastating to my senior teammates and me than last year's because the opportunity to beat Mayfield and win a championship had disappeared.

The accolades that I received from the Mayfield game did not compensate for losing, but it did make me realize that my goal to play college football seemed more attainable. Along with Mayfield's Dave Hoehnen, I made the Cleveland News Dream Team, an award given each week to the top 11 performers from the metropolitan Cleveland area. I also made the Cleveland Press Star honorable mention for the third time and received praises from Mayfield Coach Gene Schmidt.

"Somebody in there was giving our kids a good going over. I think it was Palmer, but I'm not sure. Whoever it was, he sure was tough." The Wildcat mentor told Tom Place of the Cleveland News. The columnist, after talking to Coach Quesinberry reported, "It was Palmer, a big, solid 6'3", 205 pounder." All-star game nominations and many letters from colleges resulted from the honors.

Later in life when I saw the achievement level reached by Mayfield's Daryl Sanders, whom I collided with almost on every play, it made me proud that I performed so well against him–a future All-American and also a professional football player.

The Mayfield game took so much wind out of our sails that a team with a losing record, Solon, upset us the following week, 18-13. Our effort in that game epitomizes the football terminology "flat." If we had beaten Mayfield, an unbeaten season would have been likely. Having lost the title game had a lingering effect on our emotions; in addition we were playing a team that considered us their archrival.

We rebounded the last game and for second straight year beat Orange the team that we considered our archrival, 19-6.

I played in 23 high school games during my three varsity seasons. The Tigers record in those games–20 victories and 3 losses. All three losses were close, hard-fought games decided by a single touchdown. In each of those games one big play would have enabled us to be unbeaten for two consecutive years.

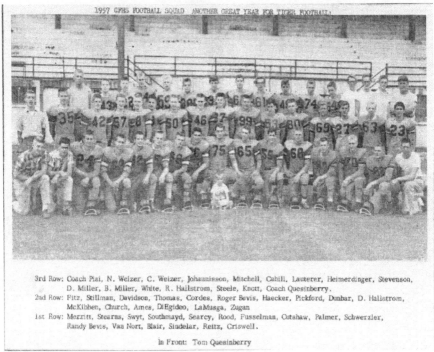

3rd Row: Coach Piai, N. Weizer, C. Weizer, Johannisson, Mitchell, Cahill, Lauterer, Heimerdinger, Stevenson, D. Miller, B. Miller, White, R. Hallstrom, Steele, Knott, Coach Quesinberry.
2nd Row: Fitz, Stillman, Davidson, Thomas, Cordes, Roger Bevis, Haecker, Pickford, Dunbar, D. Hallstrom, McKibben, Church, Ames, DiEgideo, LaMusga, Zugan
1st Row: Merritt, Stearns, Swyt, Southmayd, Searcy, Rood, Fusselman, Outahaw, Palmer, Schwerzler, Randy Bevis, Van Nort, Blair, Sindelar, Reitz, Criswell.

In Front: Tom Quesinberry

Football may have been the single most significant event in my life. It made me who I am. Gary Palmer, #75, front row middle. The role model in my life: Coach Ralph Quesinberry, back row right, wearing baseball cap.

Meanwhile on the home front: With basketball in full swing, and the happiness and glow of the 1957 Christmas season in the air, Florence came downstairs to ask me if I had worked on my term paper. I told her about my immediate concerns; the upcoming Holiday Invitational Basketball Tournament at Eastlake North High School and watching a couple of my favorite TV shows. I remember telling her I had "The whole Christmas vacation to work on my term paper." Florence insisted that I do some work on my paper each night, so I went upstairs to do as I had been told, but instead of working on my paper I listened to pop music on the radio. Later that evening before turning in, I came downstairs to get a snack and found Florence lying on the living room floor in front of the couch with Stanley kneeling by her side. Grandma Davis had just called the ambulance.

"What's wrong with Florence! What happened?" I asked.

"Stay back," replied Stanley.

Stanley lifted Florence into his arms. Unconscious, her lips were slightly moving as though she wanted to tell Stanley something. When the ambulance arrived to take Florence to the hospital Stanley told me to stay home and not to worry. I spent a teary-eyed, sleepless night praying for Florence and thinking about how much I loved her. I heard a car pull in sometime in the wee hours of the morning. Stanley and Florence's brother Frankie walked into Davises' living room. Fearful and depressed, I stayed in bed, but could hear them talking about the shocking events that had unfolded so quickly.

"It's a good thing she didn't come out of the coma. The doctor said she probably would have been a vegetable if she survived the hemorrhaging," said Stanley, obviously deeply saddened, but not the type to show a lot of emotion.

Stanley's words, the most devastating I had ever heard, turned my world upside down. Thoughts of dying so I could be with Florence crossed my mind. For the past eight years Florence had been the heart and soul of my existence; she gave me a reason to be alive, and now just like God had done with Grandma, he snatched Florence away from me.

I wanted to leave the Davises', but I didn't have a place to go. I knew it would be difficult to stay with Stanley and his mother the remainder of my senior year. I also knew it would be a nightmare for Stanley without Florence. The next day my foster father spoke about Florence's death.

"Non had a cerebral hemorrhage. That means blood vessels in her brain broke and caused massive bleeding. High blood pressure caused it," said Stanley.

Stanley spoke kindly, because I knew that many of Florence's pressures resulted from my stubbornness and aggravations. My poor grades and uncertain future had become a big concern to her.

I wish Stanley would have told me something at the time, but he did manage to tell me years later, "When I was holding Non in my arms, I could see her lips moving, she was trying to tell me something, I could just imagine what it was, 'Take care of Gary.'"

Stanley didn't think I'd qualify for a football scholarship because of my grades. Florence had worked at a local florist saving everything she made to help me with college. When Stanley didn't mention anything about a savings account for college, it signaled to me that I better get used to being on my own at age 17. I realized then that the dreams I had for my future depended on one factor, and one factor alone: how I would respond to the adversity in my life, past, present and future.

Chapter XII
Hope and Determination

Survival and wondering what might happen to me now that I had once again lost the person closest to me, dominated my thoughts, even more so than when my grandma died in the spring of 1948. Back then I was a helpless child, but now I could take care of myself.

It would be difficult living at the Davises' without Florence, but where would I go in the middle of my senior year? No offers came my way to live elsewhere, but I didn't express my feelings of unhappiness either. I didn't want people feeling sorry for me or offering assistance.

Stanley and I didn't get any closer when Florence died; instead it was pure agony for both of us. She had been the glue of the family—the sole reason that I had come to live at the Davises'. It was an incredibly unpleasant time in my life and also in Stanley's life. With graduation only a few months away, I would have to gut it out; then I planned to meet the challenges of the world on my own. Maybe I would join the Navy and sail across the world, so I could get far away from what now had become a nightmare existence.

I never felt comfortable talking to Stanley and I rarely did, unless he spoke first. Looking back, I wish I had talked with him more often. He might have loosened up, and probably we would have gotten along better. There were some things Stanley told me in later years that I wish I had known when I was younger. He told me that a man came to the Crawfords' when I was very young and claimed to be my father; I was living with the Davises at the time. Supposedly, the man asked John Crawford if I lived there and John told him that I didn't. Bee denied that this happened, so possibly the man had spoken to Stanley. Stanley may have felt guilty because he denied me the opportunity to meet my father; maybe that's why he claimed it was John that turned the man away.

I had always felt close to Florence because I knew that she loved me. Her caring words after the 1956 Mayfield football game and her attitude in general inspired me. I never forgot her encouragement to find lessons, even in defeat, and use them to become a better person. Florence's prediction of future success based on my determination, and her five words of encouragement elevated my self-esteem more than any I can remember: "I am proud of you."

I had many regrets about Florence's passing, but three of them have never gone away. I regret the last words I spoke to her, an angry display of discontent when she asked me to do my schoolwork. I regret that I didn't get to tell her, "I love you." Lastly, I regret that Florence never had a chance to know my wife and children.

When Florence died, it looked as though I might have been headed for a lifetime of trouble. Some of my classmates didn't think I would graduate from high school. One of them, the former Joan Matthews, always reminds me of this at our reunions: "We (I guess she means her and her friends) didn't think you were going to make it."

After Florence's death I got into trouble not only in school, but also with the police. When the police came to the Davises' and got me out of bed at 3:30 in the morning for playing musical statues with anybody that had one in their front yard, I thought Stanley would kick me out of his house.

Besides continuing to be a troublemaker, my grades had been constantly slipping like a cat trying to climb a greased pole. I stayed in school because of sports, Florence's confidence in me, and Coach Quesinberry's encouragement. With Florence gone and my poor academic standing getting worse, I knew that college was out of the question. Florence had been working for several months at the local florist shop; she told me she took the job to help me with college. Stanley didn't mention anything about Florence's college savings plan, and since it wasn't officially my money, I didn't feel it was my place to bring it up.

The Eastlake North Holiday Basketball Tournament began a few days after Florence's death. I conferred with Stanley, Reverend Parr, Bee Crawford and Coach Gallagher before deciding to play. I should play because that's what Florence would want became the consensus opinion. Through the years I've learned that Christians often feel their own choices have been approved– or mandated–by God.

Stanley's brother Earl and his family lived nearby and attended the Eastlake Holiday Tournament. Stanley, still in shock over Florence's death might have been at the game also, I just don't remember. If my foster father were in attendance it would have been the only time that he saw me play basketball. He did come to one football game–my last high school game.

Between quarters and during timeouts I glanced into the stands and saw Stanley's relatives; they lived nearby. I'll never forget the sadness on their faces. They felt the pain of Florence's death; I could tell their hearts went out to me. Possibly they were thinking along these lines: "Poor Stanley and Gary, what will they do without Florence? What a strain this will put on Grandma, Stanley and Gary. Florence and Gary were close, what will he do now? I hope he gets through school. Aunt Non, she was one of a kind, what a lady and what a great mother for that kid."

Our game against the Eastlake North Rangers did not resemble an athletic work of art. Coach Gallagher appeared sympathetic about my loss, but he was upset with the way we were playing.

"That was the most unemotional first half of basketball that I have ever seen."

Coach Gallagher continued his debasing remarks in an attempt to instill the drive that we obviously lacked.

"People are going to start calling you the gutless wonders. Gutless because you don't have any guts and wonders because everybody wonders why you're even out on the court."

Coach Gallagher, as did Coach Quesinberry, sometimes tried to inspire by intimidation and insult. It stood as a common practice for coaches in the 1950s to question people's courage when things didn't go well.

I learned one useful lesson from Coach Gallagher's occasional burst of negative rhetoric: It is far more productive to build people up than to tear them down. Later in life I put this theory into practice. When I taught and coached I tried to inspire people by getting them to believe in themselves. I did this through repetition of fundamental skills, positive reinforcement, and something I learned from Coach Quesinberry–a high level of physical conditioning.

Coach Gallagher's attention to detail and his emphasis on fundamentals left a lasting impression. Once while scrimmaging at Cuyahoga Falls High School, Coach Gallagher stopped the action, "Take those two points off the scoreboard!" he told the scoreboard operator.

It happened right after I found the bottom of the net on a long-range jump shot against the state's then fifth ranked Black Tigers. My lack of follow through on the shot caused this unusual request. My form did not fit the parameters of a fundamentally sound shot.

After winning basketball championships the past three years a win over Orange in the final game of the regular season would have given us a share of another title. The Orange championship game came down to the final second. We led in a ball possession defensive struggle, 39-38, with about three seconds left. A Nick Kavourius tip in at the buzzer gave Orange a 40-

39 win and for the third time in four years, the varsity league title.

I walked slowly to the locker room thinking about how another championship had slipped from our grasps. My teammates and I sat in the locker room, listless, dispirited and drained of energy and emotions. I saw Parks standing by the locker room door waiting for the right time to come in. You could hear a pin drop when his tall, athletic frame began to slowly walk across the room. He stood next to me with one hand grasping the top of my locker. Again he waited for the right time and then he spoke. His words were soft and sincere.

"Gary, you have nothing to be ashamed of. You played a great game. You and Steve and the rest of this team are winners, regardless of what the scoreboard says. You played a great game," said Parks, his voice trailing off.

"Great" had certainly been a stretch of Parks' imagination. He extended himself as a friend after a heartbreaking one-point loss. I scored a game-high 13 points, but that didn't matter, I had good position under the basket and still failed to stop Kavourius from making his game winner at the end. I should have fouled the former West Tech star hard enough to prevent the ball from going in, forcing him to the foul line with all the pressure on his shoulders. But I didn't–maybe if I became a coach some day I would learn from that experience.

When the basketball season ended, and before baseball began, there was a void in my life for female companionship. I always wanted a steady girlfriend, but I lacked confidence, never feeling very worthy of most girls, especially the more popular girls in my class. But the older boys, especially the athletes, awed the younger girls. Judy Cummins, an intelligent, pretty, horse-loving freshman cheerleader remedied my lack of female companionship. She was a darling girl that brought happiness to my life– someone I will never forget. I was touched when I read about Judy's passing in the alumni newsletter in 1996.

Florence's death and my low academic standing left a lot of uncertainties about my future. Several colleges were interested in my football talents, but at least for now, college was not an option. During the spring of my senior year the high school counselor called me into his office.

"What are your future plans?" my counselor asked.

"I'd like to go to college," I responded.

"Gary, you're not college material. You would just be wasting your time and money," he replied.

"I don't have the money to go to college, but I have several football scholarship offers," I replied and then continued. "I'd like to play college football and graduate from college, but I know I'm not ready now. I'm thinking about going in the military first, and maybe go to college when I get out."

The disbelieving look in my counselor's eyes said it all, and then he began talking: "From what Coach Quesinberry says I don't doubt that you can play college football, but I think academics will be a problem for you. I think you should focus on other things."

Florence and Coach Quesinberry had encouraged me to attend college. I desperately wanted to prove them right, but I knew that I would flunk out of college at this point in my life.

Stanley didn't pull any punches, "These colleges don't want goddamn dummies playing for them. They don't want people like you."

Stanley was right, but some day I wanted to prove that my counselor and Stanley were wrong. So maybe the disbelievers did me a great service. In the words of Walter Bagehot (1826-77), a renowned English social scientist and banker, "The great pleasure in life is doing what people say you cannot do."

In upper middle class Chagrin Falls during the 1950s, 85-90% of high school graduates attended college. For public schools that percentage was probably among the highest in the state. College was definitely the norm for kids from Chagrin Falls. I always felt that college would be the only path to a happy and successful life. The attitude about college and success was one of the reasons growing up in Chagrin Falls was so beneficial to me. But for now, immaturity, lack of confidence, money, and of course poor grades, stood in the way.

Nevertheless, Coach became a walking, talking endorsement of my football talents through his promotional deeds with college coaches. I didn't think I deserved all the attention from college recruiters, but it did get me thinking that I might be good enough to play college football, a lifelong dream.

One day during the recruiting season when college coaches actively visited prospects, Coach sent me a note to meet him at a specific time in his office. Miami University Head Football Coach, John Pont, wanted to speak with me. After being introduced to Coach Pont, Coach Quesinberry began talking.

"Coach, he'll do the job for ya'! He can play anywhere on the offensive and defensive line and he's the best center I ever coached!"

What a difference a couple of years make! I remembered the sideline incident my sophomore year, and when I first got switched to center my junior year, Coach told me, "You're the worst center I ever coached." And now Coach Quesinberry emphatically endorsed my football playing ability to someone who became one of college football's most successful coaches, John Pont. But things had changed: I had added some weight and muscle and now had football playing experience.

"He's competitive and he's gonna get a helluva lot bigger. His best football days are ahead of him. Gary's an all-around athlete. If you wanna look at these films again, take 'em with you," said Coach.

Coach Pont thanked Coach Quesinberry and said he had seen enough game film. Coach Quesinberry glanced at me before continuing his conversation with John Pont.

"His biggest problem has been the books, but he likes football so damn much he'll make himself a better student."

Coach Pont, a Canton, Ohio native, later coached at Yale, Northwestern, Indiana and Mount St. Joseph, and stands as the only coach to take the Hoosiers to the Rose Bowl (1968). The Redskin mentor looked at me and said, "Gary, we'd sure like to have you at Miami! I'd like you to visit the campus. I'll stay in touch with you, son."

In spite of graduating near the bottom of my class, Coach Quesinberry still encouraged me to give college a try. But, my immediate objective was to get away from the Davises' and build a life of my own. I decided to join either the Navy or the Marines.

My buddy, Bill Cutshaw, was in the same boat as me. Cutsh was recruited to play college football, but struggled in the classroom. We hung around together a lot, especially during our high school years. Bill was a big, strong farm boy; born in east Tennessee he was two-years old when he moved to Chagrin Falls in the early 1940s. The Cutshaws were dirt poor, but the entire family including Bill's sisters, Wilma and Lois, and his mother, rumored to be a full-blooded Cherokee Indian, were likable people. Bill's dad, a "city farmer," sold produce at roadside stands. Fred Cutshaw taught me how to milk a cow, and he spoke often about his business dealings. Bill learned a lot about business from his father, and eventually Cutsh became a very successful businessman.

Cutsh and I were the antithesis of the typical upper middle class kid growing up in Chagrin Falls. Neither of us talked about our backgrounds and upbringing, but it was obvious we were different. In school, athletic achievement was the only thing that made us feel equal in any way. Now that we had finished high school and since we were not college material, serving our country was another way to feel equal, on the way to achieving our goals. We didn't talk about our goals or announce them to the world, but we knew what they were—success in life.

Bill and I didn't go into the military right after graduation. My buddy and I wanted to enjoy the summer and play in a post-season all-star football game before we lost our freedom. Also, I didn't want to leave Judy too soon after graduation. I continued dating her during the summer months and helped her father build a horse barn.

But Bill and I looked forward to serving our country, learning a trade, growing into manhood, meeting beautiful girls from around the country and the world, and being independent. First, we had to make some decisions. I went to see the Marine Corps recruiter in Bedford, Ohio–then Cutsh and I both visited the Navy recruiter in South Euclid.

The Navy recruiter insisted that we could learn a trade, see the world and take college extension courses for credit. Since the draft remained in effect in 1958, we could do this while serving our country and fulfilling our military obligations. The Navy recruiter drummed home the fact that if we didn't go to college, Cutsh and I would have a technical skill to fall back on in civilian life.

The Marine Corps recruiter offered basically the same package, but the adventure of seeing the world did not seem as promising. I imagined myself seeing the inside of a foxhole or bivouacking for weeks on end in remote places, away from stadium football lights and beautiful girls. At the time, I didn't realize how closely connected the Marine Corps was to the Navy.

Bill Cutshaw and I became obsessed with sailing around the world, so we decided to take the test for the Navy. Our high school diplomas and military test scores guaranteed that we would be assigned to a technical training school after boot camp.

A requirement for enlistment, a birth certificate, caused some disruption in my plans. I contacted the county and the state birth records department, but they had no record of my birth. The only hope of coming up with a birth certificate seemed to be my mother whom I had not seen since the sixth grade. I got my mother's phone number from my brother Kenny and talked to her about my birth certificate.

"I'm joining the Navy and I need a birth certificate. The state and county have no records of my birth," I said.

"Oh you can get a birth certificate anytime, just go to Cleveland," replied my mother.

"You don't understand. I've been to Cleveland and I've written to the state. There are no records of my birth. Do you know anything about my birth certificate?" I asked.

"I don't know why you can't get it. I got mine," insisted my stubborn 46-year-old mother.

"Your birth was registered. That's why you got your birth certificate; mine wasn't. Was I born some place other than Chagrin Falls?" I asked.

"Nooo, you were born in Shag-err-in Falls," she maintained.

"Then where the hell is my birth certificate? This is a crock of shit!" I added, in the manner of a 17-year-old.

"Old Doc Cameron delivered you. He was always drunk. You can ask anybody in 'Shag-err-in' Falls about Old Doc Cameron. Whyyy he was nothing but a drunk. When he came to deliver you he was drunk," replied my mother.

"Did you think of asking Old Doc for a birth certificate? Stanley said by law he had to give you one," I commented.

"He (Dr. Cameron) wouldn't know anything about that," replied my mother.

"What the hell kind of a doctor is he? He's drunk all the time and he doesn't register births. Did a midwife or someone else, maybe Grandma, deliver me?" I asked.

"No, Old Doc delivered you. He was too drunk to remember a birth certificate," she muttered.

"Did you ever think of changing family doctors?" I asked, half jokingly.

"You couldn't do that! The only other doctor was young doc and he was never around," rationalized my mother.

"This sounds like a bunch of bull to me! My problem is, I'm trying to enlist in the Navy and I need a birth certificate. If I don't come up with one, Stanley says I'm going to have problems my entire life!" I responded.

"Well, you're here aren't you?" replied my mother.

Getting information out of my mother paralleled trying to get top-secret military information from President Eisenhower. I returned to the Navy recruiting office to inform them that I could not get my birth certificate.

"What did your mother say about your birth certificate?" asked the Navy recruiter.

"She said she doesn't know anything about it, and then she said, 'You're here aren't you?'" I replied.

"Were you baptized?" asked the recruiter.

"Yes sir," I answered.

"We'll accept your baptismal certificate for enlistment. Bring it to me as soon as you can," said the recruiter.

"Thank you! I'll go to my church and get it tomorrow," I responded.

After getting my baptismal certificate, big Bill Cutshaw and I decided to serve our country and see the world during these non-refundable young years of our lives. When most of our friends had gone to college, we joined the Navy on the "Buddy Plan," a recruiting program that guaranteed we would be stationed together during our initial training period–the ten weeks of boot camp.

Cutsh stood about an inch shorter than me at 6'1", but he was strong and tough, and a good football player. When we joined the Navy, Cutsh outweighed me by at least 20 pounds.

"Cutsh, maybe the boot camp base in San Diego has a football team. We can kick some butt like we did in the all-star game back in July," I proclaimed, in reference to our 13-6 victory over the Geauga County All-Stars.

"Yeah that would be nice, but I heard in boot camp they keep you so busy you're lucky to have time to shit. Four o'clock in the morning comes awful early. I hope we're doing the right thing," said Cutsh, trying to keep from smiling.

"Cutsh, you've been up at four o'clock to milk the cows since you were five years old. This'll be a snap for you. The recruiter told me we get up at five o'clock, but he also said we stand guard duty on rotating shifts throughout the night. That could knock the hell out of a good nights sleep, ha! ha!"

"Okay Pume, you're not going to be laughing when we get to San Diego."

I talked briefly to Stan about my plans. He didn't have much to say about my decision to join the Navy, but he told me I could keep my belongings at his house until I finished my tour of duty. I left some clothing, a collection of baseball and football cards, a knapsack, and some sports equipment at Stanley's.

Grandma Davis had nothing to say about my decision to join the Navy. Agnes was still a sturdy old gal at age 76–calloused from hard work and just as ornery as ever. It was an embarrassment when my friends would call and she would answer the phone. I always knew when the call was for me. In a very harsh and angry way, she would always say, "Just a minute!" But, now I was leaving for good, and I didn't need to concern myself with those and other embarrassments ever again, "Hallelujah!"

On October 2, 1958, the same year Alaska entered the union as the 49th state, Bill Cutshaw and I boarded an American Airlines 707 jet out of

Cleveland Hopkins Airport for our cross-country flight to sunny southern California. We declared our independence and willingness to step forward in the world on our own and the United States Navy became our new home.

When I lifted off the ground at Cleveland Hopkins Airport a feeling of adventure streamed through my veins. I felt good about the decision I had made, especially after seeing and talking to a couple of pretty stewardesses. At this point in my life, I didn't care if I'd ever see Chagrin Falls again.

Russia increased their edge in the space race in 1958 when they launched a satellite weighing 3,000 pounds, Sputnik III. We countered that same year with Explorer I, an artificial earth satellite weighing in at a burly 31 pounds.

The cold war technology and the race for military superiority between the two superpowers accelerated to full throttle in 1958 and we had some catching up to do. The United States, embarrassed by the Soviet Union's accomplishments and paranoid over the ramifications of Russia's technology edge, established the National Aerospace Scientific Administration. Beating the Russians in the scientific exploration of space became NASA's immediate objective. NASA, established itself in Washington D.C., on October 1, 1958, the day before my buddy and I joined the Navy.

Chapter XIII
The Challenge of the World

After Bill and I went through Navy boot camp together, he got shipped back East to Sonar School and then joined the Atlantic Fleet. I stayed on the West Coast all four years in the Navy, serving two years on land and two years in the Pacific Fleet.

After boot camp in December of 1958, I came back to Chagrin Falls for Christmas. It was the only time that I came home during my four years in the Navy. Stanley welcomed me to stay with him during my two weeks of leave, but coming back to Chagrin Falls was bittersweet. I felt like a guest in my own hometown, even more so when I met a girl who had moved to Chagrin after I left ten weeks earlier. But that feeling didn't keep me from spending a few nights with her during my leave.

I returned to San Diego for Radio School and then the march began. I served one year at the Navy's early warning communication station on Midway Island, where the battle that changed the course of the war in the Pacific took place in early June of 1942. On the way to Midway, I spent a few days transient in San Francisco and then at the historical Pearl Harbor Naval Base in Honolulu. I had the fortune of being in Honolulu on August 21, 1959, the first official day of Hawaiian statehood.

The year I spent in isolation on Midway away from the opposite sex is not something that I would recommend to anyone, but it did help me focus on my future. I began a rigid program of weight lifting, running, exercising, and playing sports. I also took a college extension course offered through the University of Wisconsin. I made up my mind early on, that I would attend college at the end of my tour of duty and that I would earn a scholarship playing football. Despite my meager military salary, the financial lift from being isolated on an island helped me save for college. Throughout my four-year stint, money was deducted from my salary and invested in the Navy's Paymaster Savings Plan. On Midway, I was able to save money in addition to my automatic deductions.

Beginning in August of 1960, after a year on Midway, I served on the U.S.S. Samuel N. Moore, a destroyer out of Long Beach, California. The

Moore, commissioned on my fourth birthday, 24 June 1944, received several decorations for heroic action in World War II, Korea and Vietnam.

The U.S.S. Maddox, the ship reportedly attacked by North Vietnamese torpedo patrol boats in the Gulf of Tonkin in 1964, served as one of the Moore's sister ships in Destroyer Squadron 23. The attack on Desron 23, nicknamed the Little Beavers, stands as the provocation that began our large-scale involvement in Vietnam.

Early in 1961, I transferred from the destroyer squadron to an amphibious assault aircraft carrier, the U.S.S. Princeton. The Princeton's motto, *Every Man a Tiger* fit the sailors and Marines that served on our ship perfectly, and especially fit me. I was a former Chagrin Falls Tiger with a tiger-like attitude that sometimes got me into trouble.

A big chance to prove if we really were tigers came in April of 1962 when we got the call from President Kennedy for a top-secret mission. With two helicopter companies of Army advisors we deployed from White Beach, Okinawa, for parts unknown. Only a handful of the 800 sailors and 400 Marines aboard the Princeton were privy to our destination. Several months later we found out about our deployment in Southeast Asia. We had spent several days in the Mekong Delta area of the Republic of South Vietnam. The advisors that we took aboard were deployed to Soc Trang, near the Mekong Delta. I had guilty feelings watching my countrymen go ashore possibly for the last time and not be able to go with them. Not everybody felt that way, many had the attitude better them than me, but I never felt that way. Later in life when I learned about the military history of my ancestors, going back to the Revolutionary War, my feelings became understandable.

Besides San Diego, Long Beach, San Francisco, Hawaii, Midway Island, Okinawa and South Vietnam, my Navy adventures took me to Mexico (Baja California), Hong Kong, the Philippines and Japan.

When I think back on my Navy days, many memorable experiences enlivened my four years of service, but frolicking at the beach and socializing with the tanned girls of the Pacific became my favorite pastime. Even though I spent just as much time weight training, running and exercising, in preparation for college football. A Marine shipmate, Ed Leon, and I started a weight training workout room aboard the Princeton in 1961. We purchased the weights at Kadena Air Force Base in Okinawa.

My aggressive and immature personality got me into a lot of trouble during my Navy days, mostly fights. Most notably, in 1959 I got thrown in the slammer in Tijuana with a Marine buddy from Camp Pendleton. We caused a major ruckus in a bar and came uncomfortably close to being gunned down by the Mexican Policia.

The weight training and rigid exercise programs that I religiously engaged in were assets when I got into ruckuses. In addition to lifting weights and running I did endurance swimming, and every night before turning in I did pushups and sit-ups. The only nights withstanding were the nights when I had too much to drink or those rare moments when I hit the beach for a hot date.

After returning to the states from Southeast Asia in the summer of 1962, I visited my childhood friend Parks Odenweller and his family in Menlo Park, California. Parks had graduated from Yale and lived with his mom, dad and younger sister Vicki, a student at nearby Cal Berkeley. I enjoyed renewing old memories and talking about recent experiences and future plans with my old friend. I felt proud of Parks; what a brilliant future he had in store. I remember hoping that some day I would have a college education and a good job so that he would also be proud of me.

My release from active duty on September 7, 1962, 25 days early so that I could start the fall semester of college, ranked as one of my happiest days. I looked forward to the next chapter of my life.

The decision to return to Ohio had been swayed mostly by my acceptance to Ohio University, a school located in Athens in the foothills of the Appalachians in southeast Ohio. I had heard a lot about Ohio University, and had received football-recruiting letters from them while in high school, but I had never seen the campus. But attending a state school in Ohio was a more affordable option because of in-state tuition. I had mixed emotions about leaving a very pretty girlfriend, the warmth and beauty of California, and the beaches of the Pacific Ocean that I had fallen in love with. Nevertheless, I had made up my mind that nothing would stand in the way of my goals. Leaving California also gave me an out from marrying my Texas-bred girlfriend. Her focus was on getting married; mine was on getting a college education. My priorities were getting an education, landing a professional position, and then if I met the right girl, maybe I would even get married.

My confidence level to achieve in college grew a few months before my discharge when I found out I had scored in the 86th percentile on the OSPE college entrance test. But, in spite of my test scores I knew that earning a college degree would be a long, hard struggle.

Through the Navy's savings program and my mustering out pay, I had enough money for one year of college. I would have to earn a football scholarship and find a good-paying summer job in order to fund the remainder of my education. During this time period, unlike World War II and Korean veterans, we servicemen and women did not receive the G.I. Bill to help subsidize our education.

In September of 1962 when I got back to Ohio, I only had a couple of days before my four-hour bus ride to Athens. It gave me enough time to see Kenny and his family in Cleveland, and then go back to my hometown, Chagrin Falls. I planned to see Stanley Davis, Coach Quesinberry, and some of my friends from high school.

With Kenny's borrowed 1956 Ford, the old farmhouse on North Main Street became my first stop. I couldn't wait to tell Stanley that I got accepted at Ohio University. My visit to the Davises' in September of 1962 would be the last time that I would see Grandma Davis. She died during my college years. Since Stan and I were not in touch, I didn't find out about her death until after college.

I never wrote or called my former foster father during my stint in the Navy, so he was no doubt surprised by my plans. When I broke the news to him he sat silently in his easy chair and showed little or no emotion. I imagined what raced through his mind, "Herman, in college?" He always thought that I would be wasting my time in college and fail in the pursuit of my endeavors. I relished the thought of proving him wrong.

Stanley probably thought that I would return to a job similar to my high school summer job at George Arthur's Coal and Supply. I certainly wasn't allergic to hard work, but I wanted to spend the rest of my life in more productive and satisfying pursuits.

Even though Stanley wasn't convinced that I would amount to much, he may have been thinking that Florence would be proud. She always wanted me to attend college and become a successful person, but unfortunately I could only tell my plans to Stanley.

"Well Stan, I'm going to surprise Chagrin Falls and make something out of my life! I know that's what Florence wanted. I've been accepted at Ohio University. I'll be trying out for the football team as a walk-on. I spent the last four years of my life preparing for this opportunity. In order to stay in college, two things need to happen: I'm going to have to earn a football scholarship and I'm going to have to study real hard."

At first, Stanley just sat and looked at me. Then he asked questions about the Navy and where I would be living when I came home. I told him that I planned to stay in Athens, but when I did come home I would be staying with my brother, Kenny, and his family. When I got up to leave, he wished me well in my college experience. On the way to the back door I stopped in the kitchen and spoke to my former foster father once more before leaving.

"You know something, Stanley, Parks graduated from Yale in June, and most of my high school classmates have a college degree; Steve Van Nort, Pete Southmayd, Bobby Nichols and people like that, and here I am just starting college. But I served my country, matured a bit and sowed some of my wild oats, so maybe I can hack it now! Remember my old buddy Al Sindelar, when I was growing up? I bet he goes to college when he gets out of the Marine Corps. He's probably already out," I said.

Stanley extended his hand and said, "Well Herman, I wish you the best."

Later that evening, I went to see Coach Quesinberry. His reaction about my plans to attend college and play football was quite different from Stanley's.

"I'll call Coach Hess and let him know you're coming," said Coach in his usual enthusiastic manner.

Coach Quesinberry promoted me as if I would be an All-American. He had a way of exaggerating the talent level of his former players. Coach called Bobcat mentor Bill Hess late that evening. He never paid much attention to clocks and things that interfered with what he thought to be the right thing to do. Coach mentioned my name only at the introduction of the conversation and then began his promotional jargon.

"He's one of the best players I ever coached; one of the best players to ever wear a Tiger uniform! He lifted weights and got himself in top shape when he was in the Navy. He's got a tremendous amount of drive and determination. He could have gotten a scholarship to Miami right out of the service, but he chose to play for you because you didn't guarantee him a thing; you told him he would have to prove himself, after four years in the Navy. I remember when you tried to recruit him back when he played for me. A helluva lot of schools tried to recruit him. He won't let ya' down. Give'im a good look Bill," said Coach, along with other undeserving superlatives.

Forty-five days after my discharge and just over a month after I enrolled at Ohio University, the Cuban Missile Crisis brought us to the brink of nuclear war with Russia. On October 22, 1962, when the Russians backed down in the face of our naval blockade, it enabled me to stay in college rather than be called back to service.

The Cuban Missile Crisis did not interrupt nor end my college career, but I decided that if I had to leave Ohio University because of academic and or financial reasons, I would return to the West Coast, declare California residency, and enroll at a junior college.

Just as I had expected, college became a big challenge for me, academically and athletically. I managed to earn a football scholarship for two of the 4½ years that I spent at Ohio University, and I acquired some good paying summer jobs that enabled me to stay in school. I worked construction for two summers, building sidewalks one year and installing in-ground swimming pools the other. The last two summers of my college career I had the best paying summer job of all. I joined the Teamsters Union and worked long hours for a moving and storage company in Cleveland—it was not unusual to work 60-70 hours a week. I loved it because the overtime made me feel like a "happy baker," you know, rollin' in the dough.

Besides earning a football scholarship for two years and having good paying summer jobs, the other good thing that happened to me in college was meeting Barbara Foderaro. Our up and down relationship began in 1964 in a dormitory parking lot at Ohio University. I was in a car with a friend when he spotted his girlfriend Donna and her roommate, Barb, driving through the parking lot near their dorm. When Tom pulled up next to Donna's car, Barb and I made eye contact. She was a beautiful girl and now I had a point of reference when I decided to call her for a date.

Our first date was not a classic one that made her yearn to date me again, at least for a while. We decided to go to nearby Lake Hope and I was loaded for bear, no pun intended because we were in a place where black bear were often seen. I brought a blanket, radio and a six-pack of beer, and in Barb's words, "I thought this was supposed to be a study date." On the way back from the lake I poked fun by pretending to run out of gas in the forested foothills of Appalachia, and I continued to poke fun when I told "Barbie" that I was from Denver, Colorado. Besides her beauty, I liked her purity and innocence right from the beginning. Little did either of us know that four years later we would be married!

In August of 1966 during my senior year at Ohio University, my brother Kenny informed me that "Dad," at age 62, had a heart attack and died at Saratoga Racetrack in Saratoga Springs, New York. In the years preceding his death, he lived with my brother, George, in Aiken, South Carolina and worked with him at the Clark Estate. It was fitting that he died among the thoroughbred racehorses since he spent most of his life working with them.

Kenny said if I intended to go to the funeral I could drive him and his wife, Mary, and my mother, in his station wagon. Kenny said I could do the driving because no one else, except Mary, could drive, and she had never done any long distance driving. My mother had never been able to drive and Kenny claimed to be too nervous. I decided to go because I wanted to pay my respects to the man that people said was my father. Surely, if Kenneth Palmer weren't my father they wouldn't invite me to the funeral, at least not without first telling me the truth or at least they would tell me the truth along the way. The real reason they invited me was because I could drive, and if Kenneth Palmer really wasn't my father, they could continue to play their game of secrecy and not tell me anyway. It dawned on me that possibly, after all this speculation, this runt of a person named Kenneth Palmer might be my father after all. It seemed too unbelievable and cruel for these people to know the truth but still not tell me, especially after Kenneth Palmer died. But knowing my family, nothing would surprise me.

After the funeral, I put the feelings about my identity aside so I could focus on completing my education. I accomplished three goals while in college: I played football, something I had dreamed about most of my life; I received a football scholarship for two years; and I earned something else that I had dreamed about most of my life–a college degree. I majored in physical education and received a Bachelor of Science degree from the college of education in January of 1967.

My next goal, becoming a physical education teacher and football coach, also became a struggle. The last semester of my senior year, due to the uncertainty that surrounded my future, I broke up with Barbara, my favorite college girlfriend. I applied to 100 school districts in seven states and did not get one interview. The education market got flooded with qualified teachers, many of whom wanted to be deferred from the Vietnam War.

Discouraged by the lack of response from the flood of teaching applications that I sent out, I took a job as an insurance adjustor trainee in Atlanta. When the training ended and I got my assignment to return to Cleveland, I decided to resign my position and hit the beaches of Florida during spring break of 1967. I headed south with everything that I owned packed away in my 1962 Ford and $350 in my wallet.

After less than two weeks sleeping in a $10 a night room at a boarding house in Daytona Beach, roaming the beaches, hitting the bars and partying with some pretty co-eds, the well had run dry. I didn't even have enough money to get home. It seemed unbelievable that I had realized my dream by earning a college degree, yet I would soon be penniless and homeless. I tried unsuccessfully to get a job in Daytona Beach and then I called my brother George in Aiken, more than 300 miles away. I had only seen George twice the past 21 years, but I had stayed with him a few days and got acquainted a little when I attended my father's funeral. Anyway, George invited me to come up, and he said they were hiring at the Savannah River Nuclear Power Plant, just outside of Aiken.

I enjoyed visiting George and his family, and especially liked playing baseball with his son, Gregory, an 11-year-old little leaguer. I applied at the Savannah River Nuclear Power Plant, but did not land a job. I talked to George and Marge about my identity, but George, like everybody else in the family, denied any suggestions that Kenneth Palmer might not be my father.

George also said, "Dad kept your picture in his wallet, you know, when you were in the Cleveland papers for football. He was real proud of you." On several occasions when we discussed the family, I remember Marge saying, "Blood is not thicker than water." The level of confusion about my identity did not change when I visited George. It only made me think that maybe I was way out of line thinking that Kenneth Palmer might not be my father.

George suggested that I stay in Aiken, get a job and live with him until I got on my feet. However, when I decided to go back to Ohio, he lent me $50 to get home.

Upon returning to Cleveland, I went to the shores of Lake Erie and became a longshoreman. I worked in the holes of the Great Lakes freighters unloading and loading everything from toilet paper to steel girders. It reminded me of the work parties during my Navy days on Midway Island.

Barbara and I started dating again, but I felt insecure about my future and certainly didn't want to get married. In the summer of 1967, I made a decision that would change the course of my life. I decided that if I did not have a teaching and coaching position by August 20th, I would return to military service. But this time things would be very different. Since I had served in the Navy as an enlisted man, if I qualified, I wanted to become a Marine Corps or Army field officer. I had already spoken with the recruiters and told them of my willingness to serve in Vietnam. My biggest concern about returning to the military centered on passing the tests in order to qualify for Officer Candidate School. I was disappointed when the Marine Corps recruiter told me I had just missed the age cutoff (26 years old) for OCS–I turned 27 in June of 1967.

When I told Barb about my plans, I knew for sure that I wanted to spend the rest of my life with her. I'll never forget her words; "Whatever you decide to do is fine with me because I love you!" Up until that point, I felt pretty insecure about relationships. I wasn't sure anyone was capable of loving me for the rest of my life, and because I was so goal oriented, I wasn't sure I could love anyone else either.

Barb and I had some religious issues to resolve, but the religion differences didn't turn out to be as much of a problem as I thought they might be. The important thing was that we thought alike about core issues–saving our money, buying a home and raising a family, and job security. Initially, because of our upbringing we had different opinions about religion. She didn't relish my suggestion that we compromise between Methodism and Catholicism and become Episcopalian.

In retrospect, I believe subconsciously I was looking for a girl more like Florence and the very opposite of my mother, someone that I could trust without question. Inwardly, I wanted someone who would be faithful and resourceful–outwardly, someone beautiful and intelligent. Barb fit the bill for these criteria, and when she didn't flinch at the thought of me re-entering the service and even when I told her about telling the recruiters of my willingness to go to Vietnam, that convinced me that she was the girl I wanted to spend the rest of my life with. Lesser women, those that were conscious only of their own comfort level, would not understand commitment, patriotism or duty.

As fate would have it, sometime around August 15th I received a phone call from the Cleveland Board of Education. They offered me a position teaching driver education and coaching football at one of Cleveland's inner city high schools. I became the offensive and defensive varsity line coach and the junior varsity wrestling coach at the now obsolete Lincoln High School. Teaching in the inner city was like sitting next to a keg of dynamite waiting for it to explode. I was a 6'2", 245-pound teacher and coach and it wasn't in my makeup to take crap from anybody. I learned quickly that it was sometimes necessary to be a warrior in order to protect my students and myself from intimidation.

Only one confrontation that I was involved in was physical, but there were other incidents that were on the verge of exploding into violence. On one occasion, the unlikely villain that I confronted in defense of my students and myself was the Cleveland Police Department. Another time it was a motorcyclist that I came close to decapitating with a parallel parking standard. Then there was an unruly student that I slammed against the wall because he absolutely refused to move from a seat that I had assigned to someone else. And finally, there was a student that I took to the office to search because he refused to take off his outerwear, giving me a reason to think that he might have a concealed weapon. When we searched him, a loaded automatic pistol was found.

Through all the chaos, Barbara Ann Foderaro and I became engaged in November of 1967 and got married June 29, 1968 at St. Bartholomew Catholic Church in Middleburg Heights, Ohio. Getting married was quite amazing for me. It was hard for me to trust anyone because of all the things that happened to me when I was younger, but with Barb I was sure I had the right girl. Our makeup and backgrounds were miles apart, but once we decided to get married, we were on the same page with our plans and dreams, and most importantly, our love for each other.

In August of 1968, two months after we got married, I began teaching in the Parma City School District; the same school system where Barb taught. At the time, Parma ranked as the largest suburban school district in northeast Ohio. It was a real change from the explosive, hostile, inner city environment where I had taught and lived for a year.

Also in August, halfway through her second year in the classroom, Barb became pregnant and because of the bylaws at the time, had to resign from her teaching position. In May of 1969, eleven months after we got married, she gave birth to our first son, John, and three years later in May of 1972, to our second son, Jeff.

John's birth occurred the same year the United States, led by Neil Armstrong, landed men on the moon, and one year before the May 4, 1970 National Guard shootings at Kent State University.

The births of John and Jeff changed the whole focus of our lives. Holding those healthy babies in my arms, my own flesh and blood, and knowing that I had the capability and responsibility to help control their destiny, was the greatest feeling that I have ever experienced. I made a promise to God that my children would be the focal point of my life; that I would do everything in my power to protect them and to enhance the quality of their lives. I also vowed that I would never forsake my wife and children, as I had been forsaken. Loving my family would be eternal for me, so help me God.

Barb became the key factor that opened the doors to a happy, healthy and productive life for our family. A very family oriented, dedicated and loving person, she was the perfect mate. Barb, along with her younger sister and brother, Carole and Richard, spent a great deal of their childhood with their father's closely-knit Italian family. Barb's grandmother and aunts and uncles played a big part in her developing into the kind of person that she became. Being the first grandchild and the first niece, she was showered with attention and love from her father's side of the family. Some people would call it being spoiled—love is a more appropriate definition of the way her father's family cared for and took care of her.

Barb's dad, Tony, was the oldest of six children from a family that moved to Cleveland from Farrell, in nearby western Pennsylvania. The Foderaros were descendants of Italian immigrants, the grandfather being a tailor by trade. They were mostly self-educated, successful, professional people. Barb's father, a design engineer for Picker X-ray, was responsible for the development of many patents on x-ray machines. My father-in-law was a brilliant man; he was unable to attend college during the hard times of the Depression but attended night school at Case Institute of Technology to attain his career qualifications.

Barb's mother, the former Beatrice Kraus, came from a family that was quite different, and resultantly, her mother was quite different than her father's side of the family. Beatrice's mother was French and her father German. The family was not close and there was much resentment over Baptist Beatrice marrying not only a Catholic, but also an Italian. Beatrice had a tough childhood, moving from place to place and being raised by people who lacked passion for their family; the same people that masqueraded as Christians, but in reality looked down their noses at anybody who was different than them. The trend that the Kraus family had established continued after Barb's mom and dad were married. Barb hardly knew anybody in her mom's family. Despite their close proximity, she only saw them on rare occasions, and when she did, they seemed like strangers, not family. The Foderaros were a blessing for Barb and made a real difference in her life.

The upside, as strange as it might seem, is that Barb's mother and her family might have caused her to relate to me more easily than others related to me. Because of her mother's family she knew about people that were self-serving, cold and bigoted. When we met that fall day in 1964 and I briefly discussed my background, she didn't flinch.

In January of 1973 two significant events happened. The signing of a cease-fire agreement ended the Vietnam War. Neither side surrendered, but even though we didn't accomplish our objective in Vietnam, the United States military forces won every major engagement. In shear number of casualties, and with one hand tied behind our backs, we outdid the enemy in Vietnam.

The second event in my life in 1973 was shocking. After five and a half years of teaching and coaching in The Parma school system and eight months after Jeff's birth I got a phone call from a former high school basketball teammate, Bob Williams. He was a year ahead of me in school, and someone that I always liked and respected. When I heard the tone of Bob's voice I knew that something had happened.

"Gary, I don't know how to say this, but I (there was a short pause), I called to tell you that Parks died."

For several seconds I could not respond to what Bob had just said. Tears trickled from my eyes, as I grew numb and saddened by the bad news. Parks, a friend through the adolescent years of my life, a 32-year-old Yale graduate, the father of two young children, an IBM executive with a brilliant future, died of colon cancer in a New York City hospital. After speaking briefly with Bob and thanking him for calling, the trickle of tears gathered momentum and became streams rolling down my face.

My pleasant memories of Parks came to life. I thought about the New York Giants baseball cap that he always wore; the games we played together; his thin-wheeled racing bike; the smile that he always managed to have on his face; going to the NFL Championship game and the Major League All Star game with Parks and his father in 1954; his brilliance; the bright future that he once had; his outstanding athletic ability and academic prowess; playing in the NCAA Basketball Tournament in 1962; and my last visit with him in Menlo Park. My sympathy went out to Parks' wife and their two very young children.

Now Parks was gone, swept away just like my grandmother and Florence. But my memories of all three and the way that they have inspired my life will never go away. My grandmother died at age 54, Florence at 45, and now Parks at the age of 32. A popular song from the 1960s came floating into my mind, *Only The Good Die Young*.

Two other sad events happened during my 14-year teaching and coaching stint in Parma. My brother Kenny's beloved son, Michael, lost his life to muscular dystrophy in 1978 at the tender age of 17, and Barbara's dear grandmother, Francesca (Francis) Mary Foderaro died the following year at the age of 88. A widow for 44 years, she had been a family oriented, loving lady that had much to do with the type of person that Barb became.

Michael's passing and the suffering that he and his family went through, ever knowing that he would only live into his teens seemed so unfair. Kenny's wife, Mary, told me that Michael liked me because I always treated him as normal despite his handicap.

The loss of people that you love is not easy, but I know that they want us to carry on and lead happy and productive lives, and nurture the children that we so dearly love.

Adversity in my life added energy and purpose to my determination that John and Jeff's upbringing would be very different than mine. Barb and I knew that success inspires people and builds confidence. Her academic approach and my emphasis on athletic achievement resulted in confident, successful, happy children and adults. I have always believed that success in any endeavor, academic, athletic or other life experiences exudes confidence and that becomes the backbone of nurturing.

Despite the satisfaction and feelings of accomplishments that I experienced being married to Barbara and raising a family, some unsettling feelings began to surface again in my life. My uncertain identity had been an issue for most of my life. My father coming to say goodbye in 1948 when I lived at the Davises'. His words had echoed through my mind for 43 years, "I'll probably never see you again; you be a good boy."

Knowing how much I loved my children, telling them I would never see them again would be worse than death. Then I wondered what kind of a man would beat up his wife and abandon his family. Clear and simple, it was a man without character, driven and controlled by the bottle; a man that put drinking and gambling ahead of his family. Having said this, I would not be disappointed if Kenneth Palmer is not my father, but if I knew my father, I probably wouldn't accept him either.

I always wondered what caused me to be different than my biological family. After writing this memoir, I know the answer: The people in my life that nurtured me caused me to be different than my family. The nurturing from those wonderful people from Chagrin Falls came at a time when I needed it most.

In August of 1977 with eight-year-old John and five-year-old Jeff, Barb and I set off to discover more about Kenneth Palmer, the man that everybody in my family wanted me to believe was my father. I contacted a brother and sister of his, both of whom lived in New Jersey. They were very open to seeing my family and me. When we met them they seemed very cordial, especially Uncle Richard. But maybe they had been prepped to be tight-mouthed like everybody else; a question that I should have asked when we visited, but I didn't. Even though they might have been forewarned, my guess is they weren't. But knowing how strongly my mother and Kenny felt about keeping the family secret, maybe they contacted Richard and Ginny. Although, neither of them seemed to suspect that I wasn't related to their brother, especially Richard. I've had an uncle-nephew relationship with him and his wife Ersilde that has stood the test of time. Every year I send a Christmas card with a note about my family, and I get the same from Richard.

What really leads me to believe that Kenneth Palmer's relatives in New Jersey think I'm their brother's son is my remembrance of Kenneth Palmer's comment in court back in January of 1949, "My mother in New Jersey can take Gary and raise him."

But Barb and I did not see any family resemblances between Richard, Ginny and myself; they were considerably smaller than me with very different features.

My mother and brother Kenny knew about the trip to New Jersey; another perfect opportunity for them to tell me the truth, but they continued to protect the secret. Maybe they felt that I didn't deserve to know the truth about my identity or possibly having something over on me gave them a sense of power.

Once in Kenny's backyard, he came close to breaking down and telling me the truth, but he couldn't bring himself to do it. I could tell by his body language that he knew I should be told the truth, especially when he hung his head after I told him I knew that his dad is not my father. And he hung his head lower when I asked him if he knew the identity of my father since our mother had a lot of bed partners. But my brother chose to remain silent; for some reason he didn't want to be known as my half brother–he didn't want to give up the title of "brother," even though that seems too selfish to be true. What really seemed strange about this whole thing was that Kenny never told Mary about our conversations. Maybe he didn't want her to think that I cared about knowing the identity of my biological father. In reality, nothing could have been further from the truth.

My mother, the main clog in the search for my real father, swore Kenneth Palmer was my father and whenever I pressed her for the truth, she avoided conflict by saying such things as, "You're here aren't you?" "Let the dead be buried," and "Let sleeping dogs lie." These statements reinforced that Kenneth Palmer wasn't my father, but I still did not know the identity of my father. It seemed strange that my mother didn't think I could possibly be smart enough to figure things out.

In 1982, the identity issue became the least of my worries. My career in education ended when the Parma schools announced massive reduction-in-force layoffs. The announcement that I would be losing my job did not come as a surprise or disappointment and had nothing to do with my performance as a teacher. Ironically, I rejoiced because for two years I had thought about other challenges in my life. I wanted to enter the business world, but the 15 years that I spent teaching and coaching had certainly been rewarding. During my tenure in education, I taught 13 grade levels (K-12) and three subjects: physical education, health education and driver's education. And I coached four sports: football, basketball, baseball and wrestling. I knew that the rewards resulting from the emphasis on preparation, commitment, discipline and an unyielding determination to win would carry over into other endeavors in life. It paralleled the same philosophy that I had in mind for my own children. The carry over value to the young people that I served, including my own sons, gave me a purpose, a reason for existing. I looked at the particular sport that I coached or class that I taught as a foundation, a proving ground for living a happy and productive life. I really felt that the lessons from my teachings would help create the building blocks for great things in their lives, and also in mine. Some people, those that haven't been in the trenches, may have looked at this as naivety and idealism, but needless to say, I certainly didn't.

I planned on testing my principles in the world of business. I knew that failure would precede success, just like it always does when people venture into new things or put themselves on the firing line. Michael Jordan put it best when he said, "I have failed over and over and over again–that's why I succeed."

I didn't have a job to step right into so I had to really swallow my pride. To get by until I was able to land a position in sales I stood in line at the unemployment office. It was not a shameful thing because losing my job was not my fault, but it hurt my pride more than I can ever put into words. What got me through besides the thoughts that I would inevitably prevail were the encouraging words, and the attitude and confidence of Barbara.

The world of business began for me in 1983. I tried a couple of sales jobs including operating a small company selling imprinted sportswear. A friend of mine, Fred Frey and I started the business and it lasted for a year. In terms of dollars earned, it wasn't a success but it turned out to be a great learning experience. A real opportunity for me came in 1985 when I became a field rep for a national company selling imprinted and embroidered sportswear, primarily to college bookstores.

I struggled initially because of my inexperience and my refusal to miss seeing John and Jeff's involvement in sports and other school activities. But by 1988 I had built a solid customer base in a three state territory and I became one of my company's best field reps. I began selling nationally in 1988; during my career I sold sportswear in 25 states. In August of 1991, I was promoted to regional manager, but I continued selling nationally, and maintained a home sales territory that had grown to twice its original geographical size. Besides selling, I had the responsibility of hiring, training, and managing people in my Midwest region.

The Persian Gulf War loomed as the major world event in 1991. It took the United States and its allies only a few weeks to destroy the Iraqi war machine. Since we had two sons in college, Jeff was 19 years old and John, 22, Barb and I were happy the war ended so quickly and that casualties were very minimal for the U.S. forces and our allies.

The year 1991 took on added significance when I decided once again to try to take on the challenge that had escaped me my entire life, discovering my identity. I needed to do something while the parties that could help me were still alive. Having given up all hope that my mother and brothers would tell me the truth, and with Barb's encouragement, I decided to make a big push to find out once and for all the identity of my father. I began a last ditch search for the truth during my annual Christmas visit to Stanley's, back where the mystery of my identity all began, in that quaint little village that I called home. . .Chaggy, I mean Chagrin Falls.

When I left Chagrin Falls to join the Navy I wasn't sure I would ever see Stanley again. When I went to college and during my early years of marriage I felt the same way. Growing older and knowing that Florence would want me to visit Stanley, and even care for him if need be, I found myself occasionally stopping to see Stan, especially around Christmas. At first there were several years in between my visits, beginning in the early 1980s. With the passing of time I began seeing him about once a year. But the visit I made during the Christmas season of 1991 was different than the other visits. I needed to see people who could help me discover the identity of my father before it was too late–*Chagrin Falls, I'm coming home, not to stay or to bail hay but to find my way.*

Picture was taken at Byers Field in Parma, Ohio in August of 1968. I was coaching football at Parma's brand new Normandy High School. The local newspaper that took the picture mentioned that I had played on Ohio University's 1963 Mid-American Conference Championship team. I was 28 years old, 6'2" and 248 pounds. Barbara and I had been married for just over a month when football practice began.

Chapter XIV
The Search Goes On

It had been 33 years since I lived with Stanley and a year since I had last seen him. The years had taken its toll on the former high school athlete, amateur boxer and outdoorsman. The listless, 88-year-old skeleton of his old self was no longer the hunter, fisherman, and tractor-trailer driver that had once been my foster father. It made me realize how quickly the years had passed and how those years had worn on him.

The wrinkles in Stanley's face had gotten deeper, his snow-white hair thinned, his stomach hung over his belt from lack of exercise and poor eating habits. His frail body crippled by arthritis, moved slowly through his dilapidated house, a house that was deteriorating all around my former foster father, a house that was no longer fit to live in.

After some probing by Stanley to find out if I had become successful, his eyes bulged with amazement when I began to tell him that life had been good to me. Unlike Florence, his expectations for me had never been high. He remembered what a poor student I had been and my propensity for getting into trouble, and like so many others, he thought that I was destined for failure. It prompted me to realize how wrong it was to label people. Obviously, I had some kind of drive, some kind of hidden agenda that Stanley and most others did not see or even sense. But certainly Florence, my high school football coach, and maybe some of my friends were enlightened by a glimpse of character. Without question, sports gave me hope and helped build the foundation of my life.

"Regional Manager, you're gettin' to be one of those sassy fat cats, Ha! Ha! But you don't look like it's gone to your head; you look like you're in good shape; big as a goddamned house, but in good shape."

I got a kick out of the spunk that he still had at his age. But I felt sorry for Stanley, and I knew that Florence would be turning over in her grave if she knew the way he lived. The kitchen ceiling had crumbled from water seepage, the toilet didn't flush; dust covered everything except the chair where he sat, cobwebs hung from the ceiling in the corner behind his chair, and the living room rug was soiled and worn thin. The wallpaper peeled from the walls like rusted paint rolls off of steel, and the spotted, discolored kitchen floor linoleum had split apart at the seams. The winter winds whistled through the old storm windows in the living room sounding much like a steam engine blowing its warning whistle. The whistling winds and lack of insulation caused the temperature in Stanley's house to dip well into the 60s. The nearly 100 year old farmhouse had deteriorated to a point beyond belief. The only sign that indicated life was the high stack of *National Geographic* magazines next to Stanley's 50 year old worn-out, turquoise-colored overstuffed chair. There he sat, sporting a heavy, checkered flannel shirt, staring at me through the lens of his very old bifocals.

I offered my help overseeing the necessary repairs, but Stanley immediately let me know that he didn't have any interest in my help or advice. Thirty-four years ago when Florence died the wheels of life stopped for my foster father, and he was only 53 years old at the time.

I looked through an album and found some old pictures from the late 1940s and early 1950s of Florence, Stanley, Grandma Davis and Tipper, as Stanley used to call his beloved springer spaniel. After looking at the photos, I turned to Stanley and offered help the way that he had once helped me. With Florence in mind, I made the offer for him to come and live with us, but I knew what his response would be.

"Stanley, you're more than welcome to come and live with us. If you're not willing to get these repairs done, you shouldn't be living here. You and Florence took me in after my grandma died. I had nobody and I was living in some pretty awful conditions, like you are now. I didn't have a pot to piss in when you and Florence took me in. You'd like it where we live, you'd have your own room and TV and three squares a day," I said.

"Ha! Ha! Ha! Much obliged! But I'm not leaving this place. Hells Bells! Herr." He started to say Herman out of habit but caught himself and suddenly stopped before continuing, "I'll stay put, right here."

My former foster father looked at me with his mouth partially open, and his eyes again gazing at me disbelievingly. During my youth when I lived in poverty across the road, Stanley probably felt sorry for me, now I felt sorry for him, so sorry that when I later drove away from 230 North Main Street, tears were rolling down my cheeks.

I came to visit Stanley this Christmas season for reasons other than to merely wish him Merry Christmas and give him a present. I needed to find clues and inevitably answers to my true identity. I wanted to find out if I had a father or at least discover that I had been dropped from Krypton or some other planet. I grew tired of people not willing to tell me the truth, a conspiracy by some to deny me a basic right because they had chosen to do so. Someone had to have the common decency to help me, and Stanley could certainly start the ball rolling.

Stanley, Aunt Goldie and Uncle Harold had grown to be pretty old, so I had to be aggressive and persistent or it would be too late.

"Stanley, remember when you told me about that man who came to the Crawfords', asked for me and said he was my father? Can you tell me again what John (Crawford) told him, and anything else about the man that you can remember John telling you?" I asked.

"Well, I know John told him that you didn't live there. I can't remember too much but I remember he said he was your father."

"Was I living here at the time?" I asked.

"Yeah, you were here," Stanley responded.

"Did John tell him that I lived here?" I questioned.

"I don't think so," replied Stan.

The tone of Stanley's response indicated that he didn't want to elaborate on the incident. I later found out from Bee Crawford about the stranger's visit. Her response caught me by surprise.

"John never talked to a person claiming to be your father. He would have told me," said Bee.

If that's the case, it's quite possible that Stanley talked to the man and told him that I didn't live with the Davises. I'm sure that whoever talked to the man claiming to be my father, did what they thought was right–I strongly suspect that it was Stanley. But that's only speculation; I'll never know for sure.

I needed Stanley to tell me more so I continued probing. I didn't want to come on too strong out of respect for his heart condition. But I needed to talk to him seriously; he and my aunt and uncle stood as my last hope. Kenny, George, and my mother's conspiracy to keep secret the truth from me left me with few choices.

"Stan, I'd like to find out who my father is. I'm certain that Kenneth Palmer is not my father but I need proof. I need to find out who my real father is. I'm fifty-one years old; it's a real embarrassment not knowing my father. I don't know what diseases I might be prone to or anything. I also need to know for peace of mind," I said.

Stanley sat quietly for a few moments with his head down. Then he looked up directly into my eyes and began speaking.

"Non was in juvenile court when they were prosecuting your father and mother for abandonment and neglect, and all those other goddamn things. Your father stood up in court and said, 'Gary is not my son.' I know how Non felt about this. You had such a tough go of it from people that had the balls to call themselves human beings; you didn't need any more trash in your life. Non would have told you, but her life got cut short before she could. I didn't think it was my place," said Stanley.

Wow, what a mouthful Stanley just said! The can of worms was slowly opening.

"Can you tell me anything else. . .anything that might help me find my father?" I asked.

"Hell, I wish I could help you more but that's all I know!" he said.

"Stan, you told me a lot! I just need more clues so I can keep searching. Thank you! You don't know how much this has helped. If you change your mind about living with us, you've got my number. I need to visit Aunt Goldie and Uncle Harold. I'm gonna call and see if I can stop by their place. They live in a condominium out in Bainbridge, about ten minutes from here," I said.

"Be my guest," responded Stan.

Fortunately, I caught Aunt Goldie and Uncle Harold at home. Understandably, my aunt seemed surprised by the call and sounded anxious to see me. Careful not to reveal the true intent of my visit, I told Goldie I was at Stanley's and would like to stop by and wish her and Uncle Harold a Merry Christmas. The quick visit would not allow a bullshit dress rehearsal by Goldie or a conversation with my mother or brother about what to tell me or what not to tell me. I wanted the truth from Goldie and Harold so I could find my father.

While driving up snow covered Bainbridge Road (now called Chagrin Road) on the way to visiting my aunt and uncle for the first time in over 25 years, memories from a turbulent past drifted through my mind. I thought about my mother being beaten into submission by her husband, and other domestic turmoil that haunted the Palmer family in the early and mid 1940s. I thought about my grandmother being left to die in a shack, and how the very people that I was on my way to visit, turned their backs on her. I may have been a shy and cruddy, pathetic little kid, but I had an elephant's memory. I also realized that the grudges against my family that are instilled in me are not going to get me through the Pearly Gates.

After thinking about the negatives of the past, my thoughts switched to more pleasant memories of my aunt and uncle. I thought about the Christmases long ago that I had spent with them in the rural horse country of Gates Mills. I didn't see my aunt's family very often, but most Christmas days between 1946 and 1957 had been spent with them.

The Christmases past, filled with the smell of cut pines and freshly baked cookies floated through my mind. The center of holiday spirit, the tree, had always been decorated with large colorful bulbs, shiny tinsel, and glittering lights. Cochise, the Bywaters' Dalmatian, sat next to me and insisted on my attention by repeatedly snapping his powerful tail against my legs.

Visiting the stables that formed an L-shape connection to the four-room living quarters is my favorite Christmas memory at Aunt Goldie and Uncle Harold's. I went to the stables to feed and pet the horses and to watch my uncle care for them.

I remember fantasizing about coming back to horseback ride at my aunt and uncle's in the summertime. I imagined the wind working its magic on my face, and rearranging the mane of a dashing stallion or mare while they were gracefully jumping over creek beds and streaking across fenceless fields. The hardest part of coming to my aunt and uncle's had been trying to talk cousin Susan into letting me ride her horse. She never let me ride her horse out in the pasture just inside of a small training corral. And she only let me ride if I adhered strictly to her rules and her directions. She protected her mare as if it would melt if someone else jumped into the saddle and got too far away from her.

Uncle Harold was the caretaker of horses for the wealthy owner of a large country estate. I especially remember sometime during my high school years a conversation I had with Uncle Harold.

"Uncle Harold, how did you learn how to handle the horses like you do?" I asked.

"Well Gary, horses have a good sense of what's going on. When you break 'em in ya' have be firm, but you have to be consistent and at times you have to be perfectly still and quiet. You have to know what they're thinkin' and they have to know what you're thinkin'. They have to sense that you're on their side, but also that you mean business," answered my uncle.

Uncle Harold also bred foxhounds and trained them for hunting, and he played polo until age 75. When he lived and worked on an estate in Massachusetts, he helped train the United States Olympic cross-country equestrian team. Uncle Harold's horsemanship gained him a lot of respect, especially from his peers.

When I got closer to my aunt and uncle's condominium, I began driving slower, gathering my thoughts for perhaps the last opportunity to find the identity of my father. I didn't expect this to be easy; my aunt and uncle are strangers; they've never even met my family. The last time I saw them was 1966–they didn't even attend our wedding. But I prayed that they would help me. I needed to be firm and persistent, but in no way did I plan on begging for the truth. So that Goldie and Harold would open up, I decided to pretend that I knew more than I actually did.

Seeing my aunt and uncle after all those years became a real eye opener. They looked like the grandparents of people I used to know, making me realize how old I must have looked to them.

Both had been grounded by the misfortunes of poor health. Uncle Harold's feet and ankles had swollen and discolored so badly he could hardly move his legs. Because of the severe pain from lack of circulation in the lower part of his body, Harold never stood up during my visit of several hours. He sat in an overstuffed chair with his feet extended on a footstool; his eyes fixed on mine.

I gazed around the white-walled, modern, well-kept condominium and noticed familiar looking pictures of horses, foxhounds, and my uncle on horseback. The colorful photographs represented pleasant reflections of his prideful past.

With no signs of the Christmas season and due to my aunt and uncle's old age and failing health, it stood as quite a contrast from yuletide visits long ago.

After some brief conversations about Christmas, the weather, my family, and reminiscing over Uncle Harold's memorabilia, I wanted to get to the main event.

My uncle sat motionless in his chair and continued to look at me in a curious but friendly way. It appeared obvious that he had focused on every word that I said. My intuition told me that he wanted to ask or tell me something, but didn't know quite how to do it.

Aunt Goldie used a walker to get around. It stunned me to see her crippled by old age because I still had this image of Goldie from her younger years. She had been an attractive woman with long blond hair and sparkling blue eyes. Her sloped posture and rounded shoulders were more prominent now and made her look shorter than she did in her younger days, but one thing hadn't changed–her personality.

"Look at that old fart! He has no circulation in his legs. He can't walk or do anything. Have you ever seen such a wreck?" Aunt Goldie asked, while laughing and looking at me for approval.

Uncle Harold just sat in the chair and didn't waste his breath on the old hag. But occasionally he shook his head from side to side; the same way he had done 40 years ago.

I quickly changed the subject by asking, "How's Susan doing?"

"Susan's coming over later to see you," said Goldie, who agreed at least temporarily to the cease-fire.

I commented about my cousin Susan, an only child, divorced, and eight months younger than me.

"I haven't seen Susan in the past 30 years," I commented and then added with a smile, "We're such a close family, aren't we?"

My aunt laughed out loud and my uncle chuckled to himself at that one. At my aunt's request, when Susan and her boyfriend stopped by, I bought a couple of pizzas. Goldie had never been shy about asking people to spend their money.

"Gary, would you mind treating us all to pizza? How about it, you like pizza don't you?" she asked.

"I'd really enjoy treating everyone to pizza, Aunt Goldie. Go ahead and order a couple of large ones, get whatever you'd like on it; salad and beverages would also be nice," I said, realizing that the longer I stayed and the better we got along, the more likely I would get the information I wanted.

After about an hour of small talk and pizza, Susan, and according to my aunt, her married boyfriend, left. There was never much chemistry between my cousin and me, and that didn't change after all these years. I was relieved to see her go because now I could roll up my sleeves and hopefully find some answers to my questions.

"Aunt Goldie and Uncle Harold, I need some answers from you about my father. You know there's been a cover up my whole life. You have to help me because you're my last hope to find the truth. I've known for a long time that Kenneth Palmer is not my father, but that's all I know. I found out some interesting things lately but I need your help. I'd like to find my father before it's too late. I'm fifty-one years old; how much longer should I have to wait?"

Uncharacteristically, Aunt Goldie sat quietly, staring at the floor; after a short pause, Uncle Harold looked into my eyes and spoke. "I knew your father; he was Italian."

"Italian! Why do you say that? You're kidding. . .Italian? My father's Italian? You mean after all these years, I'm half Italian?" I asked in utter amazement.

Uncle Harold became the first and only person to tell me anything about my father's nationality. I must have appeared stunned because I certainly felt that way. Previously, I only knew one thing about my nationality; I'm German and Irish from my grandmother's side of the family. This Italian thing blew me away; Barb is half Italian and now I may also be half Italian. Of course, that also means that John and Jeff are half Italian. I knew the four of us had a lot in common, but I didn't realize to what extent.

I thought about the handful of people in my life that have said, "You look Italian," which I laughed at because it seemed so ridiculous. I am taller than most Italians and I have blue eyes. In my wildest dreams, I never thought about the possibility of being Italian. But I did know that the northern Italians are taller, and many of them are blond and blue eyed. Shortly after Uncle Harold threw the Italian curveball at me, I thought of something else–through the years I've always had my share of Italian friends.

After Uncle Harold watched and listened to my reaction to his statement, he threw a compliment at the man that he claimed to be my father.

"I knew your father well. He was a successful businessman. He owned race horses and a nightclub in Westbury, New York," said Uncle Harold.

"What's his name?" I asked.

"John Barelli, most people called him Jack," replied Uncle Harold.

"How do you spell Barelli?" I asked.

"B-A-R-E-L-L-I," responded my uncle.

"You're not going to believe this, the company that I work for is located in Westbury, New York," I said.

At this point Aunt Goldie joined the conversation. Even though I wasn't ready to take anything to the bank, especially from Aunt Goldie, I listened to her comment.

"Your father was a real ladies' man. He was handsome, a good dancer and very successful. Your mother and him danced together quite often; that's how they met. He was quite a bit younger than your mother you know," said Aunt Goldie.

"How much younger?" I asked.

"Oh I don't know, six or eight years I guess."

Then she looked directly into my eyes and waited for a response.

"How do you know that this man is my father?" I asked.

"Oh, you look just like him!" she answered.

"I look like a lot of people," I responded.

Then a very strange thing happened, but because of whom I was dealing with, I was not surprised. Goldie got a billfold out of her purse and opened it up. She handed me several pictures and pointed to the one on top, a 5 and 10 Cent Store photo from the 1940s.

"This is your father when he was in his twenties," she said.

"Why do you have his picture in your purse after all these years?" I asked.

She avoided my question by saying, "Oh, I've had it for a long time. I knew your father quite well."

"Why should I believe this man is my father after being lied to and deceived all my life?" I asked.

"Your mother should have told you," said Aunt Goldie.

When Goldie showed me the pictures, I made another discovery that also didn't surprise me in the least. Staring me in the eyes loomed another family cover-up that everyone except me had been privy to. A man appeared with Barelli in several of the photos that Goldie had shown me.

"Who's the other man in these pictures?" I asked.

"That's Jim Moorhouse, a friend of your father's; he was your father's best friend," she said.

While continuing to look through my aunt's portfolio of pictures, I found another photo of Jim Moorhouse. I looked on the back of the picture to hopefully get more information about Moorhouse. The back of the photo read, "Susan's father." I didn't need to comment or ask anymore about Barelli's best friend.

When Goldie saw me read the back of Moorhouse's picture she snatched the photo out of my hand, grabbed a pen from her purse and scratched out the words that she had once written on the back, "Susan's father."

Since people in this family consider honesty a weakness, I didn't jump to any conclusions about Barelli being my father. But I knew without question that Uncle Harold was not Susan's father. The family trend of dishonesty continued later in the evening when Goldie discussed Susan's visits to New York.

"Susan's first trip to New York was right after she graduated from high school. She went there as a guest of your father; it was her graduation present. Your father wined and dined Susan in some of New York's finest restaurants. Jack only dined at the best places," commented Aunt Goldie.

Now the bullshit was really flying. Susan had been invited to the Big Apple to be wined, dined and entertained by my father...as a graduation present nonetheless. Certainly my father, for whatever reason, had nothing to do with me when I graduated or at any other time in my life for that matter. But Goldie tried to throw up a smoke screen about Susan's trip to New York; she wanted me to think that my father had a special affection for Susan.

A moron could figure out that Susan went to New York to see her own father. The back of the photo that read "Susan's father" unveiled the cover up. Obviously, Goldie, in true character, tried to elevate Susan, make me feel less important in order to disguise the real reason Susan went to New York, to visit her father, Jim Moorhouse.

It's difficult to believe anything that people in my mother's family say, including the information about the identity of my father. They don't have a conscience about anything. Possibly, Harold is the one exception; he seemed sincere about what he had told me. Between Harold, Goldie and Susan, Harold had always been my favorite, although I always thought he took too much shit from Aunt Goldie. It's hard to understand why he stayed with such a lying, cheating, unfaithful woman, all those years.

This Italian-Romeo Barelli guy might have been my father, but I still needed proof. Since I had no other leads, I had to pursue the evidence at hand in spite of the fact that bullshit flew around Bainbridge, Ohio, like frisbees at a dog show.

"How can I get in touch with this man you claim to be my father?" I asked.

"He passed away several years ago," replied Harold.

Oh no! Just exactly what I didn't want to hear. But I still wasn't sure I had heard the truth. I had to get enough information from my aunt and uncle to continue searching for the truth. This would be hard, but I didn't plan to leave Goldie and Harold's until I had enough ammunition to continue the fight.

I asked every question that I thought to be pertinent; questions such as:
How do you know that he died?
When did he die?
Where did he die?
Do you know the cause of death?
What was the name of the nightclub that he owned?
How many children did he have?
What are their names?
Does he have any other children out of wedlock?
What proof do you have that he was my father?
How successful was Barelli breeding and training racehorses?

Were both his parents Italian?

Was he born in the United States?

Were his parents born in the United States?

Uncle Harold tried to answer these questions, but struggled with some of them. But, he felt confident about answering one question.

I asked my uncle, "What was your affiliation with Barelli and how did my mother know him?"

"Kenneth Palmer, your mother and Goldie and I went to Westbury quite a bit because of the horse business. We worked with your father's thoroughbred racehorses and we stayed at his house and ate and drank at his restaurant; it was also a nightclub. His horses were trotters and people came to his restaurant from miles around for his mother's Italian cooking and for the nightlife in his club. There were no handouts, but when he took us out on the town he was a generous man. He paid for food, drinks and everything, but it was different when we came in his place. He ran his business the right way...there were no free drinks or free food, but the food was good," said Uncle Harold.

I continued thinking to myself...I had heard that Goldie and my mother made trips to Westbury together. Now I understand why. Everything came into focus. Poor Uncle Harold, he's such a nice man; he didn't deserve someone like Goldie.

What made Kathryn and Goldie so dysfunctional? Obviously, their loose sexual behavior stemmed from low self-esteem. Maybe the ultimate taboo, abuse by their father, Fred Jones, caused them to be the way they were. Coincidental it might be, but from old pictures I noticed a striking resemblance between Kenneth Palmer and my mother's father.

While driving home late that cold, wintry evening, I was anxious to tell my family about my recent discovery. Even though I remained skeptical about the findings, I was grateful to Uncle Harold and Stanley for their contributions to my identity search.

Because of declining health, I felt fortunate to have visited Stanley and Uncle Harold when I did. In September of 1992, nine months after my visit, Stanley passed away. Uncle Harold died in April of 1993, seven months after Stanley's death. I attended both of their funerals; I sincerely appreciated their contributions to my life and the information they had given me during my identity search. Getting the information from Stanley and Harold a short time before they died had spiritual overtones. I could feel an unexplainable force pushing me to see them, just in the nick of time. People can say it was luck or good timing or whatever, but I am certain it goes beyond that.

Stanley and Harold helped more than anybody in the search for my identity, and thanks to God, they lived past the life expectancy for males in the 1990s. Stanley had reached his 88th birthday seven months prior to his death, and Uncle Harold died a few weeks prior to his 85th birthday. Stanley's estate went to his three nephews, but he did leave me a small token amount of money. It was probably the money that Florence had saved for my education before she died in 1957.

When I broke the news of my identity findings to Barb, John and Jeff, they acted quite stunned. There were many questions and a sense of excitement over the prospect that after all these years there's a possibility that I had found the identity of my father.

Because their lives unfolded so much differently than mine, Barb, John and Jeff had always thought that I got the short end of the stick. Maybe in some respects I did, but I was making up for it now. Something in my makeup and Barb's attitude toward love, devotion and family enabled me to focus on the task at hand–taking care of my family and being the best father and husband that I could be.

Since John and Jeff were both in college when I discovered the information about my identity, life in the business world was still my main focus. But what I had found out about my probable biological father became such a big event in my life, I needed to prove or disprove what I had learned from Stanley, Uncle Harold and Aunt Goldie.

More than ever before I thought about and discussed with Barb how different I was than the people that I was genetically connected to. I also thought how fortunate I was to have gotten away from my mother and her abusive husband at an early age. I became the antithesis of them; the happiness, success and prosperity of Barb, John and Jeff were the reasons that I existed.

A lot of things were happening during the months that followed my Christmas visit to see Stanley, Aunt Goldie and Uncle Harold. In 1992 on Easter Sunday, Buffy, our family dog died. With John and Jeff in college and no family pet, a real emptiness loomed in our house, and now there was added stress because of the uncertainty about my identity. It seemed that whenever Barb and I weren't working we discussed my past and my identity problems. We especially talked about things I needed to do to bring closure to the "Who's my father crisis?"

In the mean time I began suffering from mild depression, something that was out of character for me. For several weeks I took anti-depressant medication. Barb was a pillar of strength, as usual, helping me through the down time in my life. We decided on something that became an overnight cure-all to my problem. In October of 1992, we purchased a female golden retriever puppy from a farm in Dalton, Ohio. Izzie, like Tippy had been during my youth, became my pride and joy, and my favorite companion. My new floppy-eared hunting dog was just what the doctor ordered. My short bout with depression quickly ended and I stopped taking medication. Izzie improved the quality of my life, which in turn improved the quality of Barb's life.

My level of physical activity and also Barb's got a big boost. There was an instant bond with our new pup: daily walks and hikes in the woods, swimming at the lake, and good, solid fun playing together. I started walking two to three miles every day, began lifting weights regularly, not just occasionally, and started writing my life's story in a journal. I was so inspired by my new companion, everything in my life started getting better. Except for company business, Izzie came with me everywhere I went.

Chapter XV
The Irony of Westbury

Taking care of both company business and personal business came to the forefront in my life. Because I had a strong feeling that my mother would deny my findings, I called Kenny first to inform him about my discovery. I spoke to Mary, and after telling her what I had recently learned, she was not happy. Her concern seemed to be, who let the cat out of the bag? Her initial response, "Who told ya?" said it all. Then I talked to Kenny and he was also unimpressed by my findings. I could tell by the sound of his voice that he was not thrilled, and that feeling was reinforced when he said, "How did ya find out?" Even though I knew they would figure out who told me, my response to Kenny and Mary was, "I'd rather not say." That went over like a room full of termites.

Knowing that Kenny would warn my mother about my discovery, I immediately called her so she could not organize her lies. No one except my mother could confirm what I had learned from Goldie and Harold, but true to form, she denied everything. My mother called my findings a bunch of lies and refused to even discuss the issue.

The next plan was to call New York and try to make contact with Jack Barelli's sons. Thanks to Uncle Harold, after several phone calls I had enough information to reach Pete Barelli, one of Jack Barelli's sons. Pete owned and operated the nightclub that had once been his father's. Pete Barelli and I had some interesting conversations, and I wrote down everything that he told me. It amazed me that he did not seem surprised or offended by my findings concerning his father. Barelli indicated that his father was no angel. Many of the things we talked about on the phone would later be discussed in person.

There stood a twist of irony about all this horsing around in Westbury, New York, a community located in west central Long Island 20 miles from uptown Manhattan. The company that I work for during the struggle for my identity had its corporate headquarters in Westbury. On my next trip to New York in March of 1993, I would be tending to more than just company business.

The man that Aunt Goldie and Uncle Harold claimed to be my father had four children with his wife, and several other children out of wedlock. Pete Barelli told me this in one of our phone conversations.

It was strange being 51 years old, finally discovering my probable identity, then being scorned by my mother and her entire family. I remember my cousin Susan calling and telling me how awful and upsetting it would be to the Barellis if I decided to contact them and bring them into the mess that I had created. But how could I expect anything different from people who have always been numb to my feelings?

The attitude from my family that I should feel guilty for trying to find out the truth about my identity, spurred me on. It made no sense why these people never wanted me to know the truth, especially my mother, who was now 81 years old. Nonetheless, I had too much information for my mother to continue denying everything. I called her several times to tell her that I knew all about Barelli and that we needed to talk in person. It took several months, but finally, under pressure from my demands, she agreed to an interview. I'm certain that if Barelli had still been alive, she would have refused to discuss the issue.

I also believed that my mother held out for so long talking to me about Barelli for two reasons: initially, she thought that I would eventually go away; and when I didn't, she might have gotten advice or encouragement from other family members to hold out until I offered her money for giving me the information. My mother and her family always had a scheme about how to get money from people because they don't have the ambition or the ability to earn it on their own.

My mother lived at the corner of a busy intersection in a three-room apartment in a very old section of Cleveland Heights. She had lived by herself for the past 46 years: in Cleveland, Mayfield Heights, and at her present location for more than 25 years. She was living on her social security check and since she and Kenneth Palmer never got divorced, she had been drawing his social security since his death in 1966. I had always suspected that in her younger years she had an illegal side profession, possibly prostitution, but that was never confirmed. Her past living habits and material wealth didn't add up to the minuscule income that she earned as a waitress. But in retrospect, until she got old and as long as she could, she always made sure she dated men that could provide for her. That itself is a subtle form of prostitution.

To document the important conversation with my mother, I concealed a tape recorder in my briefcase, but to keep her from seeing the recorder I positioned the open end of the briefcase away from her. This muffled the sound of her voice and destroyed the quality of the recording, but that didn't stop me from getting the information that I needed.

My mother gave in to my continued demands for the truth by finally admitting that Jack Barelli, deceased New York businessman was indeed my father. She was visibly upset over me finding out about Barelli and she didn't want to discuss anything else about their relationship. When I asked my mother the reason she never told me the truth about my father, her answer was a typical lie: "I was going to tell you who your father was before I died."

The next time I saw my mother, several years later, ended up being the last time that I would see her. I visited her in the hospital where she lay penniless, dying a lonely death from colon cancer. Not many people, including my brothers, came to her funeral service to witness the burial of her ashes in Chagrin Falls. Kenny and Mary, who lived in Mississippi, visited her a few weeks earlier in the hospital, but supposedly he and Mary were sick and couldn't come back for the funeral. Kenny was the executor of her will but his daughters, Linda and Ellen, who lived in the Cleveland area, made the funeral arrangements. Except for all the clothes that she had, her estate could not have been more meager: a few pieces of furniture, some framed pictures, and $600 left over from the insurance money that was designated to bury her.

One unforgettable, but not surprising incident took place at the cemetery, in the middle of the burial ceremony. Aunt Goldie came to the cemetery in a wheelchair in Susan's boyfriend's van. When the doors of the van opened, my aunt began hollering at me, "I don't care what you say! That woman is your mother! Do you understand? She's your mother!" My aunt's words were too pathetic to even respond to. I did the same thing that most other people did; I glanced over at her and then looked away. One side of my brain felt sorry for the old bitch, but the other side didn't.

During the remaining ceremony I thought back to what my mother said when I asked her why she wouldn't tell me the truth, "I was going to tell you who your father was before I died." Then I reflected on what my half-brother Kenny said when I asked him the same question. In an effort to make me feel sorry for him, Kenny had a sheepish and rather selfish response; "I thought you wouldn't look at me as your brother anymore."

I believe Kenny felt he had some kind of older brother power that he would lose if the truth came out. He also wanted to stay in his mother's good graces because I'm sure that she convinced him that I should never know the truth. Also, Kenny may have been embarrassed because of his bigotry toward

Italians.

"Goddamn dagos!" he used to say.

"That goddamn dago brother-in-law," is what he called Mary's sister's husband. The name-calling had a lace of irony. Kenny's brother-in-law always stepped forward and volunteered to help with repairs and projects around my brother's house.

Since Kenny believed Barelli to be my father and never thought that I would find out, not only did I view the name-calling as bigotry, but also as a telltale show of disrespect toward me.

As a little boy I remember Kenny teaching me what I thought to be the Notre Dame Fight Song: "Cheer, cheer for ole' Noter Dame, the dagos and Jews have stolen your fame."

At age 12, when I bought my first and only record, *A Medley of College Fight Songs*, I learned the real words to the Notre Dame fight song.

Kenny's biggest drawback was being a Palmer. He didn't finish high school and as a result never had anything but a minimum wage job. When he got married he was a gravedigger, then he worked at a lumberyard as a yard hand. While in his forties, when his family desperately needed an income, he stopped working altogether. He said he couldn't work anymore, but it was more a case of wouldn't. Besides not being educated, he also lacked the confidence to try new things and the desire to try and improve his financial situation for the benefit of his family. Alcoholism played a major role in my brother's downfall, and my mother added to his problem. She contributed to his drinking addiction and poor work habits by always making sure that he had money for cigarettes and beer. Kenny was addicted to both alcohol and nicotine, and my mother, who always seemed to have money for Kenny, nurtured his bad habits. It enabled her to be controlling and to feel important, and she loved the recognition from Kenny. My mother and Kenny were not concerned about food on the table for my brother's family, and self-respect as human beings. Mary didn't like what was happening, but for some reason allowed it to continue. After Kenny stopped working, if not for the financial help from one of Mary's brothers and her employment as a hospital aid, I don't know how my brother's five children could have been cared for.

Despite Kenny's problems he had a good side to him. When I lived with the Crawfords, he always remembered me at Christmas and on my birthdays. No one in our family, except Kenny, came to see Grandma during her bout with cancer when we lived in the most deplorable conditions imaginable. He served his country and fought in the Korean War. He let me stay with him whenever I came home from college, and I know he loved his family. Sadly, my brother died at the age of 70. The last few years of his life, he lived in Walnut Grove Mississippi, a town much smaller than Chagrin Falls.

In March of 1993, I went to Westbury to train a new sales representative. I planned to engage in business during the day and to pursue my identity leads at night. It's amazing that Westbury, New York was the home of my company and also the home of the person that now has the label of being my biological father.

Our first business appointment was at the United States Military Academy, a place I had always dreamed of seeing. The tradition, history, mystique, and beauty of the fortress on the Hudson were very special. Army had been one of the schools that I revered and dreamed of playing football for during my younger days.

Navy was another one of my favorite teams, going back to 1947 when I played imaginary Army-Navy football games in my grandma's front yard. With those memories in mind, I had a marketing idea for the 1993 Army-Navy football game. I presented the idea to Agatha Gerardi, the bookstore manager.

"Agatha, I have an idea for a shirt to commemorate the next Army-Navy football game. The all time series is tied at 43 victories apiece and 7 ties. How about a shirt recognizing that the biggest rivalry in college football is presently a tied series. The Army mule and the Navy goat could be squaring off with the words BREAK THE TIE below the mascots," I suggested.

"Break the tide?" asked one of Agatha's assistants.

"I was thinking tie, T-I-E," I said, spelling it out before continuing, "but I like the tide idea also. How about 'Break the tie and send the Navy out with the tide,'" I responded, without volunteering information about my Navy background.

Agatha cracked a smile over my suggestion, but did not comment any further, nor did I. She liked our merchandise and bought several items, but I couldn't sell her on the commemorative shirt idea.

Knowing a couple of the Cadets was another reason why my trip to West Point was special. Phil Lenz, a junior Cadet and one of the Army quarterbacks, had been a high school classmate, teammate and friend of our youngest son, Jeff. Barb and I often sat with Phil's parents at the St. Vincent-St. Mary football games. But due to Phil's rigid schedule, I could not make contact with him.

Jim Cantelupe, a second cousin of Barb's was a plebe at the academy.

Jim, an honor student and All-Ohio football player at Trinity High School in Garfield Heights, Ohio, had an outstanding career at West Point both academically and athletically. He lettered four years in football and captained the Cadets his junior and senior seasons.

After my business appointment at the West Point bookstore, I called Jim in hopes of getting to see him. He had a duty assignment and could not leave his post, but I talked with him on the phone. After speaking with Barb's second cousin, my thoughts changed to someone who might be my half brother.

Later that evening on March 16, 1993, I visited the nightclub owned by Pete Barelli. If Pete's father was also my father, we had a lot to talk about. Because of the cold and snowy weather I took a cab to the nightclub, located about two miles from my motel, the same motel where singer Connie Francis had been raped several years earlier.

I didn't tell Pete Barelli about my plans, I just showed up. Warning him that I was coming might have given him a reason not to be there. Leading up to the surprise visit, many thoughts raced through my mind; I didn't know what to expect.

From the get-go, I wanted Barelli to know that my visit was not motivated by money. Then I wanted to state and reinforce the purpose of my visit: Initially, peace of mind became the objective; I wanted to find a link that would prove or disprove the truth about my identity. And since I have reason to believe that Jack Barelli was my father, I wanted to gather information about the medical history of the Barelli family.

When I arrived at the nightclub the first thing I saw was a canopy over the front entrance. The club was rather nice but not as upscale as I thought it might be. When I opened the door and an attractive young hostess greeted me, I asked to speak with the owner, Pete Barelli.

"Can I have your name, sir?" she asked, before calling Barelli's office.

"Yes, will you please tell Pete Barelli that Gary Palmer from Ohio is here to see him?"

While waiting for Barelli I felt anxious but not nervous. I wondered what he would look like and whether he would be as nice as he seemed on the phone. When Barelli came to greet me he was blatantly nonchalant, showing no emotion whatsoever. I probably appeared the same way to him because I certainly didn't feel warm about this whole thing–anxious to hopefully find the truth but not warm.

We shook hands and I said, "I'm Gary Palmer. I think we may be related."

He remembered my name from our phone conversations. "Let's go back to my office where we can talk," he said.

We walked through a long, carpeted area that connected the front door to the nightclub, engaging in small talk along the way. He asked me how long I've been in Westbury, where I'm staying and if I had plans to go uptown. I told him that I planned on going to Manhattan tomorrow night for dinner and maybe to a Broadway Show, and then I complimented him on his nightclub.

Pete was not as tall as I expected him to be; he may have been 5'11" or 6'. He had dark hair, light brown eyes and he appeared to be in good condition; he probably weighed about 175 pounds. I didn't notice a striking resemblance between him and me, but I wasn't really expecting him to look like me either. Maybe a third party might look at us differently and say, "Gee, I can see the resemblance," but I couldn't.

Pete's grandfather immigrated to the United States from the seaport city of Genoa in northern Italy and his grandmother hailed from Naples, in southern Italy.

I knew from phone conversations with Pete that all the Barellis were younger than me, and that Pete had two brothers and one sister. I also knew that Pete's father died of a heart attack in 1984, at the age of 68. I didn't waste time getting to the point.

"Pete, from our phone talks you know that I am reasonably sure that your father is also my father. I can't prove it, but there's some pretty strong evidence. I have a confession from my mother that I recorded without her knowledge. Have you ever heard anybody in your family mention a person named Kathryn Palmer?" I asked.

"No, I haven't," Pete responded.

"What about Kenneth Palmer?" I asked.

"No, I don't think so, but my dad had a lot of friends," answered Pete.

"Have you ever heard of Jim Moorhouse?" I asked.

"He was a friend of my dad's," he said, shaking his head up and down to emphasize that he knew Moorhouse.

I proceeded to tell Pete the whole story, as I knew it. Pete repeated some information that he had given me on the phone, but added more and spoke very openly.

"My father took advantage of every good looking woman that came in here. Women came here and still do, looking for a good time. I don't know if we're related, but I wouldn't be surprised. There are others that claim to be related to me too. In fact there are twins that claim my father is also their father. Like I said when we talked on the phone, my father was no angel," he commented, and then waited for my response.

"Tell me about the twins," I asked.

"I don't know a whole lot, but there are female twins claiming the same thing that you're claiming," he said.

"Can you tell me anything else about them?" I continued.

In an effort to change the subject, he looked away and said, "I don't know much about them."

"What else can you tell me about your dad?"

"Well, he had an addiction to women or maybe I should say an addiction to sex. There's one of his pictures," he said, pointing to a photo of Barelli with one of his horses.

I noticed from the picture that Barelli was quite heavy, not obese but overweight. It indicated to me that later in life he probably spent more time around the nightclub drinking beer and eating pasta than at the stables with his horses. It also made me realize that I didn't want to look like him when I hit the sixties age bracket.

Realizing that it might be the last time that I would see Pete I tried to stretch the conversation so that I could learn more.

"What was your father's relationship with your mother like?" I asked.

"Well, it wasn't a traditional type of relationship. For a good part of their marriage they never even slept in the same bedroom. My father wanted to hold the marriage together and so did my mother, but they didn't have much to do with each other," Pete said, and then he hesitated before continuing.

"This business (the nightclub) didn't help my father's problems. The ladies liked him and he liked them. The problems he had are a big reason that I would like to get out of this business. There's a lot of bad memories here," Pete Barelli said.

I found that interesting because Barelli had remodeled and added on to his restaurant. If I had considered getting out of the business, I probably wouldn't be investing more money in it. But maybe he knew that he could sell the club for a lot more by remodeling, or possibly he didn't really intend to sell it. Maybe he just wanted me to know that he didn't want to fall prey to the same temptations that his father had fallen prey to.

Even though Pete Barelli gave me information about his father, I had this feeling that he thought that I might be there for reasons other than peace of mind and medical history.

I certainly understood those suspicions; I would have felt the same way. Beginning with our phone conversations, I put myself in his shoes and tried understanding things from his perspective.

I always thought that New Yorkers had a superiority complex. They try to act worldly, but when you get to know them their mindset is very provincial. I tried to get inside of Pete Barelli's head and guess what he might have been thinking.

"Who is this hayseed from the Midwest? Ohio, I'm not sure if that's east or west of Indiana. I wonder if this guy's real purpose is my father's inheritance. He's taller than the rest of us and his eyes are lighter, but who knows," raced through my mind when I tried to guess at his thoughts.

When I talked to Pete on the phone I remember him telling me something about his father that struck my interest. I asked Pete if his father had served in the military during World War II. Pete's answer revealed some interesting information about his dad.

"He was in the Merchant Marines during World War II. A German U-boat sank his ship on one of their supply runs to Britain. There was something like one hundred and seventy men that went down with the boat and only nine survivors. My father was one of the survivors," said Pete Barelli.

Whether he's my father or not, Jack Barelli being one of nine survivors from the submarine attack was an amazing feat. It appeared that Barelli had strong survival instincts, much like my grandmother and her ancestors. If this man is my father, at least I had something to hang my hat on.

I wanted to find out more about Jack Barelli while I had the face-to-face opportunity with his son. And since the momentum from our conversation had kicked into high gear, I continued asking questions.

"You said you had two brothers and a sister. Can you tell me more about them?" I asked.

"Jimmy's a teacher; Julie has a hairdressing business, and then there's Mike. I think I told you that Mike's the oldest. He also has a lot of problems. Mike got into some trouble and served prison time," said Pete.

"What did he do?" I asked.

"He did some pretty bad things with horses. He and this veterinarian were purposely injuring horses, probably using wire lines to trip 'em and break their legs or some disgusting thing. They did it to collect on the insurance policies. The insurance company would see the injured horses and authorize payment after the veterinarian recommended that the horses be put to sleep. The vet was claiming through signed affidavits that he was putting the horses to sleep. But he would nurse them back to health, and he and Mike would sell them to the Amish. (Pete pronounced it Aamish with a long a). I don't think you'd want to meet Mike," he said.

"I can tell you right now if I did, there'd be trouble! I'm an animal lover. Dogs and horses are at the top of my list. I don't like your brother and I don't even know him; I don't ever want to know him! God, that's incredible what you just told me," I responded and then continued.

"Where is Mike now?" I asked.

"He's out of prison but he lost his license to work with horses in the state of New York. He's planning on going to Ohio, and get back in the horse business. There's a couple of tracks in Cleveland that he may be going to," he said.

"Northfield Park and Thistledown?" I asked.

"Those names sound familiar," said Pete.

"So he plans to bring his act to Cleveland, eh? Our paths better not cross. I better stay clear of your brother or I'm liable to end up in prison like him," I said.

"My father would turn over in his grave if he knew what Mike did. My father loved his horses," said Pete.

"How long was Mike in prison?" I asked.

"One year," Pete responded.

"That's all, just a year?" I asked.

"Yeah," he replied.

"You still consider him your brother?" I asked.

Barelli didn't answer the question, but he did respond, "We aren't close."

"Has he always been like this?" I asked.

"He was always in trouble. When he was a teenager my dad sent him to a boarding school upstate hoping he'd get straightened out, but obviously he didn't change; he probably got worse," said Pete.

"Did Mike or any of you play sports when you were growing up?" I asked.

"Mike played football at the boarding school for a while. I think he got hurt and then quit. He wasn't disciplined enough to be involved in sports. Jimmy's the one who loves sports. He's a sports junky," said Pete.

"Did Jimmy play any sports growing up?" I asked.

"Not when he was in school, but he can tell ya' everything about sports," commented Pete Barelli.

The next day I found out something interesting about Jimmy. The man that I had come to New York to train, John Tarone, a tough Italian street kid during his growing up days, graduated from the same high school where Jimmy taught. When I told the trainee that Jimmy Barelli might be my half-brother, I'll never forget Tarone's response.

"Mr. Barelli's your brother? He was my favorite teacher; he was a cool guy."

I continued asking Pete Barelli questions.

"What about Julie; was she an athlete?"

"Julie...no," said Pete.

"What the hell did you kids do when you were growing up?" I asked, not intending to be sarcastic, but probably coming across that way.

"We were always around the track, the stables or the club, but not out on the ball fields much," answered Pete.

"To each his own, but I bet you probably followed the Yankees and the Giants, and maybe some college teams. Knowing about some of those great New York teams, didn't that ever get your adrenalin flowing and make you wanna play?" I asked.

"Naah, it was exciting when our teams won, but we were just spectators not performers."

I laughed a little, but I didn't want to embarrass Pete over his lack of interest participating in sports. Because sports had always been so important to me, it always amazed me that some kids grew up so detached from athletics. When it came to sports I had tunnel vision. The excitement, competitiveness, color and fun that sports added to my life made me think that everybody should experience that kind of high. Sports made me who I am—it was the reason that I existed, the reason I beat the odds and turned out so different than everybody else in my family, and different from most kids that had backgrounds similar to mine. I wouldn't have graduated from high school if it hadn't been for sports, and probably wouldn't have been able to finish college if it hadn't been for football.

Like Jack Barelli, I also love animals and would have loved growing up on a horse farm, but when I look at the total picture I feel fortunate to have grown up in Chagrin Falls. The Barellis may have had the stables and the track, their dad's horses, the glamour and excitement of the Big Apple and a lot of money, but I had the fields, the woods, the river, sports, good friends, my loyal springer spaniel and a couple of loving foster mothers. I wouldn't have traded places with them for anything.

Before leaving, I asked Pete if he had any pictures of his father that he could spare; maybe some negatives or doubles lying around. Pete said he would send me some photos, but he never did.

Just before I left, Pete Barelli repeated a request that I had previously told him I would honor.

"I'm asking you not to bother my sister. Julie has been through a lot with my father's problems, the same kind of problems that you're talking about. This kind of stuff has been too hard on her," said Barelli, in defense of his younger sister.

I respected Pete's request to not bother Julie, but I still needed to find out if Jack Barelli had anything to do with my existence. I thanked Pete for his time and the information that he gave me. Then I began scouting the neighborhood hoping to find some information that might tip the scales in the search for my identity.

I never knew anyone in the horse business that didn't drink, so I knew where to go. I went into bars and looked for signs of horsemen. I observed the pictures on the walls, the way the clientele were dressed, and I tried to pick up clues by listening to bar talk. I soon found out that my persistence had paid off. My brother-in-law, retired Cleveland Homicide Detective Ed Gray, would have been proud of my investigative instincts.

After deciding on the bar that seemed most likely to be a hang out for horse people, I pulled up a barstool as far away from cigarette smoke as I could get, and soon found myself engaged in conversation with an elderly man and a younger woman. I discovered my new friends to be familiar with the horse business. Luck seemed to be with me this cold March evening; my new acquaintances knew the Barelli family. I found out from the woman, a pretty, casually dressed woman in her mid to late thirties, that Julie Barelli had not married (as of 1993) and is a very pretty girl.

The gentleman told me that Jack Barelli had a strong affection for his horses. I knew he wasn't making that up because Pete and Uncle Harold told me the same thing. He also told me that they should have thrown the key away when they locked up Mike. If Mike is my half-brother, the genetic link might explain why I got into so much trouble in my younger days. But, other than getting into fights and being mischievous, I never engaged in cruel, criminal type acts like Mike Barelli did. The way that he abused his horses, it sounds like he had no conscience or morals.

"Sir, can you tell me anything about Jack Barelli?" I asked.

"Why do you want to know all these things about Jack?" the gentleman responded.

"He's an old family friend, someone I heard a lot about, but never met. I'm in the city this week for business and I thought it would be interesting to learn more about him. More importantly, he may be my father," I said.

"Well, if that's the case I guess you should know as much about him as I can tell you. Everybody called him Jack; I guess his real name was John, but he preferred Jack," said the gentleman who was older than me, but younger than Jack Barelli would have been.

After he mentioned about John Barelli being called Jack, I remembered that Uncle Harold said the same thing. I knew after that statement that I was on the right track.

My new friend, Patrick Leahy, paused before he continued, offering to buy me a drink. I hadn't drunk since 1982 when I had a life-threatening problem and underwent surgery for a bleeding ulcer. But, in retrospect, I was very fortunate that I never became addicted to alcohol because drinking problems ran in my family. Since I was bloated with Diet Coke and water, I bought him and his friend a drink instead. Being metropolitan New Yorkers I didn't expect them to say thank you, but I got surprised. The lady said thank you and the gentleman raised his glass. He gave the Irish toast in gaelic, slainte (slawn-cheh) and then began talking.

"Jack was quite a horseman! He bred racehorses...trotters. Like all good breeders he was particular about where he placed his stallions and mares. One of his fillies or mares jumped the fence and got in with the wrong stud. Jack was angry when he found out about it, but when that foal was born he was like a proud Papa. I think he had a special attachment to that horse."

This is one of those things that people say that you never forget. Besides Barelli's experience surviving a submarine attack, I liked hearing something else good about him. The good side of a person is much more interesting than the dark side, especially if he's your father. The Irishman's comments helped me to further develop an image of Jack Barelli.

My thoughts ran deep on that frigid New York evening in 1993. What Mike Barelli had done made me angry and sympathetic to the poor horses that he abused. I had this feeling that because I'm so different from these people, I can't be related to them. But it's not unusual for me to have that feeling; I also felt the same about my mother's side of the family. And even if I am related, there certainly is no chemistry or similarities in the way we think, act or live.

I didn't know Jack Barelli, so I guess it doesn't matter anyway, but the horse story told by the friendly gentleman at the bar did bring a smile to my face. It also made me reflect further.

Sometime in the late 1940s or early 1950s, did Jack Barelli come knocking on Davises' or Crawfords' door? Was Jack Barelli's disappearance from my life a result of bribery by my mother so that I would never know my father? Did Aunt Goldie contact Barelli and try to extort money from him in January of 1949 when she took me away from Florence? Did Goldie turn me over to the county welfare authorities because she couldn't get money from Barelli? Is Jack Barelli, former horseman, entrepreneur, and the Don Juan of Westbury really my father? Did the filly or mare that jumped the fence to mate with a different stud, and the foal born to a different father, serve as a reflection of some people's lives?

I'll never know for sure the identity of my father, but there are two things that I am certain of: Two ladies from Chagrin Falls and a springer spaniel built the foundation of my life; and one lady, two sons, and a golden retriever, have made the fortress more secure.